Long Hard Road

LONG HARD ROAD

American POWs During World War II

THOMAS SAYLOR

Minnesota Historical Society Press

www.mhspress.org

The Minnesota Historical Society Press is a member of the Association of American University Presses.

Manufactured in the United States of America

10 9 8 7 6 5 4 3 2 1

∞The paper used in this publication meets the minimum requirements of the American National Standard for Information Sciences—Permanence for Printed Library materials, ANSI Z39.48–1984.

International Standard Book Number 13: 978-0-87351-597-9 (cloth)
International Standard Book Number 10: 0-87351-597-8 (cloth)

Library of Congress Cataloging-in-Publication Data
Saylor, Thomas, 1958–
Long hard road : American POWs during World War II / Thomas Saylor.
p. cm.
Includes bibliographical references and index.
ISBN-13: 978-0-87351-597-9 (cloth : alk. paper)
ISBN-10: 0-87351-597-8 (cloth : alk. paper)
1. World War, 1939–1945—Prisoners and prisons, German. 2. World War, 1939–1945—Prisoners and prisons, Italian. 3. World War, 1939–1945—Prisoners and prisons, Japanese. 4. World War, 1939–1945—Personal narratives, American. 5. World War, 1939–1945—Concentration camps—Europe. 6. World War, 1939–1945—Concentration camps—Pacific Area. 7. Prisoners of war—United States—Biography. 8. Oral history. I. Title.
D805.A2S28 2007
940.54'7208913—dc22 2007021569

Book design by Christopher Kuntze
Composed in Scala and Scala Sans for the text
with Grotesque Condensed for display

Contents

	Preface	vii
	Acknowledgments	xv
	Maps	xvii
	"It's Never Going to Happen to Me"	3
1	Captured!	5
2	Prison Camps	39
3	Guards and Escape	77
4	Relations Between Men	104
5	The "Other"	130
6	Forced Marches Across Germany	149
7	Hellships and Slave Labor	176
8	Liberation	202
9	Long Hard Road	233
	Reflections	260
	Prisoners of War Interviewed for This Book	269
	Notes	278
	Sources	285
	Index	289

Preface

Captives have been taken for as long as organized warfare has existed. Yet laws guaranteeing decent handling of fighting men who laid down their weapons is a relatively recent idea, little more than a century old. In times past, prisoners sometimes were ransomed; at other times they ended up as slaves or simply were killed.

The origins of regulated, humane treatment of prisoners in the west came in the aftermath of the 1850s Crimean War and 1860s American Civil War. Wholesale and needless suffering during those conflicts attracted the attention of determined reformers. Their work culminated in the Hague Conventions of 1899 and 1907 and more specifically in the Geneva Convention of 1929. By 1939 this latter document, which contained specific provisions governing the treatment of captured enemy combatants, had been signed and ratified by all principal warring powers—the only exceptions being the Soviet Union and Japan.

Military campaigns during World War II swept across continents, and almost all nations, including the United States, saw large numbers of their armed men taken prisoner. During 1941–45, more than 110,000 American marines, soldiers, airmen, and sailors were captured by the forces of Germany, Italy, and Japan. These men languished in prisoner of war camps large and small, and some endured unspeakable hardships. The treatment in some camps followed the 1929 Geneva Convention, while in others its articles were crassly ignored and men mistreated, abused, and killed. Between 12,000 and 14,000 American POWs did not survive their time in captivity.

Yet despite the scale of this tragedy, and of the crimes responsible for it, comparatively little research has been done and hardly any narrative histories have been published on this subject. Few efforts have been made to research and publicize the hundreds of POW camps that once dotted the continents. Little visual evidence exists, either: camp locations worldwide have virtually disappeared. Visitors to Germany can tour several concentration camp sites, but of the numerous former POW camps, none remain—merely a handful of markers or plaques to indicate what existed there during 1939–45. In Japan, nothing remains at all; the historical slate has been wiped clean. We thus face the risk that this enormous human catastrophe will simply fade away after the last survivors die. *Long Hard Road* is a contribution to the ongoing attempt to ensure this does not happen.

THIS BOOK EMERGED from a 2005 oral history volume I authored about the human experience during World War II. That book, *Remembering the Good War,* assembled and presented a broad representative sample of the experiences of Minnesota women and men, civilians and service veterans, during 1941–45 and the immediate postwar period. In conducting interviews for that project, I spoke with nearly 140 people throughout the state and collected much interesting and valuable data. Early on, I interviewed several prisoners of war, from Europe as well as from the Pacific. It immediately was clear that their range of experiences was far beyond what *Remembering the Good War* sought to document, whether during or after the war.

Yet these were compelling, at times tragic stories, important chapters of World War II that needed to be part of the permanent historical record and shared with a wider audience. After consulting with colleagues, I decided to establish a second, separate project, one dedicated solely to the experiences of Americans held as prisoners during 1941–45 by the Japanese or the Germans. With the POW Oral History Project I endeavored to collect and permanently preserve individual prisoner of war experiences and to select the most compelling of these stories as the basis for a book. During 2002–5, I conducted in-depth interviews with nearly one hundred ex-POWs. The great majority have ties to the Upper Midwest and still reside there, but others now live in distant locations, from California, Oregon, and Washington to Pennsylvania, Florida, and Georgia. *Long Hard Road* contains their stories.

THIS BOOK ATTEMPTS to address several needs. As a historian, I believe we have a societal responsibility to create a permanent firsthand record, one that future generations can research and refer to. To learn from our past, though, to employ history as a decision-making tool, we must assemble the historical record—and the time for doing so with our World War II veterans is very quickly passing. Men interviewed for this project were born between 1914 and 1925; the youngest already has passed eighty as I write these words. Compelling firsthand accounts risk being lost forever unless concrete steps are taken—and taken now—to record and preserve them and make them accessible.

Long Hard Road also is designed to raise awareness about the varied experiences of the more than 110,000 American prisoners of war of 1941–45: their wartime plight but also their postwar struggle to adjust and find acceptance in a society that after 1945 sought a heroic, victorious narrative of World War II. Long overlooked or given minimal coverage in the majority of standard war-era histories, the POW story is an important part of that period, of this nation's World War II tapestry, and must be considered in the construction of any balanced assessment. There has been an enormous output of works in English on World War II, dealing seemingly with any and all aspects of it: individual battles and military figures, the air war and battle at sea, politicians and the home fronts. Yet aside from accounts of Bataan or high-profile escape attempts from German camps, precious few narrative histories detailing the POW experience exist. Popular perceptions of World War II POWs are of strong, confident men who sought ways to resist their captors, even in the camps, always looked for opportunities to escape, and rejoiced in their liberation before seamlessly resuming their civilian lives. The story, I learned, is much more complex and nuanced than this.

Even scarcer are books that employ oral history evidence—that is, the words of the POWs themselves. This book contributes to that literature. Furthermore, *Long Hard Road* is virtually unique in presenting both European and Pacific POW experiences in a single volume. This approach adds perspective and reveals points of comparison as well as points of contrast: in important ways, being a prisoner of war was strikingly different depending on where one spent time in camp and when.

Through the interviews for this book, many difficult memories emerged. Uncomfortable as they may be, we must acknowledge them and include them in the historical record. On one level are sadistic guards and slave labor details, civilian lynch mobs and starvation diets, terrible interrogation procedures and myriad diseases. But there is another level: among the POWs themselves, darker sides of human behavior also surfaced. Thus we see the strong preying on the weak in the struggle for food; men killed by fellow prisoners in the hot, overcrowded holds of Japanese cargo vessels; long and difficult postwar adjustments that destroyed families and left psychologically crippled men.

Finally, and this is unfortunate, the theme of prisoners and their treatment is not just a historical subject or a study of the past. Even though the 1929 Geneva Convention articles relating to prisoners of war were amended in 1949 and again in 1977, since the end of World War II prisoners have been taken and held in conflicts around the globe and in many cases abused or tortured in violation of existing international law. Heated debates in the aftermath of the post-2001 U.S.–led invasions of Afghanistan and Iraq, specifically relating to the subsequent imprisonment and interrogation of suspected terrorists, demonstrate that a study of prisoners taken during armed conflict is as timely as ever. To make informed decisions and policy choices, it is crucial to understand the debates from the past, to examine the ways POWs have been treated in past conflicts, and to witness the longer-term ramifications of prisoner abuse.

Long Hard Road is organized in chronological fashion, with the experiences of POWs in Europe and the Pacific running parallel to each other. Stylistically, the goal is always to keep the focus squarely on the narrators, on their words, with minimal authorial intrusion. Thus, each of the nine chapters has but a short introduction to provide readers with necessary thematic context; within the chapters, brief comments set up narrator voices.

An initial vignette reveals that ground troops and airmen in both theaters of war were, almost without exception, unprepared for being taken prisoner and had given little if any thought to what life might be like behind barbed wire. Chapter one details the capture moment: on Bataan and Corregidor; after being shot out of the skies over Germany and Japan; on battlefields in France and Italy; at sea; and many other places. Wherever the location, emotions of fear and uncertainty were present; in some situations, tensions were magnified as men were assaulted by angry civilians. In chapter two, interrogation methods and transport to permanent camp locations are the subject matter. Men speak of feeling helpless and alone, at times terrified; some talk openly of physical and psychological abuse.

Chapters three through seven take readers into the camps, in sites across Germany and throughout Japan's empire, and then beyond. The conditions in which men were forced to live, sometimes brutal work details, and the suffering endured by certain Pacific captives are presented in chapter two. In chapters three and four, men talk about their guards, reveal their thoughts about escape, discuss how prisoners related to one another, and acknowledge what could and did happen when severe hunger framed every minute. Chapter five considers what it was like to be "the other" among prisoners. The final two chapters in this section detail the human tragedies of the war's last year, 1944–45. Packed into the blistering holds of so-called hellships in the Pacific, marching aimlessly through the bitter German winter, performing slave labor in Japan—literally thousands of American POWs perished during the death throes of the hellish regimes in Berlin and Tokyo.

A final section documents the experiences and emotions of liberation, then accompanies the now ex-POWs on their return to civilian lives and what for many became a lifelong adjustment process. For some, this path featured few hurdles; for others, though, it truly has proved to be a long hard road, with multiple difficulties.

Interviews are at the heart of this project. All interviews were conducted individually, the vast majority in person. They generally took place at the narrator's residence; a handful of others were done at my university office or other locations. The goal was to find the place most comfortable for the interviewee. Following this plan did mean miles on the road traveling to locations near and not so near, but the benefits of personal contact were the ability to sit across the table from someone, to have a face-to-face conversation, to build a level of trust.

A few men preferred to speak by telephone; with others—those on the West Coast, for example—this method proved the only way to bridge the miles. Three elected to participate by post only, as they were not comfortable talking about their experiences but wanted to preserve their memories. A few chose not to participate at all: some invitations went unanswered; others who were approached declined, saying their memories were too painful to resurrect in detail. But difficult as the interviews were at times, many a former POW afterward said or wrote that he appreciated having someone who wanted to listen, who cared enough to ensure that his individual story would be preserved.

The interview process began with a telephone conversation during which I shared information on the project, talked about general themes for the interview itself, and asked some biographical questions. With background on the narrator I then could research more specifically his military unit, prison camp locations, and other details prior to our face-to-face meeting. During interviews I worked from a list of themes, tailored to each person's experiences. The idea was to carry on a conversation, gathering information in a relaxed manner. Audio recordings were made of every interview and then transcribed, ensuring that the historical record contains the precise words of the men themselves. The average interview produced slightly over two hours of material; some ran shorter, others longer.

Because human beings can internalize and remember experiences, even similar ones, in vastly different ways and also verbalize shared experiences in their own unique voice, no two interviews were the same—even, for example, when men were captured at the same time and place, spent time in the same prison camp, or were liberated together. Some men had spent days before our meeting thinking back on their POW time, perhaps reviewing personal documents or photos, anxious to begin. Such interviews often required little guidance from me; at times the memories just poured out, and my job was limited to ensuring we stayed on track and covered our agreed-upon themes. On other occasions we spent long hours together, with pauses to reflect or collect thoughts. Such interviews could be emotionally draining for all involved.

As with my earlier oral history volume, the excerpts presented in *Long Hard Road* are the interviewees' own words. To make the excerpts read smoothly and transition clearly from one thought to the next, some necessary editing has been done. All *uhs, ahs,* and repetitions of words have been eliminated, unless the latter changed the flavor of what was said. While a theme may have been discussed more than once in the course of a conversation, yielding some shorter pieces of several sentences that could stand alone, I generally selected those pieces that dealt with a single topic and wove them together into a single longer narrative. My questions and responses have been removed to further provide an uninterrupted piece of text. Despite these caveats, every attempt has been made to preserve the original style of the interviewee, that person's particular way of speaking. Anything added for context stands in block parentheses.

In this attempt to portray the broad range of prisoner experiences, eighty-five interviews, no matter how exhaustive, cannot hope to include every story, every emotion. After all, there were more than 22,000 American service personnel held as prisoners by the Japanese and more than 90,000 as POWs of the Germans. These men spent time in literally hundreds of prison camp or work camp locations. Thus, not every German *Stalag* is covered, and certain Pacific camp sites do not appear. That said, my sincere hope is that the choice of narrators does justice to the larger POW experience and that nothing in these pages misleads, distorts, or misplaces emphasis. With this in mind, I wish to thank everyone who participated in the project, especially those whose individual stories do not appear in this volume. Your contributions are very much appreciated.

In selecting excerpts for this book, I endeavored to verify information provided by narrators. Unit histories and reference works supply helpful background data; discharge papers confirm dates of service, awards, and duty stations; and other interviewees can corroborate some recollections. But there are important limitations to what can be verified. Discharge papers do not list information on time spent as a POW, neither dates nor locations. Primary source data from the camps themselves, including prisoner rosters, is very incomplete, if existent at all. Ultimately, it is simply not possible to confirm everything shared in the course of these interviews. Thus, errors, intentional or unintentional, are almost certainly contained in these pages.

But *Long Hard Road* is oral history, not an academic monograph or traditional piece of historical research. It is conceived primarily as a memory book, a book of recollections. And memory through its very nature presents its own difficulties. Donald A. Ritchie, a leading scholar in the field, writes, "dealing with memory is risky business." The eminent oral historian Studs Terkel once put it more simply: memory is fallible. Ritchie reminds us that "not every perceived event is retained in memory" and that biases, the passage of time, and other factors can affect how and what interviewees recall. But he rightly concludes, "the memories of direct participants are sources far too rich for historical researchers to ignore."[1]

How best to work with these memories? Noted scholar Samuel Hynes, author of *The Soldiers' Tale: Bearing Witness to Modern War*, asserts that a participant adds her or his own relative truth, and it is by considering the aggregate of these recollections that we are able to arrive at "the sum of witnesses, the collective tale." In writing this book, as with my earlier *Remembering the Good War,* I followed the approach of the collective tale. Here the goal is to present a representative mosaic of the prisoner of war experience, based on men's perceptions of what was happening to them and around them, their reactions to events large and small, their feelings about particular situations, their emotional responses—all elements of oral history and part of its enduring power. The collective tale of *Long Hard Road* will by necessity constitute an imperfect record, but as we are unable to question every actor on that faraway stage, now more than sixty years distant, it is the best we are able to compile.[2]

AFTER WORKING closely for more than three years with nearly one hundred ex-POWs, I can say this has been the most demanding research and writing I have ever undertaken. Interviews dealt with emotionally charged topics, physical and psychological pain, and moments of terror. But there were ample rewards: getting to know some wonderful men, and having the opportunity to preserve their memories and increase public awareness for prisoners of war.

Acknowledgments

Numerous organizations and individuals provided assistance as the POW Oral History Project grew and developed, and I take this opportunity to express my sincere thanks. The project received major financial assistance from the Archie D. and Bertha H. Walker Foundation and the Minnesota Historical Society. Additional financial support came from the faculty development program at Concordia University, St. Paul; Hiawatha Chapter (Minnesota) of American Ex-POWs; Lakeville (Minnesota) Lions; and VFW Post 210 of Lakeville. Thanks also to Bob Heer, Herb Kohnke, Bob Michelsen, and Deb Norton.

My partners at the Minnesota Historical Society Press have my heartfelt appreciation. Special thanks to editor Shannon Pennefeather, a real professional; as with our first collaboration, *Remembering the Good War,* this book is a more polished product because of her guidance. MHS Press director Greg Britton provided encouragement and helped secure some needed funding; Christopher Kuntze put his talents to work on graphics and layout; Jim Fogerty of the MHS oral history office answered questions as they arose.

The American Ex-POWs organization gave invaluable support. Thanks especially to Minnesota state commanders Vernon Bigalke (2003–4) and Dick Carroll (2004–5) for providing me with invitations to the state convention in 2003 and 2004 and for their assistance in developing a list of Minnesota interviewees. Vince Crawford of the St. Paul Veterans Administration also lent his strong backing to this project.

I am deeply indebted to the POWs of the Japanese lunch group for allowing me the privilege of joining them for their monthly gatherings. Just listening taught me so much. Bill Connell, Stan Galbraith, Al Kopp, Harold Kurvers, Alf Larson, Ray Makepeace, Bob Michelsen, Byron Pope, Kenneth Porwoll, Irv Silverlieb, Howard Swanson, Don Vidahl, and Jim Whittaker—thanks a million, guys.

Al Muller used his extensive contacts among veterans to bring new men to the project. During a 2007 research trip to Japan, I was fortunate to receive research assistance and feedback from members of the POW Research Network Japan. Greg Hadley of Niigata University shared his research on B-29 prisoners, took time to show me former POW camp sites in Niigata, and helped with sources and photographs. In Tokyo, Tsuyoshi Ishihara of Waseda University was a gracious host.

My friend and university colleague Paul Hillmer helped ensure that my teaching schedule allowed some time for research trips and writing. Paul also read sections of the manuscript and provided feedback; I benefited, too, from the insights of Kay Madson, Steve Morgan, and Kimberly Johnson. Concordia president Robert Holst has been a consistent supporter of my work, as has my friend John Jensvold.

Assistance also came from Jim Gerber, John N. Powers, and ex-POW Russ Gunvalson. Many POWs throughout the region invited me to their homes and were very generous with their time and hospitality. Former POW Bob Michelsen, whom I first met in 2002, has been a friend in many ways; lunch with him is always a pleasure. The staff of Oxford University's Bodleian Library helped me locate obscure books during my summer 2006 residence. Linda Gerber is, quite simply, the best transcriber ever—fast, ahead of deadline, and always accurate. Renata Fitzpatrick again did excellent indexing work. Trevor Saylor took the author photograph on the book jacket. Keith Williams supplied the maps.

My family provided moral support, encouragement, and patience; I couldn't have completed this without them. Thanks to Kimberly, Natascha, and Trevor and my folks Marge and Len Johnson of Mount Joy, Pennsylvania.

ABOVE ALL, thanks to all the former prisoners of war from across the region and the country who shared their memories, even as doing so proved often difficult and at times painful. It is to them that I dedicate this book.

Maps

POW Camps in Germany

CAMPS FOR ENLISTED MEN

1	Stalag II-A	Neubrandenburg
2	Stalag III-A	Luckenwalde
3	Stalag III-C	Küstrin
4	Stalag IV-B	Mühlberg
5	Stalag IV-F	Hartmannsdorf
6	Stalag VII-A	Moosburg
7	Stalag VII-B	Memmingen
8	Stalag VIII-A	Görlitz
9	Stalag IX-A	Ziegenhain
10	Stalag IX-B	Bad Orb
11	Stalag XI-B	Fallingbostel
12	Stalag XII-A	Limburg
13	Stalag XIII-C	Hammelburg
14	Stalag XIII-D	Nuremberg-Langwasser
15	Stalag XVIII-C (317)	Markt-Pongau

CAMPS FOR NAVY, MERCHANT MARINE, AIRMEN, AND OFFICERS AND HOSPITALS

16	Stalag Luft I	Barth
17	Stalag Luft III	Sagan
18	Stalag Luft IV	Gross Tychow
19	Stalag XVII-B	Krems/Gneixendorf
20	Dulag Luft	Wetzlar
21	Stalag Luft VI	Heydekrug
22	Marlag-Milag	Tarmstedt
23	Oflag 64	Altburgund
24	Lazarett IV A	Hohnstein
25	Lazarett IX C	Obermassfeld
26	Lazarett IX C	Meiningen
27	Lazarett XVIII A/Z	Spittal/Drava

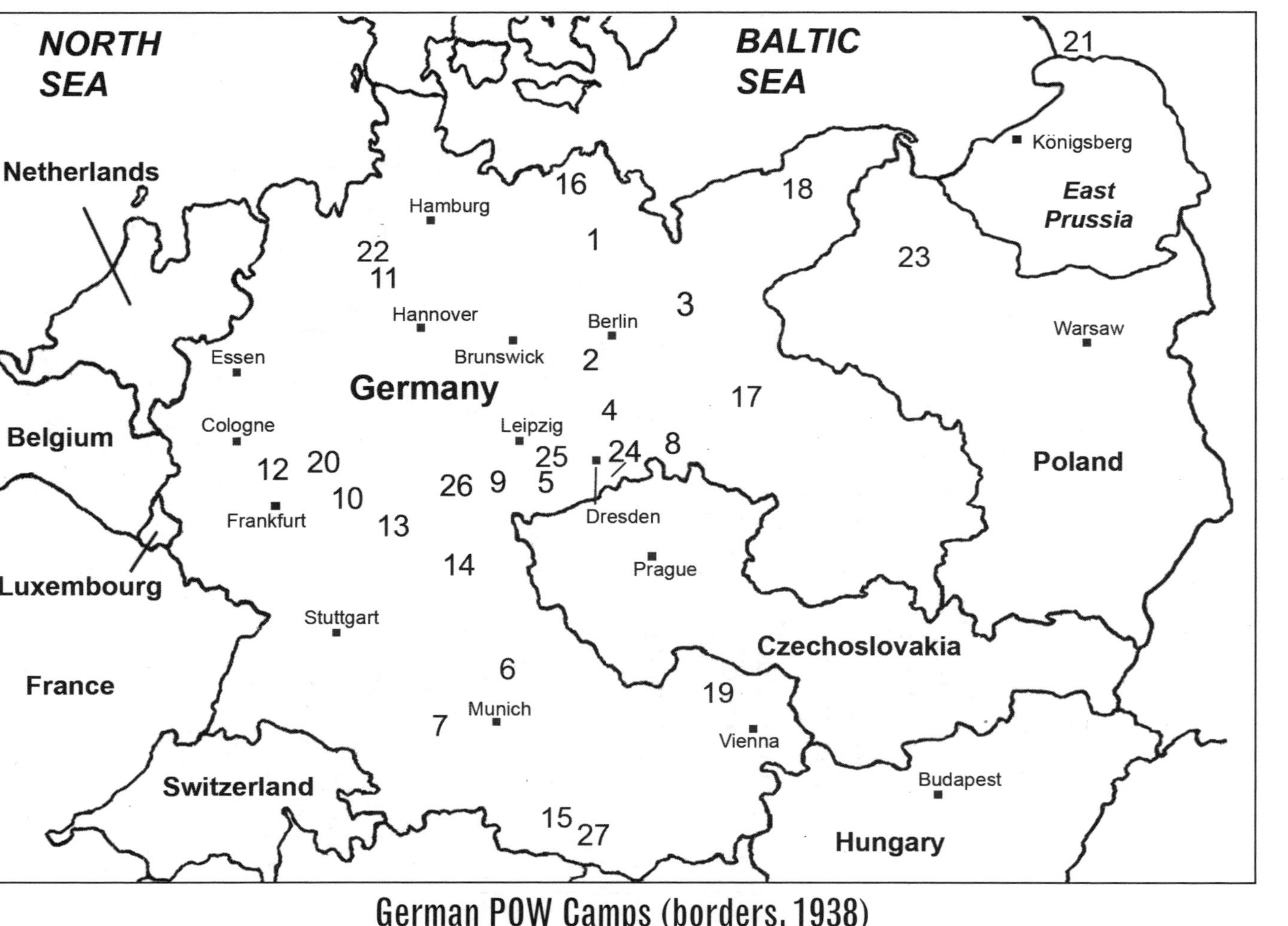

German POW Camps (borders, 1938)

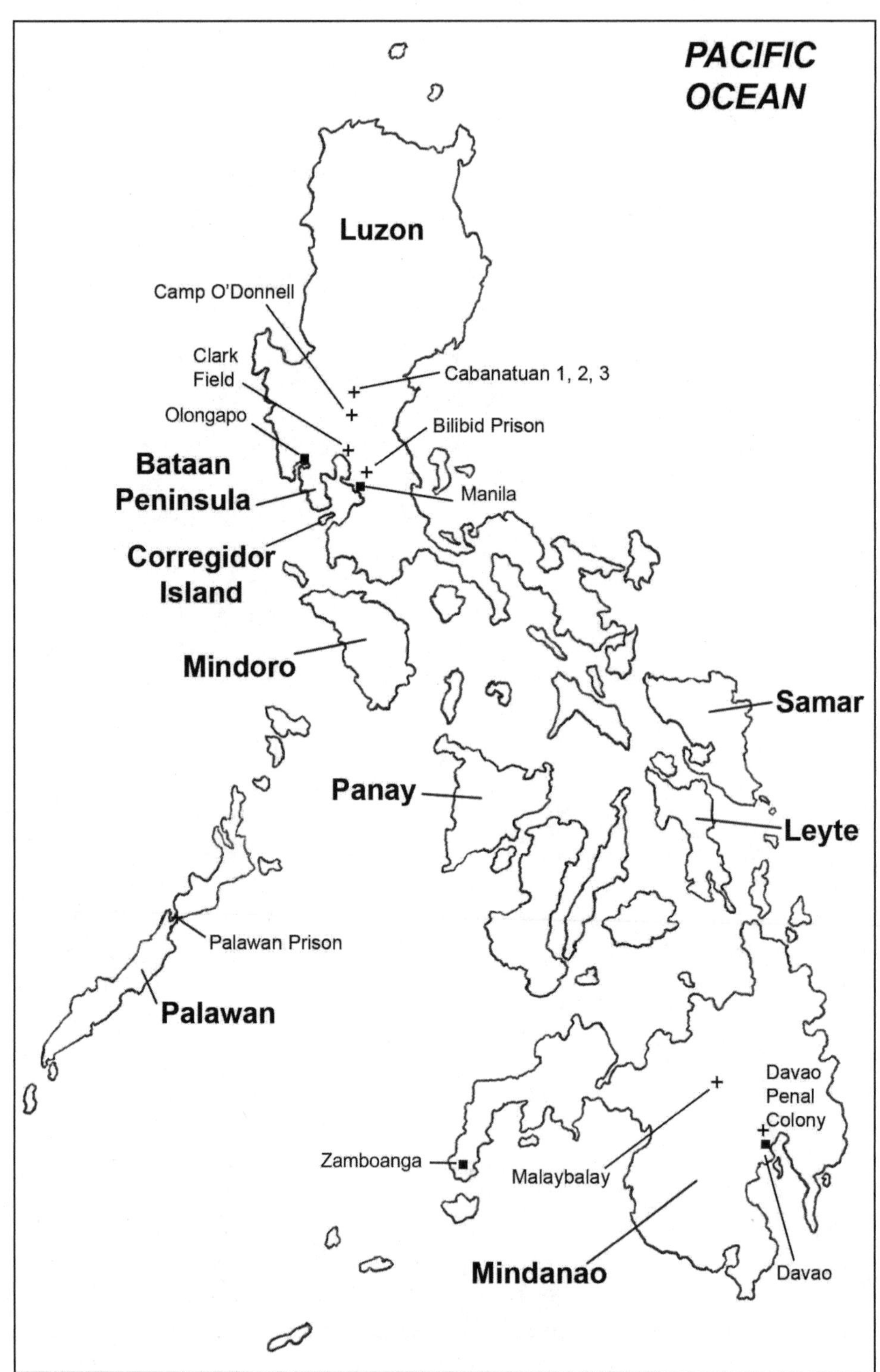
PACIFIC OCEAN
Luzon
Camp O'Donnell
Clark Field
Cabanatuan 1, 2, 3
Olongapo
Bilibid Prison
Bataan Peninsula
Manila
Corregidor Island
Mindoro
Samar
Panay
Leyte
Palawan Prison
Palawan
Davao Penal Colony
Zamboanga
Malaybalay
Mindanao
Davao

Philippine POW Camps

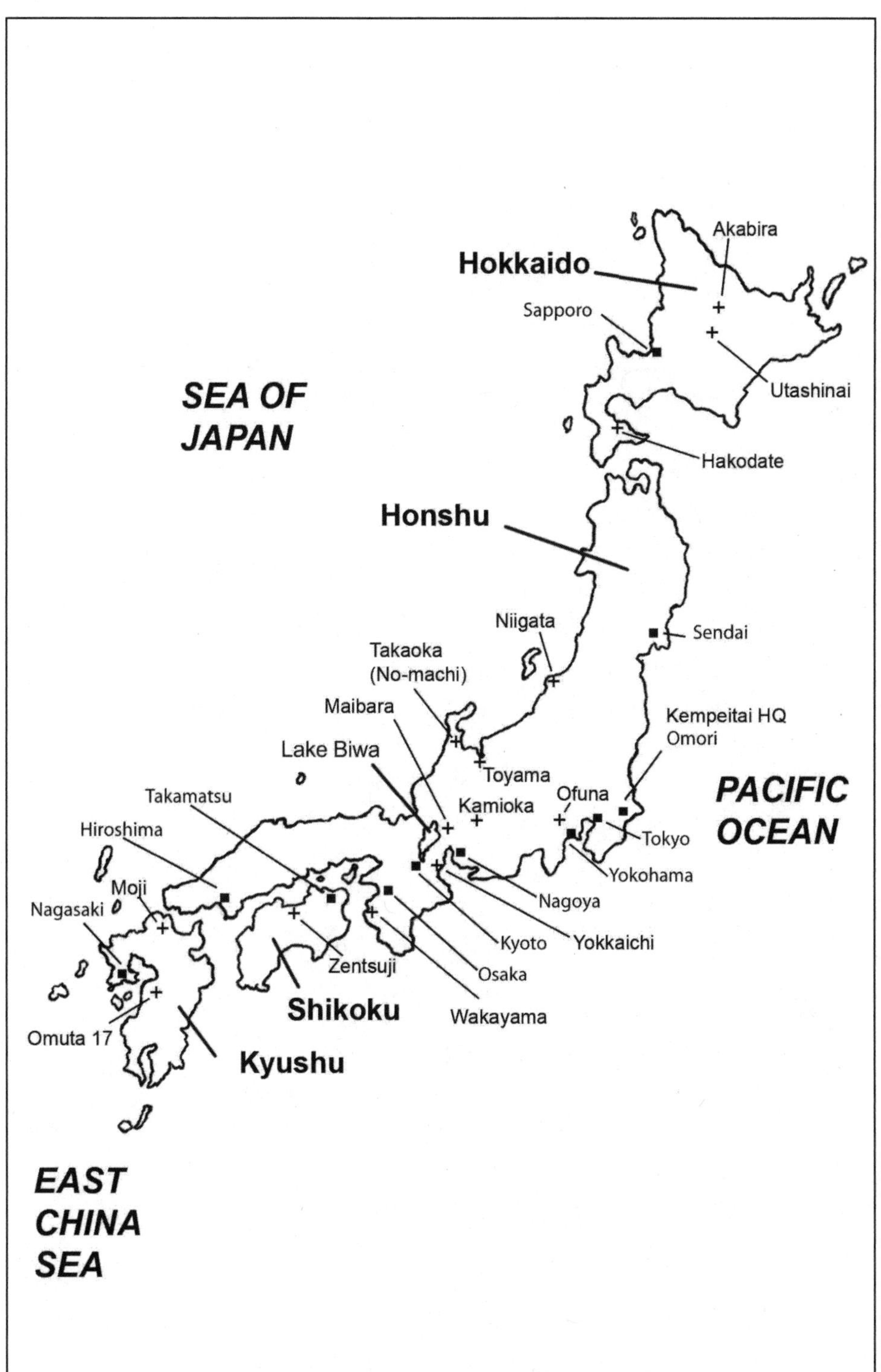

Japanese POW Camps

Long Hard Road

"It's Never Going to Happen to Me"

PRIOR TO THE EARLY 1942 DEBACLES in the Philippines and other Pacific locations—and even after—American government and military leaders did little to prepare service personnel for the possibility that they could end up prisoners of war. Some policy makers believed that even suggesting to soldiers what they might expect in the event of capture could weaken their resolve to continue fighting and make surrender an acceptable option. Not until 1944 did the U.S. War Department author and distribute a pamphlet entitled "If You Should Be Captured These Are Your Rights"; this late publication date meant most enlisted men would never read it.[1]

Most men recall little or no training to prepare them for the possibility of capture and POW camp life. Some air corps personnel do remember receiving instructions on how best to evade capture and work their way through German- or other enemy-occupied territory back to Allied control. Before each mission, airmen also received a packet containing emergency rations, maps, and foreign currency to aid them during an evasion odyssey. But regarding prison camp and existence behind barbed wire, the response was unanimous: "we heard nothing."

As historian David Rolf writes, "Every man who was captured went through a traumatic ordeal which was most personal, and his reaction differed according to place, time, and circumstance. The only common feeling was one of surprise that he should be 'in the bag' at all." Overwhelmingly, men report, they thought of being maimed or even killed. But taken prisoner? "That," said former prisoner Cal Norman, "is as *far* from your thoughts as possible."[2]

I never thought about that. You don't go into combat thinking you're going to be a POW. You live day by day. That's it. You run into combat.

You shoot at the people here and there. You live day by day, and being a POW . . . don't give it any thought. We took prisoners. But you don't think of yourself *being a prisoner.* VERN KRUSE, ARMY RECONNAISSANCE, FRANCE

Regardless of where you are, you're carrying your rifle and guys are shooting at you. You figure, now am I going to be wounded, and how bad will it be? Will I be killed? What will happen? But not once *do you think that you're going to be a prisoner.* Not once! CAL NORMAN, ARMY INFANTRY, FRANCE

I mean, you know it's there. The possibility is there. Every time you went on a mission. But you don't expect *it. I just felt that we had come as far as we had and we were going to make it the rest of the way. And you get to feeling hopeful, complacent a little bit maybe, and thought, boy, we're going to make it.* LEE BEDSTED, AIR CORPS BOMBER CREWMAN, ENGLAND

B-17 crewman James Fager, age twenty, at the family home in Minneapolis in early 1944, prior to joining his bomber crew in England.

I don't think I did [believe that I'd *ever* become a POW]. *(chuckles)* A young guy, I was going to *make* it.

Captured!

NEARLY 115,000 American service personnel were taken prisoner during World War II. There were career soldiers and conscripts, men from all service branches. The first were taken captive in December 1941, just weeks after the United States entered the war; the last were captured in August 1945, days before the Japanese capitulation.

The vast majority of American POWs were captured in Europe. Official military statistics place the number of American POWs in Germany at 92,965; of this total, 32,730 were airmen—the majority crew members of heavy bombers—and 60,235 were ground troops. Nearly 23,000 Americans were taken prisoner in the Pacific—more than 90 percent of them in the Philippines—in the war's first months. Here, too, ground troops were the majority. The brutal Pacific island battles after mid-1942 produced few captives; during these years only the occasional airman or survivor of a sunken naval vessel added to the number of Americans in Japanese camps.[1]

ARMY AND MARINE ground troops fought the war at close range; they were paratroopers and members of machine gun crews, jeep drivers and riflemen, tank crewmen and medics. Capture often meant an engagement was in progress or had just ended and the enemy was directly in front of them. Surrender involved the literal laying down of weapons and the raising of hands, and often a physical search by one's captors. The process was undignified and, many POWs recalled, brought with it a feeling of guilt: they had given up when their duty was to continue fighting. For some, being wounded intensified the stress of now, often quite suddenly, being a prisoner.

Capture played out differently for airmen. Most bailed out of stricken aircraft and were captured almost immediately after they parachuted to the ground. Some evaded the enemy for brief periods of time, and a handful actually made it back to Allied control. For most, enemy police or military were waiting near where they landed; in certain areas, particularly the countryside, however, civilians might arrive first. Here the experience of airmen could be drastically different from that of ground forces, for decent treatment was by no means assured: as David Foy recorded, the "reception could run the gamut from a demonstration of warmth and concern to verbal and physical abuse—from aid and comfort to ill-treatment and death."[2]

The likelihood of violence, even lynch justice, being directed toward downed airmen was highest in and around urban areas, the primary targets of bombing attacks; the probability of brutal treatment rose as the war dragged on and raids on German and Japanese cities increased in frequency and intensity. There are documented cases in Germany, but such practices were most prevalent in Japan. In the eyes of the public, the crew members of downed B-29 heavy bombers were immediately responsible for the incendiary campaign that had torched many cities; civilians were encouraged to "direct any hatred or frustrations they had . . . towards these demons." And direct it they did, with murderous consequences. Airmen everywhere could expect better handling from those in uniform. Indeed, there are numerous accounts of military or policemen protecting captured airmen from mistreatment or death at the hands of enraged civilians.[3]

SOME 21,500 AMERICAN service personnel were captured in early 1942 in the Philippines, nearly 12,000 at the Bataan Peninsula (April), and a further 8,700 on Corregidor Island in Manila Bay (May). The Japanese had no plans to deal with this number of men—nor with the additional 69,000 Filipino prisoners from these engagements. At Bataan, several factors contributed to what became a human tragedy: the men's poor physical condition; inadequate supplies of food and water; the blistering tropical heat; and no sanitation facilities.[4]

But primarily responsible for the wholesale loss of life on what became known as the Bataan Death March was the brutal treatment of prisoners by Japanese troops. Starving, weakened men, many suffering from dysentery and malaria, were bayoneted or shot if they fell behind. The Japanese also committed random acts of violence, simply killing or beating prisoners as they struggled along. By the time the final groups of men completed the multiday trek to the town of San Fernando, thousands of their comrades lay dead on the roads. Estimates are that between 500 and 1,000 American and 5,000 and 10,000 Filipino troops perished.[5]

But this was no isolated incident. Allied forces captured across Asia and the Pacific—the majority American, Filipino, British Commonwealth, and Dutch—consistently faced extremely brutal treatment from their Japanese captors. A primary reason is the xenophobic nationalism that took hold in Japan in the 1930s. Much that was perceived to be western—including concepts of surrender and captivity and appropriate treatment of POWs—was rejected. By 1940, Japanese soldiers were told that to be captured would bring dishonor on their family: "Never live to experience shame as a prisoner." The treatment Japan meted out to captured enemy combatants was entirely consistent with this directive. Those who capitulated "were dishonored and deserved to be treated badly."[6]

Bataan and Corregidor

Three men talk about their personal experiences on the march from Bataan. Harold Kurvers was a medic with the army's 194th Tank Battalion. After the surrender, his first memory was of the uncertainty.

We were tired, tired and beat. The thoughts . . . it was up in the air. We didn't know what was going to happen. We were thinking that they were going to take us to Manila. Even before the march, we wondered what was going to happen. Then we sat talking about if they were going to take us to Manila and we were going to be freed, you know, exchanged for enemy prisoners or whatever. It was wild thinking—rumors like crazy. . . . We didn't know what we were going into. If we'd have known what we were going into there would have been fear, but we had no idea. You'd never been in that situation before, so you didn't know what to expect.

Then the march began.

Some of them [couldn't make it]. . . . I saw my share of bodies on the side, and I think some of them were killed. I only had one experience where I thought a guy was trying to get away. And a Japanese guard walked him—there was kind of a hill—they walked around there. I heard the gun fire, and [the Japanese] came back alone, so I had to think that's what happened to him. . . . I saw a lot of bodies.

Prisoners found what food and water they could.

[I remember] being hungry and thirsty. I remember a sugarcane field. A bunch of us broke into that and got by with it, because usually when we broke out of ranks they shot. But we broke, and broke off some of that stuff. I got some sugarcane. Vividly remember that, sucking on that. You could feel the energy. In that condition, I could feel that energy surge through me.

I remember that one place, and I can't remember any other places that we were being fed. We dug up some sinkomas. They were a vegetable. It was real juicy. It was underground, and we dug it up. We ate that.

Reaching the town of San Fernando didn't mean the end of the misery.

[That was just] a gathering place for all the guys before they shipped us out. It was a mess, too. Just laying around with the other guys. Every place you stopped you saw human feces. [There were] no facilities. And it seemed that they threw up a fence around where you were, just so you couldn't get away. If they would rest you, it would be in the sun; it would never be in a shady area. It was always in the sun when they stopped.

Captured American and Filipino troops begin the march from Bataan. Note the Japanese military photographer, lower right.

Alf Larson served with an air corps materiel squadron; he had been in the Philippines since 1939.

It surprised us that they were as brutal at times as they were. Not all of them were. . . . There were some that would, I won't say they would really try to *help* you, but they wouldn't hinder you. Things like that. . . . But there were some that were, they just took delight. One incident: we were walking, and I happened to be on the outside of the line. Because they tried to keep us three, four abreast if they could. This guy, he was just swinging a bat, and he caught me right across the upper part of my legs. It hurt like sin, but I wasn't going to let him know that he'd hurt me. So I just kept right on walking. They didn't say [why he was swinging that bat at people], and nobody ever knew. And another thing I saw, where a tank had run over one of our POWs on the road. I saw the ragged aftermath of it.

The most vivid part of the whole bunch was the fact that we couldn't get water. The artesian wells were flowing right alongside the road up there, but they would not let us get water. But one of the most memorable things that I came across on the way was when we had stopped the night for camp. Camp was just lay down on the ground and sleep. They had dug a slit trench a little ways out from where we were. I had gone over there even though I couldn't urinate because I had no water. But it felt like I had to. When I got there I tried and couldn't, and this American came, and he was delirious, basically. He squatted down to go to the bathroom and he slipped and he fell in. The Japanese made this group of prisoners that was there—that had dug the trench and that—made them fill up the trench with him in it. They buried him alive in the excrement.

We didn't get any food until we got to the town of Balanga. At Balanga we got a rice ball. But from the time we left just outside of Mariveles and up to Balanga we had no food. Now there were kitchens along the way, and they said—the Japanese, we could see them eating—and they said that we were supposed to get it, but we had broken . . . they would make up some infraction, like they had searched somebody and found a gun or something. So that we weren't going to get any food. And we could see them eating on the side of the road there.

I was walking basically with people, a few, that I knew. We tried to stay together. Each one would look after the other one if they possibly could.

If something happened, if you got real weak or something, they would help him. This one fellow that I remember was Corporal Manzi. He was walking with us, and the night before we got to Balanga he lay down to rest. He took his shoes off. His feet were hurting him. And somebody, an American, swiped them when he was sleeping, so he had to finish the rest of it to Balanga, to San Fernando on bare feet. Somebody swiped his shoes. And they left a pair there, but real small. He couldn't even get into them.

I attribute the fact that I was even able to keep going to two things. I was in pretty good shape. That is, before the war. And also I had a little pocket Testament that prior to the surrender I would read occasionally. After the surrender when I saw what the Japanese were doing, I didn't want them to take it, so I took a piece of string and tied it to my skivvies and put it in my crotch. And that's where I kept it, and they never did find it. I brought it home with me

When we got to San Fernando, we were fed there. We were given a rice ball, and then the next morning they put us on the train. These little boxcars. And there were over a hundred of us packed into each one of those cars.

We had people die in there, in the car, because, what they did, they shut the door [and] . . . you were wedged in there so tight that you couldn't fall down. If you had to go to the bathroom, which very few did because we had nothing to pass, you just went where you were. It got stifling hot, because the Philippines is hot anyway. And they shut the doors on us. It was unbearable in there.

When we got up to . . . a town outside of Clark Field, they stopped the train. They opened the doors, and the Filipinos ran over and tried to toss stuff to us, and the Japanese beat them out, and then they shut the doors again. And then they didn't open until we got to Capas, up at Camp O'Donnell.

Ken Porwoll had arrived in the Philippines in September 1941. From the very beginning, Ken recalls a sense of foreboding about what lay ahead.

The one thing that really impressed us was that when the first group of Japanese soldiers came through our area, one was real flushed and red in the face as if he had fever, and before he cleared our area he fell to the ground, and the [Japanese] lieutenant in the front of the column came back and unhitched his sword and beat this man with the scabbard. Until the man got on his feet and walked off. And we said, hey, there you go, man. It told us that there is no limit to what they could do to you. No limit. *(pauses three seconds)* So you better start making your mental adjustments now.

The Japanese would pull men out of the line of march and beat them and beat them and beat them and beat them and kill them. They would then look through the walking ranks of the Americans and invite more Americans to come to help—help the person they're beating on. Then they all get the same treatment. So you learned after the first event not to go out.

That's what became a real hard part in that when you . . . I kept telling myself don't, if you want to live, Ken, don't go out there because you'll *die* out there. Then when you didn't go out, then you die a little bit inside and you say, what kind of soldier are you, Ken? What kind of a guy are you? You won't go help another American. . . . Then you get a yes, but . . . I want to *live*. And I'm *not* going out. You have to first make the decision you want to live, and then all the rest of it kind of falls in behind.

On the Bataan march, Ken shares one small positive experience in the midst of misery and death.

A very personal experience. Very personal in that I found myself walking with four other fellows that I had gone to high school with. And we'd played on the same football teams and basketball teams, and we had competed for dates for school dances. . . . You know almost everybody in the company. You know them. You know their background. Maybe you know their families. So a very . . . kind of an intimate thing. Which in one way is nice, and in another way it is rather distressing, too, when things get tough and you have to make decisions as to who gets what or who dies, who lives. And among these five men, then, including me, we made kind of an agreement to hang together. We might help one another.

Well, that very day the biggest guy [named Jim McOmis] gets a malaria attack, and then as his fever changes to a chill he loses his control and is very unsteady. So we get one on either side of him and help drag him along the road. Shoulder him up the road. We'd keep changing off about every hour or so until Jim said that we were going to have to drop him in the ditch because we won't make it if we have to carry him.

And we argued a bit. I said, "Let us keep trying a little while longer. Maybe something will break." But it didn't. And Jim again says, "You've got to drop me in the ditch." He knew when he said that that all stragglers were killed. If you were beside the road when the column passed, the Japanese cleanup squad came by and killed you. He knew that, and we knew that. And yet he insisted on shouldering his own responsibilities. And I'm helping him at the time we decide to turn him loose, and I'm apologizing to him for our friendship coming to this kind of an end. And he says, "Forget it. Forget it, Ken. I'll just have to find another way." I thought, wow! He hasn't given up. He hasn't quit. He's looking for tomorrow. And he knows his chances are 99 percent against him. But he's still looking for tomorrow. We dropped him in a ditch. And we never looked back, and we never mentioned his name again for the rest of the days [on the march].

And after eight days I end up in San Fernando, and the second morning I'm there I roll over at sunrise and I look into the eyes of Jim McOmis. I asked him, "What are you doing here?" He says, "Laying in the dirt like you are." I said, "How did you get here?" He said, "I walked, just the way you did." Then I said, "What happened to allow you to walk?" He said, "Well, when I went in the ditch and I looked up ahead I saw a culvert, and I crawled into it and slept off the malaria attack, and the second day when another group of Americans came by I crawled out and joined them." How he happened to lay down alongside of me that particular night, I don't know.

Douglas MacArthur was another of the Americans taken prisoner at Corregidor. He recalls his thoughts as the Japanese arrived.

The only thing that went through my mind was, whatever happens, I'm going to get back. And everyplace that I went, no matter what detail I was on . . . that was my attitude: whatever happens, I'll be back. I was just pure, total confidence. There was just no way I wasn't going to get back. I didn't let that enter my mind.

As the Japanese worked out what exactly to do with yet more prisoners, the Corregidor men were held for several weeks at a facility called the 92nd Garage, a rather flat ten-acre space, formerly a motor pool for a coast artillery unit. This facility simply wasn't equipped to handle thousands of men;

On May 6, 1942, just one month after the surrender at Bataan, Japanese forces captured the island of Corregidor. Ray Makepeace was among the Americans taken prisoner that day. He recalls what happened as the men emerged from the island's headquarters area, Malinta Tunnel.

There was the Japanese troops out there. As we came out, they took our watches and fountain pens and wanted to search us, see if we had any contraband on us.... You didn't do anything about it. If they wanted something, they took it. If you didn't give it up, they'd kill you. As simple as that.

for Ray Makepeace and others held there, memories of the horrible human conditions remain strong.[7]

We stayed right down close to the beach where we could go in the water. You didn't have any water to drink, but if you were thirsty and get your body soaked in water your body will absorb water, too. So I did that every day. But there was no food.

Howard Swanson served with the Marine Corps. He has distinct memories of the 92nd Garage facility.

The Garage. Ninety-second Garage area. That was a miserable damn place. The flies. And just the misery, and the heat. The *heat.* The sun bearing down. No place to get cover. No place to get cover at all. It was hot. Hot as blazes.

I don't know how many [men were there], but there were a lot. Marines, soldiers, navy men. I stayed with a group of marines. We'd go out and forage for food, if we could find some. But the food wasn't the big problem. The big problem was *water.* You can do without food, but you can't do without water. There was . . . yes, a tap. Water pipe running underground that came up like a spigot, and the lines were long to get at the water. We'd take turns in the water line. Water was scarce, and we were always thirsty.

We'd sleep right on the ground. Open ground. So when the sun came up, it just beat down on us. The thing that woke us up were the flies that were crawling on our face and trying to get up the nostrils. Oh, *God,* there were flies! Those flies! They crawl and they bite and they crawl up your nose if you let them. There were a *lot* of flies. . . . When it got dark the flies went; they didn't bother us. It was get by with this day until night comes, and the flies go away. . . . I think it's just getting through the day. Sunup to sundown.

It was just a miserable place, and the sun beating down like that, and guys getting the shits. It started right away. We dug these trenches to piss in, crap in . . . and . . . sometimes the sides caved in. There were a lot of prisoners there, and it was bound to happen where a prisoner would fall in. I thought, God, if I ever fell in one of those places I would just drown.

One wise guy made a little sign: "No swimming allowed." Because the guys fell in. There is that sense of humor there. It's very important. You *gotta* have that some way. You see that sign and . . . when I first saw that I just couldn't help busting out laughing because . . . my God!

Hundreds perished at the 92nd Garage before the Japanese finally removed the men to the Philippine mainland.

Face-to-face with the Enemy

Alois Kopp, a pharmacist's mate on the cruiser USS Houston, *became a prisoner of war on March 1, 1942, when the* Houston *was sunk by the Japanese off the coast of Java. Al recalls leaving the sinking ship.*

I was standing with another guy, and he said, "I'm going to jump." And I said, "I'll go with you." His name was Dave Williams. We jumped off the stern. The ship was really listing then. . . . There was a thick oil slick on the water, maybe an inch, inch and a half thick. And there were some fires. But not near me. Some of the guys were burned.

First of all, we starting heading for one of the rafts that were left. You throw it overboard before the ship goes down. And the Japs were strafing them. I said to Dave, "Let's get out of here. We're just going to get killed." He and I got out, and we were hanging onto things forever it seemed. It was night. This [Japanese] launch came around the bend and picked us up. Had machine guns on us, and rifles. Motioning to us and hollering at us about getting up in there. Well, I couldn't even raise my arms, let alone get up in that stupid launch. Finally they reached down and picked myself and this other fellow up and threw us in there. . . . When they pulled me out of the water, it was nine hours later. They pulled me out, and everybody looked . . . just black.

The captured men were taken to shore.

[When we got to shore] they threw me over there on a sand pile. Dave and I. They tied us together, back to back. . . . It was dark. You couldn't see, because we were so full of oil. They had us stand on the sand, on shore. There was probably a dozen or so in my little group, and then a few yards down the beach there was another dozen.

Oh, that was a mess by about ten o'clock, when the sun came up. It must have been ninety degrees right away in the morning, or close to it. I got blisters. People started hollering and moaning. They wouldn't give us any water. . . . And they wouldn't give us any medicine for the guys that were getting blisters from burns from the fires and from the oil. So that didn't help. That was a terrible, terrible experience, because guys were still dying from their wounds. They wouldn't let you go stop a guy's bleeding leg, for God's sake. They'd just kick you right in the face. They were just mean. *(pauses three seconds)* I was fully prepared to take a bullet. I really was. I thought, oh, man, what all are they going to do?

I was getting good and scared. Then I just *knew* they were going to shoot us. What else? They're not giving us any food. They're not giving us any water. They're letting guys bleed to death. They're just going to kill us all, slowly but surely. Shoot us. Yes, I was scared. You *bet* I was scared. I had *time* then to *get* scared.

Army infantryman Cal Norman was with the 100th Infantry Division. On December 3, 1944, Cal's company stopped in the small eastern French town of Wingen-sur-Moder. German units came through after dark.

Guards were posted—not an adequate number, quite obviously—outside the building, and then the rest of us, [they told us,] "Just rest now. Take advantage of the dark. It's night. Get some sleep." So I was laying on the floor, and a fellow named Bill Pebley was next to me. There was an open window, a basement window, out into the street. And after a little bit we heard some voices and some hollering and footsteps and things, and someone, it must have been a Kraut, stuck his rifle in through this window and fired into the basement. It didn't hit anything, so no one was hurt.

Then after a little bit in came a grenade. We heard it bounce. It bounced right between me and Bill Pebley. When it went up it caught me right in my backside and my leg and my foot. It was as if—I'd never had this experience before, but—as if someone had turned on a blowtorch and run it up and down my legs and my backside. I was blown up into the air and came down, PLUNK!

Shortly after that, then there was lots of hollering and carrying on outside and above us. The company com-

Wundzettel

Für Verwundete und andere chirurgisch zu Behandelnde

Nichttransportfähig:	zwei rote Streifen
Transportfähig:	ein roter Streifen
Marschfähig:	kein roter Streifen

Name:

Dienstgrad:

Truppenteil: USA

Verletzung:

Knochenverletzung?

Sonstiges Leiden:

Erhielt an starkwirkenden Arzneien:

innerlich?	Gabe	Zeit
Eingespritzt?		
Wundstarrkrampfserum?		

Wounded and captured on the night of December 3, 1944, Cal Norman was processed through German medical stations on his way to a prison hospital. While under way, he wore this Wundzettel, *or wound tag, with information about his injury and medical treatment.*

mander, I think, was upstairs in the same house we were in. The sense and feeling was, let's get out, and that the Germans were there. . . . Then everybody was just being herded out. I don't recall any Germans coming down to flush us out, but they obviously were close enough and were right there.

I couldn't walk. After the fellows who could get up and walk and get out were out, then some buddies came down and carried me upstairs. The Germans wanted me to be taken to their kind of first aid station. So they tore a door off the house and several [Americans] then put me on the door and picked the door up and carried me. I remember vividly, and I thanked both the Lord and everyone else I know for these guys. . . . They took corners of the door and carried me all the way to the first clearing station that the Germans had. It was still in the town, but it was some blocks away.

I suppose I was initially most concerned about getting some kind of assistance and help to see just how badly I had been injured. I think that the fact that the Germans were there and we were their prisoners still really hadn't taken hold the way it should have.

I go back to the first little aid station. It didn't amount to much. I think it was in the basement of a barn, because I was taken in and laid on some hay, and then my buddies who had carried me were sent away. The German who was in charge pulled my pants down and saw that I hadn't lost my balls. He said, "You're okay there." *(chuckles)* I remember that distinctly, and I guess I was pleased.

Within a week, the Germans had moved Cal to a hospital facility in the town of Spremberg, in southeast Germany, where he remained for the next nine weeks.

Vernon Bigalke was a platoon sergeant with the 65th Infantry Division. He was taken prisoner in February 1945 near the French-German border.

We were trying to capture a pillbox. The Germans got us pinned down with machine gun fire and we couldn't move; we was pinned down in the trench. We lost some of our men and had some injured ones. All we did was just lay in this trench waiting, hoping that something would happen. Maybe we could wait till night and sneak back under cover of darkness.

About 4:30 that afternoon, just before dark, four Germans came out of the pillbox. They came up to the trench and virtually stuck those machine guns down our throats, so there wasn't a thing we could do about it but surrender. After we left this pillbox, they took us back to a command post. Now whatever happened in that pillbox, these two fellows that were injured, we had to leave them there. We said the Lord's Prayer for them, and we had a medic along with us, he gave them a couple of shots of morphine, and we left them. Now whatever happened to those boys? I have no idea. *(with emotion)* I'm sure the Germans didn't do anything that night with them; they left them there, because they all pulled out of there. And those two guys were left there. So I have no idea what happened to them. *(pauses three seconds)* And that works on you. *(with emotion)* They were in my platoon.

Earle Bombardier was a paratrooper with the 101st Airborne and part of the June 6, 1944, D-Day invasion. Less than two weeks later, though, Earle was a POW.

First of all, our plane was shot down. It crash-landed, but we jumped before it went down completely. We lost almost all of our equipment. We finally got about thirty fellows together. They were in the same position we were, . . . scattered all over, and we were just trying to get a group together. So we just fought indiscriminately with small groups of Germans back and forth there in the swamp where we landed. Then we started marching through the swamp there and trying to get to the American lines. . . .

But when we approached the American lines, these Americans were very skittish. Evidently [they] had been tricked by the Germans or something. We yelled at them that we were Americans. They just opened up on us, and so we finally retreated, and then we ran into a bunch of German SS troops. They killed eighteen of our thirty men, and we were captured. In the battle there I was knocked unconscious by a concussion grenade and lost the hearing in one ear and [a] lot of the hearing in the other ear. It was a horrific experience, I'll tell you, because I was knocked out. When I came to there was a big German standing there with a machine pistol pointed at me, and I wasn't about to argue with him.

We weren't treated that badly at the front. It seems that combat soldiers have respect for other combat soldiers, even though they're the enemy. But it's when you get back into the rear echelon. That's where you start getting some of the abuse.

Milton Koshiol was an infantryman in the army's Fourth Armored Division. On March 26, 1945, General George Patton dispatched a task force of several hundred soldiers from this unit to liberate American POWs held at XIII-C Hammelburg, then still sixty miles behind German lines. The task force reached the camp and briefly liberated the prisoners, but on March 27 German forces attacked. A number of task force members, Milton among them, were captured during a firefight in a small town near the camp. Face-to-face with his German captors: this moment is burned into Milton's memory.

You've got your hands on your head and leave your firearm sitting down there, and you walk down there. That's where the guys frisk you. [One German] opened up my jacket, and he looked and he saw that I had a German combat badge [picked up as a souvenir]. This guy saw that pinned on the inside of my jacket, and he looked at me for a long time. Eyes right on me. I know . . . geez, I forgot to throw that dang badge away.

I had picked that up in Bastogne. I thought I would be killed by this guy; I really thought I would be shot. After, I don't know, it seemed like quite a while, maybe it was not such a long time, instead he closed up my jacket, and he pushed me to one of our half-tracks. Boy was I thankful for that. He could have killed me. I owe that guy. If it hadn't been that close to the war's end, I'm sure I would have been shot. He looked at my eyes for quite a while. I owe him forever.

An army infantryman fighting in France, Reuben Weber was part of a ten-man group that became trapped in a German pillbox in November 1944.

Shortly before dark a German walked in, rifle on his shoulder, and said that we were supposed to surrender. Our sergeant, he peeked out [of the pillbox], and he said, "We'll have to give up. Smash your weapons."

I was just hoping it wasn't SS troopers. I didn't know what would happen. But what was going to happen was going to happen. There's nothing. . . . I had no control over it. I walked out of there. There was a German tank right in front of us there. That's why the sergeant said we have to give up.

Then we were marched back to where tanks were lined up. . . . Even though it was getting later, it was still light out because of the artillery fire. It just lit up the whole sky. It was just constant. We went by a German tank, and the guys came out of the tank to look at the American prisoners, I guess, as we walked by. We weren't past them more than about twenty-five, fifty yards, and we could hear a shell coming in. Jumped into the ditch. Didn't ask for permission or nothing: we just jumped. We knew it was close.

The shell hit the tank that we'd just walked past and killed some of the guys in the tank. The tank commander was a little ways off, and he saw what happened. He came after us, and he had his pistol out, and he was pointing it right at me, and he was going to start shooting us guys. I fully expected him to kill us then, . . . but this German guard stepped between us. He said something about being soldiers, and he finally talked this officer out of killing us. So he said, *"Raus!"* Let's get going. So we got out of there as fast as we could.

Then they walked us, marched us back until we finally get to another German pillbox. They set up a machine gun, and they marched us right along this concrete pillbox wall, and I thought, well, now they're going to shoot us. And I remember how frightened I was, and I thought to myself it isn't going to make any difference what I do; they're going to do what they're going to do. I might as well pretend I'm brave and stand there.

Bill Hall commanded a light machine gun crew in the 29th Infantry Division. He landed at Normandy in June 1944 and was in action until October 4, when he was taken prisoner in house-to-house fighting near the French-German border.

We went on the second floor, the upstairs, and set up a machine gun in the window. . . . German infantry started coming through an apple orchard directly to our front. We had a great field of fire there and caused many casualties. But the Germans kept coming.

Then the SP [self-propelled] guns came up and started coming through the apple orchard and dispersing the troops. We saw them coming and saw this big long barrel coming toward the window, so we just started hightailing it downstairs. When he fired he blew away half the wall, and all the bricks and so forth fell on top of us. . . . We went down the basement and tried to hole up down there, and it wasn't very long until we could hear footsteps upstairs on the floor and someone in broken English called down into the cellar, "If there's anyone down there, you should come up or we'll throw a grenade down there."

Paratrooper Jack Ringgenberg was at the Anzio invasion in January 1944. Several days after the initial landing, his unit was sent on a reconnaissance mission. The Germans were waiting.

We were crossing the creek when all of a sudden we looked up, and there was a tank in front of
us and there was a tank behind us. They opened up on us. The guy on my right got killed *(voice cracks and continues in a whisper)*, and the guy on my left got killed. *(very emotionally)*...
That machine gun had to go right across me. Missed me. Missed me completely.

Within seconds, twelve of the eighteen paratroopers were dead. Jack and the others spent the rest of the war in POW camps in Germany.

There was a rifle platoon sergeant: Jim Jordan was his name. He was in charge. I asked Jim, I said, "Jim, what are you going to do? The Germans are going to blow you up here." He said, "I think we better just give up." . . . So we took kind of a poll of all the rest of them. We agreed we better tell them yes, don't shoot, we'll come up. So we did.

Bill recalls clearly what was going through his mind at that moment.

Plain, stark fear. The main reason is that we had caused many casualties in the apple orchard [with our machine gun fire]. There were dead [German soldiers] out there, and they knew we probably were part of that procedure, so we thought when we come upstairs and they see us, they're going to do the same thing to us. They aren't going to take any prisoners.

It didn't work out that way. When we got up there, we found there was a German officer who was courteous and treated us as a fellow combatant and asked us if we had cigarettes. He spoke English. I offered him a cigarette. He took one, and then I gave him a package, and he gave one to each of his guys. There were probably thirty of them. Wiped out the cigarettes till they were all gone.

It's kind of awesome. [You] come face-to-face with your counterpart, your fellow man, whether he's German or Russian or whoever he is, you have a feeling, strangely and oddly enough, of comradeship. I don't know why that is. But we felt, hey, that guy's in the same situation we are. He's just winning the game right now, that's all.

Shot from the Sky

Glen Naze was a crew member on a four-engine B-24 Liberator bomber. On June 20, 1944, he bailed out near Berlin with the rest of the crew when two engines were knocked out and the plane began to go down.

I landed in a potato field. I didn't realize how close to the ground I was until I saw the ground. Then I thought to myself, I've got to get ready to land. Because you're supposed to bend your knees and stuff. And I hit.

They were all standing there, all hoeing potatoes. Old people and real young kids. . . . One of the old men came up to me. They all had guns; I could see them. They looked about this big *(holds hands far apart)*, but they weren't. I took my parachute off, and the wind caught it and blew it away. [One] old man rolled that parachute up and gave me it, wanted me to carry it. I said, *"Nichts!"*—I know a little German—and threw it down again.

I was worried about the kids shooting me. . . . I thought they could shoot me, so that's it. *(emphatically)* I resigned myself to that up in the air. When I came down, this was it.

One German came in and took me away. He took me on this truck, and we went around to all over, picking up the dead bodies or another guy and so forth. Then they threw me into jail, in the city.

They put me in jail for three days there before they took me away to interrogation. It was a, just a cell, a jail cell. Wood bed. There was a hole in the door where they'd look in at you once in a while. The third day, they threw a loaf of bread on the floor. A piece of bread. I couldn't eat it. I wasn't hungry anymore.

Bill Schleppegrell, a fighter pilot with the 371st Fighter Group, was shot down on New Year's Day 1945 while strafing a railroad center north of the German city of Saarbrücken. Hit while near the ground, Bill remembers that events moved fast.

I stood up on the seat and then went over the side. I watched the plane crash. It was that sudden, and then I was on the ground. I was close to the front lines. I could hear artillery fire. It was an open field. There was snow on the ground. Not much snow. And I landed pretty hard. I could hear saws. There was lumbering going on in the area. I didn't see anyone, but I could hear the saws going.

My only thought was, I've got to get over the front line. I knew I had to head southwest. So first of all I got out of my chute. I started across this field, and then I saw a road, a small road. I headed for that, then took the direction that I felt was closest to southwest and started walking.

I started down this road and ahead of me, . . . around the corner—the road took a bend—came this bicycle, and it kept coming closer and closer. It turned out to be an old man. In my mind I thought, there's no place to hide. There's no place to run to. If I just look like I belonged and just kept walking, maybe he would pass me. So that all ran through my mind. But as he came closer and closer I could see his eyes—he looked startled—and he went by me. He didn't say anything or do anything, but he went by me on the bike, and I kept going. Then I heard him yelling. I kind of looked back, and he was off his bike and just yelling at the top of his voice. I just kept on walking, and I kind of got up to the bend that he had come around, and at that point a motorcycle came with a sidecar, and there were two men, two soldiers. They took me prisoner.

It was scary. I was really afraid. They weren't mean or anything. They were businesslike. . . . One of them spoke English. It wasn't very good English. He asked me where my parachute was. He put me in the sidecar and drove back to where I had landed, got the chute, and I had to carry that. But as far as how I felt, it was just scary. I didn't know what was going to happen. It was the fear of the unknown, and I guess I didn't know *what* was going to happen.

Frank Linc was a heavy bomber copilot. On April 29, 1944, his B-17 was hit on a mission to Berlin. The order came to exit the aircraft.

The first thing I remember, as I tumbled out . . . I'd be facing up, and I could see the aircraft passing over me. . . . I kept falling and falling and falling, and I started thinking of a lot of things. Silly things, like my laundry didn't get back. *(laughing)* Those are crazy thoughts.

I fell for . . . it seemed like eternity. I thought it could be that it's a low cloud and fog below that, and I won't know I'm out of the clouds until I hit the ground. So I was ready to open my chute, and things started lighting up, and I looked and, hey, there's the ground. I had a little farther to go, so I kept falling, and finally I thought it was about time I pulled the chute. So then I looked down, and I said, so this is Germany. Crazy. *(laughing)*

I saw big trees reaching for me. Missed the trees, but I hit a stump and wrenched my back a little bit. That was it. Took my chute off and rolled it up and hid it under some branches and headed off. Head east, or rather west. We had our escape kits with a little thumb-size compass and a map of the area. . . . I ran for about five minutes and saw someone ahead of me, who was my radio operator.

Hiding in a pile of brush, the two were spotted by civilians.

So we took off like mad. We started getting out of breath. We stopped, and I heard something behind. I looked, and here's a kid on a bike following us.

Then we got to a stream. . . . The only way to escape was to cross the stream. We just got into the water, and someone yelled on the other side. Took a shot at us. So we got back and raised our hands and sat down. Then the farmers came up with a rusty shotgun. That was good enough for us. *(laughing)*

B-17 tail gunner Dick Brownlee describes what happened when German fighters shot down his plane on October 6, 1944, near Berlin.

There was a red handle there [on the inside of the aircraft] that if you pulled it, it would pull the hinge pins out and the [escape] door would fly off. So I grabbed this and pulled hard, and nothing happened. And I remember thinking to myself, well, I guess this is it. And it was not a panicky feeling. It was very calm. But I was angry at the handle, and so I reached out and just really gave it a yank, and it pulled out finally, and the door flew off, and I fell out of the door. In a few seconds, when I was away, I pulled the ripcord for my chute, and I was jerked to a standing position with some great force. I felt kind of woozy, so I just kind of let myself go limp in the chute until I kind of got my breath back.

It was a beautiful, sunny October day . . . and I'm floating down all alone. Didn't see anybody else around anywhere, and [I'm] watching the German farmland, countryside go below me. Just kind of drifting down. . . . When I finally got close enough so I had some depth perception, I realized I was going pretty fast, and I remember crossing over a road, a tar road, and landing in a plowed field, kind of spinning around and going backwards. . . . I just kind of relaxed and kind of lay my head back for a moment on the dirt there. It wasn't very long. I had my eyes closed. The next thing I knew, somebody was talking to me, in English.

It was a small gathering of small-town people, and there was somebody there with a uniform on, maybe home guard or something for all I know, because it was just a farm community. With these people looking down at me on the ground, I unhooked my parachute harness and slipped out of that. I had some silk gloves on, which were liners for the electric gloves that we had to use in the plane, and I just threw those on the ground while I was unhooking my parachute. I remember when I stood up, there was this little elderly woman there who had picked these gloves up and very gently handed those to me. They were something I really didn't need, but she certainly seemed to be a nice grandmotherly-type person. I think everybody was surprised at how young I was. I was nineteen. . . . At nineteen, I guess you don't have much fear, you know. I didn't think anything bad would happen to me. I don't remember being fearful at all.

Rodney Shogren was a B-17 waist gunner. On March 8, 1944, returning from a mission to Berlin, his damaged bomber crash-landed in a marshy area near the Dutch-German border.

My radioman, I carried him out. I had a hard time carrying him. That was dead weight. He was still conscious, but he was like in shock. I mean, he couldn't walk. I got him on my shoulder and his arms around my neck, and I dragged him out. My engineer came running by me. I hollered at him to help me, to get him, so we . . . well, we probably got him about two hundred, three hundred feet from the plane because we thought maybe it would catch fire. But it didn't. I helped to get Mike covered over [with a parachute] and gave him a shot of morphine, because he was injured pretty bad. He couldn't walk, and he was bleeding all over.

[It was] every man for himself. . . . They all left me. I thought, I gotta get out of here. Because I knew they [the Germans] saw the plane come down. But where we got shot down was swamps and dikes, so you had to stay on the dike or you were down in water. It was just like you were out in the middle of an open field. Anybody could see you. Nowhere to hide. . . . I had no idea which way to go. Didn't know my directions at all. I thought I was going west, but I'm not sure.

It was [close to] dark when I got picked up. I was probably loose for about an hour before they picked me up. A *Wehrmacht* [German Army] guy. Had a gun with a rifle and a shotgun, one on top of the other. When he told me to halt, I halted.

He brought me back to . . . like a house with a hotel room in it. There was a lobby. But it looked like just a plain ordinary house. [The remaining crew members] all ended up in the same place, because we were in a small community. . . . They were just ordinary people, like in a farm community. But everybody had to come. There were strangers, you know. They were very inquisitive to see who we were. I mean, we were like from Mars or something to them.

Bill Connell, a dive-bomber pilot, was stationed in the Pacific on the aircraft carrier USS Hornet. *On July 4, 1944, Bill was on his first combat mission, flying over the Japanese-held island of Chichi Jima. Anti-aircraft fire from the ground filled the sky; one round exploded right next to Bill's plane.*

[W]hen the shell exploded, it blew the airplane right in half, so that me and the front end of the airplane went one direction and my rear seat man and the tail went a different direction. I was just falling like a leaf. Just flip-flopping back and forth. . . . I waited a minute or two, and then I bailed out. . . . Then after I fell for, oh, ten or fifteen seconds, I knew I was clear of the airplane, and then I deployed the parachute.

The Japanese were shooting at me from this ship that we were bombing. I could see the tracer [bullets] coming up to me. So I was kind of interested in that, and I didn't really spend a lot of time looking around at the scenery. *(chuckles)* But it didn't take me long to realize that I was going to land right smack in the middle of this harbor. . . . I couldn't paddle out of there. So I just realized that there was no place for me to go and that I was going to be captured.

I was in the water about, I would say, forty-five minutes at most. They finally sent a small naval boat, about the size of a tugboat. . . . There was a crew of about, oh, eight or ten individuals on this craft. When they got me up on deck, they beat up on me pretty good. Then they finally tied me up with . . . they had a piece of line about an inch in diameter, and they wrapped it around me in a coil from my knees to just about my shoulders, so I could not move my arms. I could just barely hobble. I looked like a mummy. They put me up on the bow of this vessel. Just threw me on a pile of rope, and I laid there until we went back to shore. Then they got me stood up, and they unwrapped me, and then they put handcuffs on me, with my hands behind my back. Put a blindfold on me.

On shore, Bill was placed in a motorcycle sidecar and transported a short distance.

They took me out of the sidecar, and they took me over and tied me to a tree. They tied me in such a fashion that my hands were behind my back, and when they finally kicked my feet out from under me my buttocks were still about six to eight inches off the ground. So I was basically hanging by my arms, with my arms tied behind my back. . . . The first couple of hours the pain was excruciating and I just . . . it was very, very hard to bear. But finally my shoulders just became numb. I couldn't feel anything. I hung that way for approximately twelve hours.

When they finally cut me down and I looked at my hands, my hands were so swollen that I couldn't see between my fingers. My hand looked like I had a softball in my hand. Then they moved me down the road a piece, about a quarter of a mile, to a second tree. . . . The trunk of the tree leaned on an angle of about forty-five degrees. They tied me to that tree, and at least I was sitting on the ground and I could lean back against the trunk. I was sitting there for the rest of the night. . . .

I was there sitting on the ground leaning against this tree until the next day. Then they finally came and got me, and they moved me up to the administration building.

Ray Toelle was tail gunner on a B-29 Superfortress heavy bomber; his plane was shot down on May 24–25, 1945, during one of the firebombing raids on Tokyo. Ray managed to bail out of the burning aircraft.

You couldn't see anything down below. There were no lights or anything. I unhooked my chute so that in case I hit the water I could get out of it. I was just hanging onto the part of the chute. As I was coming down, I had my hands up on the shroud lines, and I could see that my hands were burned, because the skin was hanging. I didn't realize that I had burned my legs and my face, too. I had a helmet on, and an oxygen mask. It was a good thing, because I just got burned around my forehead and my eyes. Then my legs got burned, from my ankles to my knees. On both of them. [And] I burned the sleeves off my jacket. . . .

I figured I was going to land in the water, but all of a sudden I hit the

A B-29 on a mining mission was shot down on July 20, 1945, near the western Japanese city of Niigata. Several of the eleven-man crew were killed by local civilians after they parachuted from the plane; the others were captured in the countryside, then turned over to the Kempeitai secret police. Here are five of the captured crew members, showing signs of physical abuse, huddled on the back of a flatbed truck. Kempeitai guards stand over them.

ground. The parachute stayed [in a tree], and I hit awful hard. I wasn't any more than twenty-five feet away from this house. The chute stayed in the tree, and that's why I couldn't really land the way you're supposed to. Then I just stepped out of my chute, and I saw this old man standing over there a little ways. He was an old man, and he had a big pole. Even if he's an old guy, I'm not going to try to fight. What could I do? I went over to him and gave myself up.

He just took me up . . . there were two soldiers up on the hill there. They tore my helmet off. My helmet had burned into my forehead, and they pulled that off. I had a watch on. They ripped that off. . . . I didn't have much of my jacket left, [just] where my parachute harness was. The rest was all burned away.

The pilot and copilot must have landed close to me, because they brought them over there, too. There was three of us there. And then of course they blindfolded you and tied my hands behind my back, and they tied them so *tight*. And they were hurting the way it was. Then they marched us to this little town, through a little town. . . . On the way in . . . well, of course there were civilians there. They threw rocks at you, and they hit you with sticks and stuff. The guards didn't do anything about it.

Ray remembers being taken inside a building.

They put me out in this big room. I could hear this water dripping, and I looked down on the floor, and there was puddles of water there, and I said, "What the heck is this from?" I couldn't see [because of the blindfold]. Here it was from my hands. My hands were all blistered. The blisters were breaking. Then after a while I could feel my feet were getting wet. The blisters on my legs were breaking, and the water was running out of there down into my socks.

Then after that they put me over into a building. It was like a little hospital evidently. They took my blindfold off, and they took off the handcuffs and stuff. There was two fellows in there. . . . They cut the skin off that was hanging on my hands. They let me look in the mirror, and I could see my forehead where it was burned, around my eyes. When I looked . . . underneath this blindfold that they put on I could see a little bit, but I couldn't see with my right eye. [H]ere I had gotten a piece of metal in my right eye, and it was all swelling up. So I couldn't see. But I could see out of my left eye. They cut the skin off, and they wrapped my hands up.

Lynch Justice

The troubles for Dick Lewis, a waist gunner on a B-17 heavy bomber, began when the plane was damaged on a November 1944 mission to Merseburg, in central Germany.

I was hit [in the leg] by flak previous to this, so I just crawled over to the door and slid out. . . . As I came down I realized I was going to land in a vineyard. It was terraced with brick walls and wire fences. I thought, I've got to try to protect my leg the best I could. So I held it up in the air and kind of landed on my bottom and one leg. There was a fellow working in that vineyard, so he came over towards me, and here I was like a stupid kid—I had out a pistol, and I had my map out, trying to figure out where I was. . . . I know he certainly couldn't speak English, and I couldn't speak German. I had no idea what he was talking about. I tried to keep him away from me. I was poking my gun at him. I thought he had a pitchfork or something. I thought he might be coming after me with that.

That was probably one of the dumbest things I could have done, . . . because a [German] soldier was coming from town, too. He could have shot me right on the spot, [if he saw] that I had this pistol out. Anyway, I put it away, and then when he came, this peasant told him that I had it. He relieved me of that and my map and whatever else I had. . . . He didn't threaten me at all. He was very calm about it, and I acted very calmly. I knew I had no choice except to surrender and just hope that all went well, that he would treat me fairly, and he did. He saw I was bleeding. He had a bicycle, so he put me on his bicycle and wheeled me into the town.

But before Dick got to town, he faced some difficult moments.

These old folks lining up on either side of the road and cussing at you and shaking their fist at you and spitting at you. That was a very scary thing for me to go through, not knowing what these people were going to do. We had heard so many stories before that, that a lot of times they would take the airmen and hang them to telephone poles with their parachute lines. And that was the thing that was going through my mind all the time. I was most concerned about that.

Kelly Martinson served as tail gunner on a B-17 bomber shot down in March 1944 over Belgium. Kelly and another crew member evaded capture after bailing out.

We were in this haystack, and we were there for two days. So in the second evening we decided we better start walking. . . . We tried to get around the town of Ghent. It was so dark that we'd take turns leading each other.

They stumbled upon several police officers.

They were Belgian police. We thought, man, we've got it made; these guys are going to take care of us. They took us to the police station, and I opened my escape kit, which had chocolate, gum, and so forth in it. I was giving them some gum and candy. One of them got on the phone. . . . About ten minutes later the Germans came and got us.

After being held briefly in a small-town jail, Rodney Shogren and the other members of his crash-landed bomber were transported by train to the city of Frankfurt.

There was another crew with us, too. We must have been ten or twelve. . . .

When we got off the train down there [in Frankfurt], there were people that were vicious at us there. I mean they were . . . *(trails off)*. They were spitting on us. Threw sticks at us. At the train station.

[The guards] started to walk [toward the center of town], but they hurried up and put us on a streetcar. But the guards had to hold these people back when they did that. The German guards protected us, or the civilian people would have killed us, I think.

They called us baby killers. We dropped bombs on their people. I don't blame them for being vicious at us. . . . I could understand their anger. If I was a civilian and been bombed by them, I'd probably have the same feeling. . . . Bombs, they don't hit their targets all the time. Everybody drops their bombs on the lead bombardier, so those bombs could go a long ways. Then we carried incendiary bombs sometimes. They would explode about five hundred feet above the ground and spread out. So I mean . . . well, that's not human at all.

Harold Brown was a Tuskegee Airman, a fighter pilot with the famed 332nd Fighter Group. On March 4, 1945, strafing a railroad yard near the Austrian city of Linz, his P-51 Mustang was badly damaged as he flew over an exploding railroad car. It was soon apparent that he couldn't make it back to base. Harold recalls clearly how some actions became automatic.

It was self-survival. I didn't even think in terms of the chute—will it open or will it not? I had better things to think about, like getting out. Things are happening so doggoned fast, and you're doing things automatically, because you've gone over this thing ten thousand times in your mind. You know what you have to do. So there aren't any other thoughts. It's just get out of the airplane, get the chute open. Then, *boom,* I hit the ground.

Then after I hit the ground and whatnot, snow up to my knees and so forth, now it's what do you do now? For just a second I thought, man, I'm up here all by myself. And you could hear the [other] airplanes [in my group] die out in the distance. Now you're all alone. Not a *soul* you can turn to. So I grabbed my little escape pack. . . . It had a map, a compass, and a few other little things in it. And I knew just about where the Russian lines were to the east, and I said, boy, if there's some way I could just evade, and if I can just head east and make some decent time heading east without being picked up, I just may be able to get to the Russian lines. I thought, okay, this is what I'm going to do, and I knew the direction in which I was going to go. Well, just about that time, that was when a couple of guys came up over the top of the hill. They were standing up on the hill, and they slung off their rifles. These were civilians. Constables. And they picked me up. [Started to] march me back to the village. Just a little small village.

From the time they picked me up until they got me back to the village, that took a little time. By the time—I don't know if it was thirty, forty, fifty minutes or what—we got back to the village, it didn't take long for a little mob to form. They just saw me, or word got out. A small mob of twenty-five to thirty people, magically appearing from out of nowhere. Then they start all the ranting and raving about, arguing over, how are we going to kill him? I assume that's what they were doing, from some of the symbols. *(draws index finger across neck)*

I was scared as hell. Now I guess the fear is pretty much from the unknown, not knowing what's going to happen. You don't speak their language. You got a mob of people staring at you, cursing and everything else. And you're wondering, what are you going to do? What's going to happen next? Then you start having a few thoughts about . . . you know, cases where the intelligence officer always briefs you: whatever you do, get as far away from the target area as possible because people are upset, angry.

It's now just thinking in terms of survival. I mean really *survival.* Now that it's totally out of my hands. Nothing I can do about it. I think for just a short while—I know I was in a state of shock. Only because it was hard for me to accept reality. And I know for the first couple of minutes, I was almost talking to myself. I was saying, what are you going to do? What are you going to *do?* You gotta do something. *(louder and slower)* What are you going to do? And no answers were coming. I finally said, well, whatever happens, I'll just respond to whatever they do. Whether I run or whatever. Let them shoot me or . . . I don't know. *(pauses three seconds)* I just didn't know what I would do.

Harold describes the nightmare scenario as it unfolded.

There were two of them that brought me in [to the village]. There was a third one that came up and rescued me from the rest of them. I saw the [third] guy, and I heard him behind me, and he was speaking in German, and I could hear him hit the bolt on his rifle, and that was very clear. There was this very rapid German discussion. It went on for a few seconds, and the other two guys, I saw them drop their guns, and they backed off into the mob, and he motioned to me. *(hand motion)* Come. And I got in behind him, and he and I walked back, back up into the village about . . . it was just a short distance. The crowd was following us, and he held the gun on the crowd while we backed up. . . .

We backed up into this little pub, and we barricaded ourselves in the pub. As night came on, it was getting cold and the crowd began to disperse. I am assuming it was probably close to midnight when we left that pub. We went out the back end of it, and we walked for—and I'm guessing again—roughly I would say three, four, five miles down the road, to the next small village. By the time I got into that village, it was almost daybreak.

There's no question about it. Yes, the guy saved my life. *(emphatically)* Oh, yes.

Aaron Kuptsow enlisted in the air corps in 1942 and served as a navigator bombardier, or "Mickey Man," on a B-17 bomber. On November 26, 1944, his plane was shot down over Germany. Aaron had more reason than others to be scared about what lay ahead—he is Jewish.

I didn't see anybody; however, as soon as I made contact [with the ground], I released the harness of the parachute and got out the harness and started to run. And as I started to run, I don't know where I was running, just running, and I started to hear gunshots, and I could . . . I could actually feel some things sort of whistling by me, and at that point I just stopped and put my hands up, and a couple of farmers came over and got a hold of me. As I recall there were two; I guess they were farmers. Not in uniform. Both of them had rifles. They walked me to the road . . . and they just kept me there.

Then after a short while there were other, presumably, farmers, who came marching up with others from our crew, so that we were sort of assembled on this little roadway right next to a fence, which I think enclosed the farm. When I had landed, well, being Jewish we had been told . . . we knew that the Germans were anti-Semitic. But we didn't know, I didn't know anything about the Holocaust or anything like that. If I did, I guess I would have been scared to death of what was going to happen. But I knew that they were anti-Semitic, actively committed. We had been told that our dog tags had an *H* on it, for Hebrew, so we had been told, being Jewish, if you're ever going to be captured in German territory to throw away your dog tags. And I did that as soon as I hit the ground and got out of the harness. I pulled off the dog tags and just hurled it.

While they were assembling the rest of the crew, another farmer came up holding the dog tags. By that time the police were looking at all dog tags, you know. And here I was the only one that didn't have a dog tag, and they started to say something about spy. Automatically if you are captured and you don't have dog tags it means you're not in the service, so technically they can arrest you as a spy. This fellow comes walking up with dog tags, and he said that he saw me throw it. When they looked and they saw the *H* on there, then one of the farmers started to say "*Jude! Jude!* [Jew! Jew!]," and he slapped me in the jaw pretty hard. . . . He clobbered me pretty good. But that was the only thing there. Then I had the dog tags. But even for a while after that they kept referring to me as a spy.

Dick Carroll experienced lynch justice in Hungary, a German ally from 1941 to 1945. Copilot on a B-24 Liberator heavy bomber, he bailed out over rural Hungary in July 1944 when engine failure brought down his plane. As he floated down in his parachute, he observed a crowd gathering.

The closer you get to earth, then the more you see the earth coming up to meet you much more quickly than you expected. From about four thousand feet on you see people coming out from the little farming villages, and this was on a Sunday morning, so many of them were dressed up in their Sunday best. But they all carried some sort of weapon with them. A shovel or rake. Some with guns. They weren't too far away.

Dick landed in a field and immediately faced the Hungarian civilians.

I rolled over on my shoulder, and fortunately there wasn't much of a breeze, so the parachute came down right next to me. So I gathered up the chute. . . . They weren't that far away from me, but there was no way to hide the chute or to run or whatever. You know that you have to accept whatever comes. You hope that it's not too severe. Sure, you're afraid. And you've just gone through a traumatic experience of bailing out of safe airplane that you were in, and here you are with an enemy, and how are they going to treat you? You have no way of knowing. And within a minute, I was shot.

They were coming in sort of a semicircle, actually, and walking toward me. There must have been thirty. When I was shot, the first thing is the shock of the bullet hitting you. . . . If you don't brace yourself immediately, it will literally knock you to the ground. But something that's even more obvious is, you're on fire, and you can't do a thing about it, because when you're shot through the torso, there's no way to cool it. Like if you're burnt on the hand, you can blow on it or put it in water, whatever. But when you're on fire deep within your chest, there's just nothing you can do about it.

Two men came up and held me by the elbows, because I was getting sort of wobbly, and then a farmer came in front of me. . . . He had a long-handled shovel and a lot of hate in his eyes, and he was screaming at me. And he walked around to my right, and I knew what was coming, but I couldn't do anything about it, because I was being held up. He hit me in the back of the head with his shovel.

You don't pass out immediately. You go through stages of seeing gray, getting darker and darker. When it gets towards the black, then you go unconscious, and I felt my knees turn to butter, and I was unconscious. But I remember distinctly that solid noise of the impact of the shovel hitting me on the back of the head. That may have only been a fraction of a second, but I can still recall that clearly, yes.

I was propped up against a farm tank that they watered the horses [from], out in the middle of their fields. I was gasping for air. I was obviously running a very high fever. My throat was so dry, and my heart actually was going extremely fast. [The bullet hit me in] the right lung. It went right through the lung. I asked for water, and nothing happened. Then I thought, well, somebody might speak German, so I said "*Wasser* [water]," and immediately one of the farmers took his cap off that he had worn in the fields a long time and put in into the [horse] tank. Horses drink the water—it's a big concrete tank. He brought this capful of water, and I put my head in it, and of course I didn't have much control. Somebody had grabbed the back of my head and held my head so I didn't drown. But that was the best drink of water I've ever had in my life. Bar none.

The likelihood of lynch justice increased for airmen shot down over Japan. On April 7, 1945, over the city of Nagoya, Bill Price's B-29 bomber was rammed by a Japanese aircraft. Bill, a waist gunner, and two others of the eleven-man crew managed to escape the crippled plane. Parachuting earthward, Bill had time to look around.

[W]hen I'm near the ground, I was drifting to the northeast part of the city and out in the country, and I noticed . . . a mob of people were coming after me. And they looked to be . . . I couldn't say how many, but I'd say a hundred and fifty, two hundred. Somewhere around there. Looked like the whole damn city at first. . . . They saw me coming, and they were coming after me. So when I hit the ground, I spilled my chute and I got out, and they were about three hundred yards or so away from me.

I was scared. I was scared like I've never been scared in my life. I hope I never have to go through something like that again, because . . . it was the most helpless feeling I've ever had in my life. I really didn't know what was going to happen. I thought I was going to be killed. Really. Seriously. I walked towards them with my hands up, and the first one to get to me was a civilian with a bamboo pole, and he hit me alongside the head with it and knocked me off my feet. Didn't knock me out; I more or less rolled with it. I started to get up, and I hear this yell, and here's this soldier making a bayonet charge to me. I jumped sideways, and he ran that, that bayonet went right through my flying suit, and it tore it from the bottom to the top. I was laying on the ground. . . . So at that time then they just, they beat me with everything they could get. Rifle butts, bamboo poles, kicking me. I ended up with a broken collarbone and three broken ribs, and they took everything I had. . . .

When they got through with my beating and so forth, they took and they tied a rope around my elbows and around the back, and they handcuffed me in front, and they blindfolded me. . . . We walked to a railroad station, and they set me on a bunker, and they roped off an area of about twenty yards in diameter, and inside that roped-off area they had . . . maybe four, five, six soldiers. The reason for that is, they kept the crowd from getting to me. Then for about an hour or an hour and a half or whatever it was, I don't remember, but it was a long, long time, the crowd just threw stones at me. [F]rom the ground. And I got cut up pretty bad there.

Bob Michelsen bailed out of his burning B-29 during the night of May 25–26, 1945, over Tokyo. He is convinced that Japanese soldiers saved him from a lynching at the hands of civilians after he parachuted to the ground. Yet even while in military custody, Bob endured vicious abuse from local inhabitants.

Right away my hands were tied beyond my back; immediately, blindfold and a rope around my neck. I was just hoping I'd stay alive. I don't know how far it was; it seemed to me like it was probably two hundred yards or so. But a gauntlet formed on each side. As I was dragged to wherever we were going, it was like an Indian gauntlet: people on each side, just hitting me, swinging whatever they had at me. There was no order to stop it, because it kept on for as long as we were moving. I couldn't understand them, but I could hear them. . . . I remember going to my knees a number of times, and how long I was on my knees I do not know.

I was conscious then, and I was tied to a post of some kind, and I surmised that it was close to a building because I could hear doors opening and closing. There was no light, but I could hear the door opening and closing. . . . Every time the door opened and closed, I'd get beaten a little bit. *(pauses three seconds)* I say "a little bit"—it was more than that. Thing I remember about daylight, looking down at the ground and I said, my God, I pissed in my pants. But as it grew lighter I said, geez, that's not urine, that's blood. And most of it came from my head. I did get a little shrapnel in my leg—I didn't even know it until later—but most of it came from my head.

But back to the night: it's dark, and you could hear airplanes flying over. Once in a while you could hear everybody cheer, because you knew an airplane got hit then. In the morning I heard a vehicle drive up, it sounded to me like a motorcycle, and I was placed in a trailer attached to the motorcycle, face up, on my back. My hands are still tied behind my back, and my legs are tied now, and I'm placed on my back in this vehicle. And a canvas put over the top of me. We begin to go somewhere, and about what I assumed was every block, I don't know how many feet, they would stop and give people the pleasure of beating on you. And then they'd start again and go a little while longer and stop, and you'd get beat again.

At one of the stops, while I was getting beat on, I could feel that another person was put into this same trailer and the canvas put back on top of us. Then the same: you go a ways, you stop, you get beat, and stop, get beat. During this process, I heard the grunts and the groans and everything, and they sounded familiar, and I knew it was the left gunner from our crew. So underneath this canvas he maneuvered and I maneuvered so that, although our hands were tied, we could still touch each other and hold hands. And I've thought about that a great deal. Holding hands—you know, the connotations of it are, are such, but I think that a person in fear of his life needs a friend, and I think that was it.

2

Prison Camps

THE CAPTURE MOMENT, as we have seen, brought with it a combination of anxiety, guilt, fear, and physical brutality. A permanent camp location offered a semblance of safety and security, especially in Germany. For many prisoners, between these two stages was a third: interrogation. This process took many forms.

For ground troops in Europe, the Germans often conducted any questioning on the spot; the hope was to obtain tactical information useful in an ongoing engagement. The Luftwaffe, on the other hand, had a central facility for captured airmen, known as Dulag Luft. All airmen were transported there from their capture location and remained for periods ranging from several days to several weeks, during which time the Germans questioned them and processed them for transport to a permanent camp.[1]

German Army and Air Force interrogators used a variety of methods in their attempts to get prisoners to provide information. Some of these methods were permitted under the Geneva Convention; other practices were questionable or even illegal. At Dulag Luft, methods included solitary confinement and minimal rations. A sympathetic interrogator often offered cigarettes and food in exchange for information. Rare, however, are confirmed cases of German interrogators in the field or at a central facility threatening or physically abusing prisoners. Still, such incidents did occur, almost exclusively with army troops, in the field and under the stress of combat situations.[2]

Interrogation took a radically different form for men captured in the Pacific. In the wake of the mass surrenders of early 1942, very few men recall any kind of questioning, even in the field. There were far too many prisoners for the Japanese to conduct organized questioning of all but a few officers. Survivors were just herded into camps.

For service personnel captured after mid-1942, though, there often was a formal interrogation process. The small numbers of prisoners made this feasible; need made it imperative: as Japan's position worsened, its leaders became desperate for any information. Multiple sessions sometimes stretched over weeks or even months. To this end, the navy had its own interrogation facility, at Ofuna near Yokohama, and the feared military secret police, the Kempeitai, ran interrogation centers in Japan and across occupied Asia. Interrogators at these facilities usually were trained English-speaking professionals in uniform. Many of these men had grown up and been educated in the United States.[3]

WITHIN GERMANY there existed a network of more than a hundred POW camps located throughout the country. Camps were administered by the respective service branches: thus, U.S. Army prisoners were held in camps run by the German Army, the *Wehrmacht*. *Stalags* were camps for enlisted men and noncommissioned officers, while *Oflags* held officers. Stalags and Oflags were identified by roman numerals, which corresponded to the nationwide system of military districts, called *Wehrkreise;* camps within a military district received a letter designation and the name of the nearest town—e.g., Stalag II-A Neubrandenburg.[4]

Air corps POWs, on the other hand, spent their time in the *Stalag Luft* camps, which were operated by the Luftwaffe; these were identified by roman numerals and often the nearest city or town (but not by the Wehrkreise system). After processing through Dulag Luft, prisoners were assigned to one of these permanent camps. There were seven camps for airmen; two of these, Luft IV Gross Tychow and XVII-B Krems, originally were reserved for noncommissioned officers.[5]

The Wehrmacht generally collected captured American ground troops into transit camps before moving groups of them to permanent camps. The Germans captured large numbers of men after mid-1944 but simultaneously were forced to close camps as the country gradually was overrun from east and then west: camps that remained became badly overcrowded. Living standards declined, and food often was in short supply.[6]

But conditions in German camps had never been easy. Personal space was virtually nonexistent, food was of poor quality and offered in barely adequate amounts, buildings had no insulation to keep out winter cold, and vermin—lice, fleas, and rats—plagued the men. These problems were exacerbated as the war dragged on and the Germans became less able, or less willing, to correct problems. Boredom was a serious challenge: often there was literally nothing to do in the camps. Some men created activities, while others realized the value of humor in maintaining a positive mental outlook. Not all were successful.[7]

The Geneva Convention allowed enlisted men to be delegated for work details, known as *Arbeitskommandos*. Prisoners on work details performed various types of manual labor, factory work, and repair jobs; other men toiled on farms. With regard to labor, the Geneva Convention stated, "work done by prisoners of war shall have no direct connection with the operations of the war," but away from the camps enforcement wasn't easy. German civilian overseers supervised the details: some POWs recall these men as brutal; others remember decent human beings with whom one could deal reasonably.[8]

IN JAPAN, unfettered by the 1929 Geneva Convention—which the nation had signed but never ratified—little if any attention was paid to the mass human suffering in prison camps. Rather, POWs represented a labor force to be brutally exploited. Prime Minister Tojo Hideki made this clear in a June 1942 directive to military leaders responsible for prison camp administration:

> [Y]ou must place the prisoners under strict discipline and not allow them to lie idle doing nothing but eating freely for even a single day. Their labor and technical skill should be fully utilized for the replenishment of production, and contribution rendered toward the prosecution of the Greater East Asiatic War.[9]

To this end, the Japanese organized work details. Prisoners were dispatched to sites around the Philippines, most on the main island of Luzon, to perform every imaginable kind of work: building roads and bridges, constructing airport runways, stevedoring—any task that required hard labor. Other POWs were sent to far corners of Japan's new Asian empire—to the Philippine islands of Palawan or Mindanao, to Formosa, to Burma, even to Manchuria. Locations changed; the treatment they received did not.[10]

The largest and most infamous labor detail was the Burma-Thailand Railway. As designed, the 258-mile line, knifing through dense jungle and across mountains and riverbeds, would complete an overland link between Bangkok and the Burmese port of Moulmein, allowing the Japanese to resupply their forces in occupied Burma by land and avoid the longer and submarine-infested sea route. The Japanese used more than 62,000 POWs, the vast majority from Britain and the Commonwealth, and 270,000 native conscripts to complete the railway. All work was done by hand, and conditions in the jungle camps were abysmal, even by Pacific standards. By October 1943, when the railway was completed, more than 12,000 prisoners had perished in the jungle; at least 73,000 native laborers were also dead.[11]

Interrogation

After surrendering in a pillbox and then being marched to the rear to another pillbox, Reuben Weber and the other men he was with faced interrogation by their German captors. Being an enlisted man had its benefits, he says.

They started taking us one by one into the pillbox, for interrogation purposes. It wasn't too bad. . . . I remember they asked how old I was. I thought, that can't be too big of a military secret, so I told them I was nineteen. He says, "You're too young to die." I said, "I agree." *(laughs)*

They realized, first of all I suppose, that I was a buck private, so I wouldn't be in the know of what the plans were. Of course it's intimidating, because you know it's the enemy asking the questions. But you don't know anything. It simplifies it. The blessing of being a buck private.

Vern Kruse was part of an army reconnaissance unit. He was on a mission on August 30, 1944, in eastern France when his jeep came under German fire and he was captured. The lone American prisoner at a German unit, Vern had an interesting encounter.

We finally got to where we were going, which was a German infantry outfit. They put me in a bus, or a big motor home. It belonged to the commanding officer of this particular German outfit that I was with now. He finally came in, and he says, "Hello." He could talk English. He introduced himself, and who was I, and I told him. He said, "You know what? I lived in the United States." He could talk as good English as you can. He had a snazzy uniform. We sat down, and he said, "You don't happen to have a White Owl cigar on you, do you?" And I said no. He missed those things, because he used to have those all the time in the States.... He went back to Germany, and he was called back into the service. He was just a very nice individual to talk to. It was not an interrogation. They knew as much about me as I knew about the war anyway. Probably more.

He had to leave for a bit, and he left me in there, but I walked around in there and went to the back of the bus. There was an open window there. Troops were outside. German infantry. They had a guitar, and they played American music for me. Music that I know. They were quite a jovial bunch of guys. They sang a couple of songs, and they talked to me in broken English. I could talk to these guys.

Bomber copilot Dale Peterson was at Dulag Luft after being shot down on a March 1944 mission over Germany.

We just put on a flat face and don't say anything. Name, rank, and serial number. . . . One time they didn't get any satisfaction, get the answer, so back to the cell. Then they're calling again and same questions. *(sighs)* But same thing.

Don Frederick was a second lieutenant with the army's Fourth Ranger Battalion. He was captured in Italy in November 1943. After some initial questioning at that location, Don was moved to Stalag III-A at Luckenwalde, an interrogation center for army officers. He arrived at night, alone.

It was cold, damp, windy, rainy. Two o'clock in the morning. I didn't know where I was going. They didn't tell me. I didn't know what to expect.

They threw me in a cell down there. If that thing was six foot by ten foot, that was probably it. They had one little stool in there or chair. And one little table. Very small table. They had a little window to the outside. Not very big. That was barred of course. . . . They had a little light up here in my cell, above me. It wasn't very bright. Just dim. That was on night and day.

I'm all alone. I got nothing to read. All I can do is look in that light bulb up there. The brick walls. I'm just wondering about the next move. What's going to happen now?

I was questioned the first time about two o'clock in the morning. They did it at inconvenient times. You couldn't sleep anyway. I mean, all you slept on was a bunch of straw. All full of lice.

A couple guards came down . . . and took me out. Led me down the hall into an interrogation room. [The interrogator,] his English was *very* good. Wanted to know if I wanted a cigarette, and I said no. Then he shook hands. . . . I said, "Captain, all I can tell you is my name, rank, and serial number." Boy, the old door opened, and the two guards hauled me back to my cell and threw me in there. *(finger snap)* That quick. You're out of there.

During a month at III-A Luckenwalde, Don faced several more interrogation sessions.

Dick Carroll spent nearly five months in a Budapest hospital, recovering from being shot by Hungarian civilians after he bailed out of his bomber. In December 1944, he was transferred to the Luftwaffe's Dulag Luft facility for interrogation.

We get inside of the building and this little old guard, he had a little old lantern, and he takes us down these steep steps, down into the basement, and locks us into pens. Six by eight basically. Built out of planks and a little place that's made for a bed. Just a few boards and some sort of mattress that was made out of burlap. Locked the door behind. No conversation. . . . I mean, it's real dark. There's no windows, no nothing. It's completely dark. You can see about three, four feet. And you have no idea who's next to you. And you don't want to start talking, because you're sure that there has to be a German somewhere waiting to hear what you have to say. . . . You don't talk, and at night you hear snores and coughing. But you have no idea, American or German. So it's dead quiet other than those other noises.

[I was there] four days and nights. Every morning after breakfast—which was a cup of ersatz coffee and one slice of German bread with a little bit of make-believe jelly spread on it, which is artificial taste—then about an hour later this German guard would come down again with his little lantern, unlock your door, take you upstairs. . . . They call it [an] interview, but it's clearly an interrogation. . . . Two officers that spoke very good English. One claimed to have lived in New York City for some years before the war. Pack of Lucky Strike cigarettes on the table. "Have a cigarette?" "No, thank you." . . . Obviously they're trying to get you into a talking mood.

[I was interrogated] once every day. Four times [in all]. . . . [I was] never physically [abused], but they explained that it's a shame that you have to go back down to that terrible cell downstairs and that all you have to do is talk and we can give you good food, American cigarettes, and you can live a much better life. Gentle persuasion.

Bomber copilot Frank Linc remembers his Luftwaffe interrogation as a choreographed event, one he had heard about before being shot down. He was at Dulag Luft in May 1944.

We were interrogated separately. They took me to this office, and the captain, German captain, was there. Very polite. He asked me to sit down, and we talked for a bit. He started asking questions about the B-17, about the bomb site, and this sort of thing, and I said my name, rank, and serial number. He asked a few more questions. I'm doing the same thing, and then he got mad, and he was pounding the desk and everything. . . . It got to the point where he said, "I don't need information from you, because I know everything about you anyway."

Of course, this was just for show. I knew the procedure. Our intelligence people told us about everything that would happen . . . the pattern of our interview. They had that all down pat. That they were going to get mad, and then they'll start telling you that they know everything about you anyway. So I said, "Well, if you do, prove it." So he said, "You were born in North St. Paul [Minnesota]. You went to North St. Paul High

School, and you graduated on such and such a date." All of this information. "And you took training, flight training, and you started on such and such a day. Graduated on such and such a date. Went overseas."

By golly, he knew everything. He knew more about me than I knew myself. *(laughing)* Kind of funny, because I already knew he would say this, because of our people telling us just exactly what would happen.... So I give our forces credit for having all this information for us. It made it much easier.

Fighter pilot Bill Schleppegrell spent time at Dulag Luft in January 1945 after bailing out near the French-German border.

I don't remember how long I was there. Not too long. I was in a cell where I couldn't even stand up. It was a short ceiling. I don't think [there was] a place to sit, either. I think I had to crouch. They were kind of like cages. . . .

Anyway, then they brought me into [an] office. Really fancy office.... In fact, I remember there was a woman in there, too. It must have been a girlfriend or whatever. In civilian clothes, the girl was. I told them I could only give my name, rank, and serial number, and he said, "We'll let you think about that for a while." So then they took and put me into a cell. Solitary. I was there for eight or nine days.

It was really . . . it was just a nightmare. There was a radiator in the room that came on in the morning for a little while. If I sat on it, it was warm, but then it didn't last long. At night it came on for a little while. There was one window that was painted. I could hear a clock *(sings the clock chimes)*. I knew pretty much what time it was, and I could tell when it was light and dark. There was a cot there. You had one army blanket. That was it.

And there were discouraging things on the wall. I could see that there were marks where they evidently had marked days that they were there. I didn't know if that was ever for real. But there were like twenty-some days.

After bailing out over the Adriatic in April 1944 and being plucked from the water by a German seaplane, Dick Pfaffinger and the crew of his bomber were taken to Italy; they were held briefly in Venice, then moved to Verona.

Crew members were interrogated, one at a time. After an initial questioning, Dick was moved to an individual cell, several stories down.

The room I was in was about six by six foot, with a fifteen-foot-high ceiling. Just me. I never saw or heard another guy. You didn't know if they were all gone or what happened. That's what made it tough. But it was cold in there. All I had in there was a little round stool. Then it was so damp down there I got cold. . . . I just would shake. The only thing I got was bread and water, but I was so *cold* down there. I used to shake all the time. Then they'd bring me up for interrogation probably about every eight hours. I loved that because I could get where it was a little warm.

[They interrogated me] I'd say probably about eight, nine times. They used many threats. I had no way of knowing whether the threats would be real or not. . . . The first lieutenant would ask the question and do any rough stuff or hit me alongside the head and stuff . . . usually slapped me across the head. Face. And a couple times my ear. . . . And the captain would say, "Take it easy. This guy's been through hell," and try to get on your good side. He'd tell the first lieutenant to just lay off: "This guy's had a tough go."

I was apprehensive because I didn't think there was any way in hell of getting out of there, and so I didn't think they'd let us go. Particularly when the German was questioning me and he really pounded on me. That either I fill out my answers [on the sheet of questions they gave me] or . . . "The rest of the crew has all filled out their questions and answers and stuff. You're the only one that hasn't. If you want to fill them out, you'll go along with the rest of the crew, and if you don't, you're going to stay down there until you rot. Now what do you want to do?"

Few men faced formal interrogation in the Pacific. Several who did have clear memories of what treatment they endured from the Japanese. Ted Pflueger was an officer in the army's 803rd Engineers; he was captured at Bataan.

I was singled out and told to go over to this area where they were questioning people. They had a Japanese there who spoke English. They wanted to know where the tunnel to Corregidor was. Well, there was no tunnel from Bataan to Corregidor. [But] they thought there was.

They wanted to know, and I wasn't giving them the right answers, so they started to give me the water cure. They inserted a hose into my nose, with water under pressure, . . . and started squirting the water. I took a big, deep breath and passed out.

I came to, and they did that to me twice. They pumped me out and started questioning me again. The third time they did it to me, they didn't pump me out. They dumped me out in the back of the tent there, with other bodies.

I woke up during the night. There were about ten or fifteen bodies there, in a pile. They thought I was dead, and they didn't see me crawl away from the pile. [I] moved over to where some of the soldiers were being lined up to march down the road, and I got into one of those groups and marched down the road with them.

Floyd Caverly survived the sinking in October 1944 of the submarine USS Tang. *He spent the night swimming in the China Sea before being plucked out of the water by the crew of a Japanese destroyer. The nine* Tang *survivors all ended up on this ship.*

They had a couple of officers on there that could speak fair English. They were officers, young men that had been taught English in school. They wanted to know all *kinds* of things. How many ships were in the area? How many submarines were attacking there? How many men do you have in your navy? A lot of things that we just absolutely didn't know. I couldn't tell you how many men were in my navy. I couldn't even tell you how many we had in the submarine force. I never kept track of that stuff. I had other things to worry about.

[We were physically mistreated] to some extent. . . . I know I was rapped over the head with a sword scabbard. Officer standing there with his sword and scabbard in his hand. He thought I was lying. What I was doing, I was supposed to have been making some schematic diagrams of my radios and my radar and all of this stuff. Which, God, I couldn't have done to save me! Oh, he wanted, he just wanted a *wealth* of information. When he saw how I had that drawn, he hauled off and banged me alongside the head. Of course, I've got my hands behind my back, tied to my feet, and I'm on my knees, and he hit me and knocked me over.

After a brief stop on Formosa, the Tang *crewmen were transported to Japan.*

Floyd was sent to the naval interrogation facility, Camp Ofuna, where more regimented questioning took place, with trained interrogators.

[There was] an interrogation room. It had a long table in there and some benches. They would take us up and at one end of these tables would sit an officer or two officers, interrogation officers, and then you were set down on the bench by them.

Then the interrogation people would say "Good afternoon" or "Good morning" or whatever it happened to be, and they would speak English. They'd say, "How are you today?" Anyhow, then they would say, "Let us review what you told us about the sonar." When I went up there they were after . . . primarily the electronic equipment, our radios and our sonar. Things of this sort. . . . They had captured some of our instruction books and books on sonar, and they would lay those books out, and they'd say, "Do you recognize this book?" "Oh, yes. I recognize the book." You never told them that you didn't know anything. I always told them how smart I was. That I knew all these things. . . . I got rapped a few times for not knowing what I should have known and for telling them a lie. They'd catch me at it. But I was never worked over that bad.

Bob Michelsen was nearly lynched by civilians after being shot down over Tokyo on the night of May 25–26, 1945. Saved from probable death by Japanese police, he was taken to an interrogation center.

We were taken to a building somewhere in Tokyo. We were brought into a room in that building, and there was quite a few people there; we weren't the only crew there. American aircrews.

We were forced to kneel on the floor, your knees bent underneath you and your back perfectly straight and your head bowed. If you moved your head, or slumped, or swayed from side to side, or did anything, you were beaten immediately. Still blindfolded, but you could see down underneath them, and you could sometimes see through the blindfold. Not see clearly, but you could see shadows. So it must have been sometime early morning, [but] who knows what time it was. We were in that room for the rest of the day, I believe, because the sun had set.

I had no control over [the situation]; I just refused to think about it. If I started guessing what was going to happen, I would be worse off. You accept [what] was happening then. I think I did occasionally think about my home and family and mother once or twice, I'm sure I did, but the physical discomfort was such that it was the only thing that mattered.

I didn't think at all. No, the pain in my back was so bad—sitting in that fashion for me was very difficult, because in the middle of the afternoon, I don't know how early or late, you accepted the beatings in order to bend your back and to get some relief from that pressure.

After some hours, Bob remembers being taken for questioning.

It was around sunset, or later, when I was taken in for the first interrogation. . . . You were taken by two guards, as I recall two, into a room that was dimly lit, and again on your knees, blindfolded, and hands behind you. My impression was that somebody was sitting at a table, opposite me. But before the questions, you had the accept the next beating.

The questions started, and the first was, of course, "What is your name, rank, and serial number?" I told them right away, and then the next question started. I don't recall what it was about, you know, where are you from, Guam, Saipan, wherever. And I gave them my name, rank, and serial number once more. At that, then the beatings started, and I don't know when they ended. But it was still dark when I woke up. . . .

After Bob was taken to a permanent cell location, the interrogations continued.

I was interrogated five more times, with a couple of days between maybe.... You were taken out of the cell, your hands were tied in front of you, and a rope [tied] around your hands so they could pull you by your hands, and a blindfold on. We went from the cell—we were in the number one cell, so we were next to the door—so you could tell when you go from the building into the sunlight because the light would change. Then into another building, up about half a flight of stairs, as I recall, and then of course into this same room where you were before.

There were two interrogators: one was Shorty [civilian Yasuo Kobayashi, the main Japanese interrogator], and the other we called Junior [warrant officer Kennichi Yanagizawa]. Junior was, we figured he was learning his trade, and he was not as tough as Shorty. Shorty was a lot different. When it was Junior, things were okay; with Shorty, not.[12]

Shorty, I believe *(pauses three seconds)*, was a sadist, because he, he just... everything he did was to injure and to hurt. If you were wounded and you were in his interrogating room, that is where they'd put the pressure, on your wounds. And sometimes they were very painful. We had one prisoner—his name was Bob Ring—who was injured from his hip to his knee, a really deep, deep wound. And Bob told us, instead of beating on him, they would just put their sticks inside the wound and twist and twist and twist.

Shorty would walk down the hall in front of [our cell] and tell us that the courts had decided that you are a murderer and that within the next few days, the next week, you will be . . . you're dead. You will be killed. He always carried his sword, and he'd stick his sword in the cell. And if you sat, the closer to the bars you sat, the more you got stuck.

Germany: Stalags, Oflags, and Luft Stalags

Captured in early January 1945 in eastern France, Harold Brick was one of thousands processed through Stalag IX-B Bad Orb. By the time Harold arrived, this camp for enlisted men was badly overcrowded.

Bad Orb . . . I mean, that was a godforsaken place. The building that I was in was about the size of a basketball court. . . . [There were about,] oh, two hundred and fifty [men there]. They were laying side by side. I mean, that was without blankets. The only thing we had to cover us was our overcoat. That was our shelter.

[The building] had a real high ceiling, broken windows on the side, a concrete floor, and straw on there with paths through there. . . . I was able to get a spot by the wall, which was good, because the very first night there those who had ate some of that soup [we got when we arrived], it didn't agree with their stomachs, and they had to go to the bathroom. And the bathroom was on the one end of the building, right beside the entrance. It was a one-hole toilet. After we were in that building, they turned the lights out, and it was dark. And when you're in a new place . . . you get very disoriented. Being by the wall, there weren't quite as many people falling over me as those that were more in the center.

Hewitt "Lex" Schoonover ended up at Bad Orb after his capture in Belgium in December 1944. But instead of being processed through, Lex remained until the camp was liberated by American forces in the last days of March 1945.

[I was there from] Christmas to Easter. One hundred and eight days. I weighed ninety-eight pounds when I got out.

Edwin Luoma (left) with his brothers at the family home in Eveleth, Minnesota, 1942 or 1943. A mail clerk with the army's 106th Infantry Division, Edwin was swept up with thousands of others during the Battle of the Bulge. Then came hard time at IX-B Bad Orb.

It was just horrible, I'll tell you. . . . There were quite a few men that were sick. Dysentery was prevalent. And just plain weakness, from lack of food.

Some of his strongest memories are of the squalor and the incessant lice.

We had to sleep two in a bunk to keep warm—the body heat—because they only gave us a half a blanket. There were no lights in the barracks. We got one or two logs a day to put in a potbelly stove, the only heat.

The toilet facilities during the daytime was a slit trench, a big trench outside with tree limbs that you used like a seat that you could lean against. At night it was a hole in the floor. Nobody could hit it. . . .

The mattresses were burlap bags with excelsior in, and bugs. We never had our clothes off, the whole time. We were lousy all the time. Crawling on you. It's horrible. It's horrible. It was all welts, and it itched. You scratch. You dig yourself raw. They bite. You keep scratching. And they keep breeding in the seams of your pants and in your shirt. There's really no way . . . we had long johns on, you know. It was winter.

When the weather warmed up, they let us go out in the [camp] enclosure. That was not until the end of March. We had a warm day, and then we went out and peeled down as much as we could and picked the bugs out of our clothes. The best thing was when after we were liberated they brought in some powder that killed them, and you'd dump it down your shirt, and you'd feel them come up and drop dead. *(chuckles)* That was a wonderful feeling.

LeRoy Shaw was a gunner on a medium bomber. Wounded when his plane was shot down in May 1944 over France, he spent some months in hospitals before landing at Stalag Luft IV. The camp itself was intimidating.

You can't believe what you're walking into. The fence around the outside of this place was, I'm going to say, fifteen, twenty foot tall. There were guard towers with machine guns on all the corners.

The barracks were built three foot off the ground. At night they turned a flock of dogs loose, and the dogs roamed underneath all night. During the day these same dogs . . . between the compounds there was an area that was about, maybe ten foot wide. Two dogs walked that continually, all the way around.

It was . . . you knew you were there until the end.

Air corps gunner Lee Bedsted, whose plane was shot down in July 1944, was another prisoner at Stalag Luft IV. Roll calls, he remembers, were a constant occurrence.

They would come into the compound, and they would have a German sergeant who would holler something into the barracks, and everybody knew that we had to get out and stand roll call. [We would] just stand in a column. We were probably three deep and then . . . three long columns. Then the German counted us. Then he would go and report to another noncom, and that noncom would make a total, and then if the camp commandant accepted that, then we were dismissed to go back into our barracks, or if we wanted to we could go exercise. Walk around the compound.

Captured in September 1944 in eastern France, army medic Sam Alle was a prisoner at Stalag III-C, near the small German town of Küstrin, on the Oder River, by mid-October. He remembers the housing.

[The barracks] looked like a bunch of chicken houses. If you would have taken a board off to build a tunnel, you would have frozen to death because there was just one board on the outside [wall]. . . .

There was thirty-three of us in that one room. These barracks were long; they had three rooms in each one of them. They had ten of these buildings, and they had three rooms in each one. And there was thirty-three in our room. It was overcrowded, but we made out. I mean, we slept together. Doubled up, to keep warm.

We didn't have bunks. We were on the floor. They had a bunk, and people slept on there, and there were people that slept underneath them. Me and my buddy, we slept on the floor, underneath the bunks. And there was just as many down there as there was above, I think.

Les Schrenk was ball turret gunner on a heavy bomber. His plane was shot down over German-occupied Denmark in February 1944. After a brief stop at the Dulag Luft interrogation facility, he was transported to Luft VI Heydekrug. Crowded barracks rooms had coarse wooden bunks stacked three high.

The mattress was just a great big burlap bag, almost like a gunnysack. Real coarse woven. It had about an inch or two of wood shavings in it. That wasn't the bad part—the bad part was the *bed*. It had a wooden frame and had four slats six inches wide: one for your feet, one for your hips, one for your shoulder, one for your head. It was the most uncomfortable thing you could imagine. If you were unfortunate enough [that you] didn't have the top bunk but either the second or the bottom bunk, every time the guy upstairs rolled a little, chaff would fall, filter down on you. And we had no pillow at all. One blanket. You were cold.

For sanitation [at night], all you had is a bucket in one corner of the room. It was way too small. About halfway through the night, it was already overflowing. The whole corner [of the room] was just reeking with urine.

The latrine was a long, long ways from the barracks, and all it was, really, was just a great big outhouse with a pump in it. It didn't have flushing toilets, anything like that. To get water, your buddy would have to pump water. It was cold. . . . Two different times we were allowed to take a shower. But if you can imagine taking a shower in the middle of the winter with cold water in an unheated building. But it felt good, just to have some water.

Bruce Brummond spent time in several camps after his capture in December 1944. While conditions differed by camp, there was at least one constant: vermin. They invaded clothes, bedding, and bodies.

I don't know where we picked it up, but everybody had body lice. Especially in your hair. . . . You're itchy, and of course the Germans did what they called delousing, too. They'd have a pipe they'd stick up your pants leg and shoot some powder in there and down the back of your neck and the front of you. Whether that did any good or not, I don't know. But of course you couldn't get them out of your hair. Nobody had a comb. There wasn't any water to wash your hair in.

Once in a while you feel something crawling. *(chuckles)* More pronounced at night, because you're quiet. During the day you're more or less active. This was something you had to live with, to put up with. There was no way of changing it. I'm sure if you caught a disease from it, it would be serious, but fortunately I didn't.

Les Schrenk, who spent time in several locations after his February 1944 capture, casually analyzes the differences among various vermin.

For anybody that hasn't ever had fleas, they can be absolutely miserable. You can't get a full night's sleep. All during the day and especially at night you can feel them crawling on your body. They've got real strong back legs where they kick trying to get through different crevasses of your body, and they drive you just literally *nuts*. If you go to look for a flea, about all you get is just a real quick glimpse of it. They hop.

The lice were of the more disgusting type. They were body lice, and they would affix to any hair, like under your arms or your private parts, and you would feel like a lump. When you looked, here would be a louse that had attached himself and [was] sucking blood. They would be about the size of a good-size pea and gray and very, very disgusting. When you'd squash them, you'd have a pile of blood.

We also had a few bedbugs. Bedbugs didn't pose that much of a problem. If you have a bedbug, you'll notice them, but you don't feel them crawling over your body, and they don't seem to fill themselves with blood like a louse does.

Paratrooper Ed Haider was captured in July 1943, on Sicily. In October, he was sent on a work detail to a farm in northern Germany. The building used to house the men already was occupied when they arrived—by rodents.

There were twenty-four of us. We marched. I don't know how many miles, maybe eighteen to twenty miles, to go to this Schulenberg Farm. When we arrived there, we went in this big concrete building. It formerly had been a pigsty. All that was inside was two shelves, like, along the walls. We were ushered in there. There was a little tiny stove, just a small wood stove. A table and a couple of benches. They had just put those in there prior to our moving in there.

We didn't have to work the first day. We were given one blanket for two men, and you laid on these boards. That first night we went to bed kind of exhausted. As we laid there, all of a sudden we could feel . . . and I said to this fellow next to me, I said, "Do you feel something?" He said, "Yes," and about that time somebody shouted, "Rats!" And they were crawling all over us. Numerous rats. We'd take the blanket and shake them, and you could hear them hit the floor and scurrying around.

Well, for about five nights it was battling with the rats. We laid there in the dark, and somebody would say, "Now!" And they pulled the cord for our light, and we'd shake those blankets, throw shoes, pieces of wood, anything you could throw at the rats.

We didn't sleep very much. Oh, God! You just shuddered to think that you had to sleep with the rats crawling over you.

Men who were wounded endured a longer, more difficult journey from capture site to permanent camp. Ground troops and airmen with injuries, some serious, spent varying amounts of time in German military hospitals. Dick Lewis suffered a flak wound through his knee when his bomber was shot down over Germany in November 1944. Captured in a vineyard after parachuting to the ground, he was taken to a large building nearby.

It must have been a warehouse of some sort. . . . I laid down, and I was beginning to see spots in front of my eyes. I'd lost so much blood. I probably slept or passed out or something. I guess I was there until they finally came and hauled me off to this hospital. I don't remember if I slept or passed out or what.

I wasn't sure about the passage of time, although I know it was getting to be night, because when I went to that hospital it was nighttime, and it was nighttime when they operated on me.

I remember . . . being on the operating table and these people around me. One nurse, I was trying to motion to her. Nobody could speak English, and I couldn't speak German, and I wanted to know, are they going to cut off my leg or what are they going to do? By hand motions. She convinced me that no, they weren't going to take my leg; they were just going to operate on the wounds on that leg. . . . After they operated, I came to and had a great big cast around my leg. All the way around my waist.

From there Dick was sent to German military hospital facilities, first at Meiningen and then at Obermassfeld. Many men around him were in tough shape.

A lot of infantrymen were brought into this hospital. They had been . . . the Germans had picked them up in the winter, and they had been on boxcars, so they came in and were in very poor shape. In fact, one of the fellows, the flesh had dropped off his foot and the bones were just sticking out, so we knew he was going to have [an] amputation. A lot of these guys, their feet were black. I felt surely they were going to lose their feet. They were frozen. The Germans were taking care of them as well.

I remember one hospital, they had a whole ward of these airmen who had been burned. That's terrible. They smell. Burned flesh smells so bad. And they had a whole ward of these guys that had been badly burned.

Even with a leg cast and able to get around only with difficulty, Dick recalls positive aspects of this period.

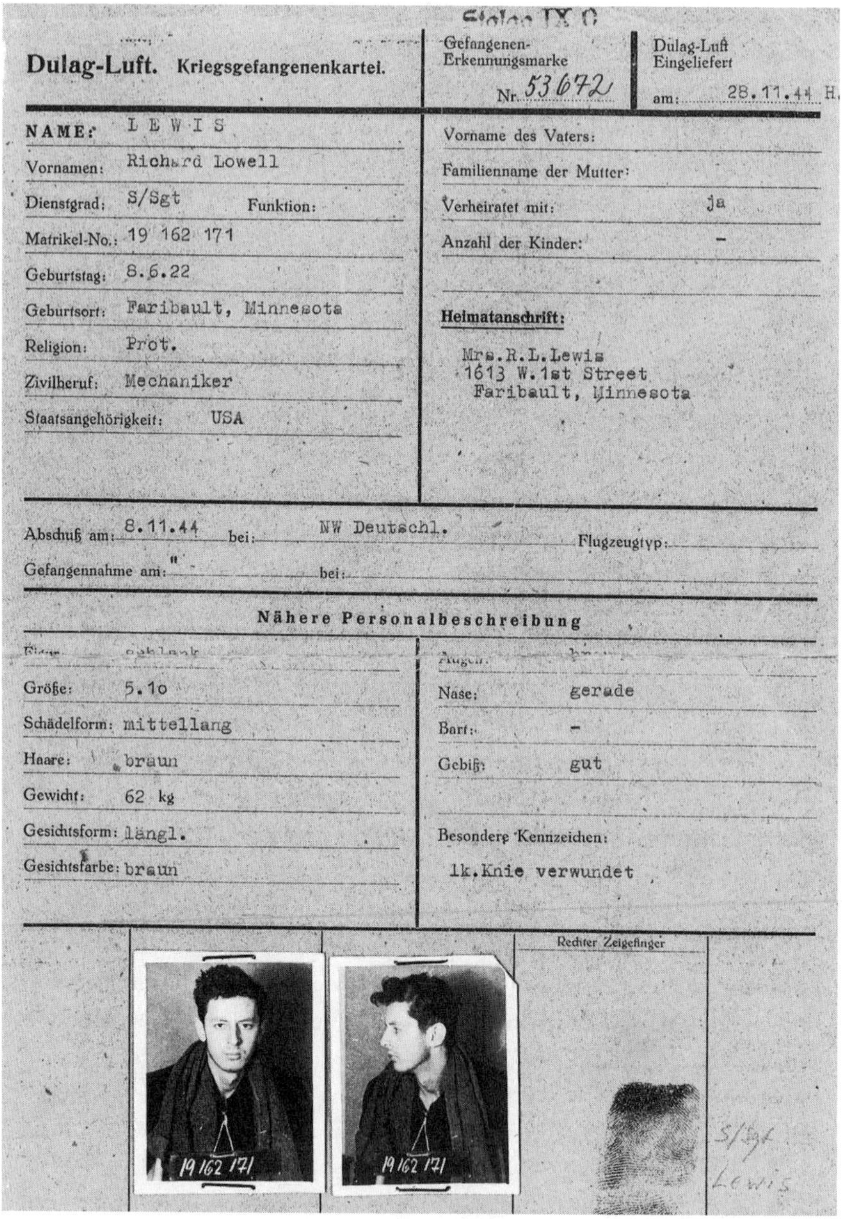

Stalag IX C

Dulag-Luft. Kriegsgefangenenkartei.

Gefangenen-Erkennungsmarke Nr. 53672

Dulag-Luft Eingeliefert am: 28.11.44 H.

NAME: L E W I S

Vornamen: Richard Lowell

Dienstgrad: S/Sgt Funktion:

Matrikel-No.: 19 162 171

Geburtstag: 8.6.22

Geburtsort: Faribault, Minnesota

Religion: Prot.

Zivilberuf: Mechaniker

Staatsangehörigkeit: USA

Vorname des Vaters:

Familienname der Mutter:

Verheiratet mit: ja

Anzahl der Kinder: –

Heimatanschrift:

Mrs.R.L.Lewis
1613 W.1st Street
Faribault, Minnesota

Abschuß am: 8.11.44 bei: NW Deutschl. Flugzeugtyp:

Gefangennahme am: " bei:

Nähere Personalbeschreibung

Figur: schlank

Größe: 5.10

Schädelform: mittellang

Haare: braun

Gewicht: 62 kg

Gesichtsform: längl.

Gesichtsfarbe: braun

Augen: braun

Nase: gerade

Bart: –

Gebiß: gut

Besondere Kennzeichen: lk.Knie verwundet

19 162 171

19 162 171

Rechter Zeigefinger

S/Sgt Lewis

At Dulag Luft, the central Luftwaffe interrogation center for captured Allied airmen, each man acquired a salmon-colored permanent record card—with photo, fingerprint, physical description, family information, and other data—which accompanied him to all future camps. This record belongs to Richard (Dick) Lewis of Faribault, Minnesota, who arrived at Dulag Luft on November 28, 1944.

In all the hospitals, wherever I was, I always had good treatment. Couldn't complain about it at all. No one abused me. They fed me well, or as well as they could with what they had.

I don't remember ever being bored. I kept this diary. I was doing spool knitting. I tried writing poetry. I worked in the library. I did some bookbinding. I was able to make my own book. So I was able to keep busy.

I was *most* fortunate. I was very, very fortunate, when I look back on the whole thing. *(with emphasis)* . . . *Always* [guys] worse off than myself.

A company aid man with the 80th Infantry Division, Sam Alle was taken prisoner in eastern France in September 1944. During the firefight, he took a piece of shrapnel in the shoulder. Sam's German captors evacuated him to a civilian hospital in the nearby city of Saarbrücken.

This nun came up to me, she took one look at me, and she said, *"Kaputt,"* meaning that it wasn't worth feeding me, I guess. Then I blacked out again, and I came to, and there was a little lady standing there. She came in, and she had a bottle of broth, and she . . . gave it to me. She didn't say anything. I don't know what it was, but it tasted good when you hadn't eaten for two days. Then I went back to sleep.

Four days after arriving, Sam was on the move again.

The Germans said that they had to move us because the Americans had bombed the maternity wing of the hospital and the population was upset. So they thought they better get us out of there. So they put me with another four guys in a boxcar. There was a lot more [guys], but they weren't anyone I knew. Then they put us in the boxcar, and they put the Germans in the bottom [of the car] and the Americans on top. So if they strafed they'd hit us, not the Germans.

I came to again in this hospital at [Stalag XII-A] Limburg. . . . This prison camp at Limburg was kind of a . . . everybody went there. Then they separated the prisoners. They had an officer's section there, air corps section. [There was a] hospital ward. . . .

There was an American doctor in there, Dr. Johnson. He said, "There isn't much we can do. We don't have the equipment to do anything." So he fed me a couple aspirins every day. Then after about ten days, I was able to go to the bathroom by myself. [I walked like this,] at an angle, you know, [favoring the injured shoulder]. He made me carry a bucket of water from one end of the building to the other. Draw water out of one and bring it to the other. I finally straightened out. You get used to pain after a while, too.

Prisoners in all camps fought boredom and tried to buoy their spirits. Each man had his own way of dealing with the overabundance of time. Taken prisoner in France in July 1944, Arnold Sprong was sent to IV-B Mühlberg. He recalls how time in camp affected him personally.

That was one of the problems—nothing to do. Literally *nothing* to do. And of course it gave you too much time to think, which was very bad at

Prisoners found creative ways to prepare food, such as cobbling together small cookstoves from odd bits of material. Vern Kruse, a prisoner at XII-A Limburg and III-C Küstrin, explains how.

Whatever we needed, we could get parts from a food parcel to build this cookstove. Two tin can covers fastened together for pulleys. Also, shoelaces were used for belts. The only thing we needed was a wood board, for the bottom. The barracks, that's a handy place to get the wood. We could go underneath the buildings and cut off a floor support—it was six inches by sixteen inches—and use that for a base. Then we'd mount the blower on that base. Easy.

that particular time. . . . Whether you were going to make it out. Whether you were going to get well. It was a psychological thing.

We felt *safe* in the camp. But the main thing was you constantly thought of food and your family back home and whether you would make it out or not. . . . You really wanted *some* activity of *some* kind.

Captured in December 1944, Floyd Dahl spent four months as a POW, all of them at IV-B Mühlberg. Finding diversions was key.

[Was boredom an issue?] Oh, yes. *(with emphasis)* Yes, yes, yes. You could sit and think and think and think. Nothing to do but go lay down on the cot, maybe all day or half a day and then try to sleep at night. Wonder what's happening at home. What's happening out in the field.

There were some books to read. You read everything that was in there. Talk, talk, talk, talk. Preparing menus. Once in a while a guy would come around after the soup at night, and they would discuss what they had done in civilian life and experiences that they had. So you learned a little bit. One of them had been a chef at one of the famous hotels in London. . . . He said, "Okay, everybody get your pencils and paper out now. I'm going to give you a recipe for making chocolate cake that you can make right here in camp. It's delicious." So he started out, you take your loaf of bread or your parcel of bread and you crumble it up. Then you take so much sugar out of your Red Cross parcels. By the time he got done, he had you using flour and eggs and sugar and stuff we hadn't seen for six months. That's how you made your chocolate cake. *(chuckles)* It was a diversion.

Another diversion they had one time . . . I thought they had a bunch of girls come into camp, and they put a play on. The camp commander was there. Everybody was hooting and hollering and whistling. They were American or English prisoners. Dressed as . . . *(laughs)* . . . dressed in drag. But it took a long time to realize. I'd never seen anything like that before. I wondered, where did these girls come from? Then it turned out they were all prisoners. *(laughs)*

Shot down in May 1944 over France, LeRoy Shaw spent much of the next twelve months at Luft IV and Luft I.

We'd come roaring back into the room after the morning roll call, and we'd go sit down. We had one little kitchen table, and four of us at a time would play bridge. As you tired of playing bridge, somebody else sat in your chair. It just rotated around in a loop.

Boredom was an issue, because there was nothing to do. It would have been nice to *have* something to do. They could have had us doing anything they wanted us to. But they didn't. . . . Well, once a day somebody of the eighteen guys in the room would go and get this pan of grub that they were given. Usually a lot of potatoes. [The Germans] must have had a lot of potatoes.

We did a lot of walking. They had like a walkway right around [the perimeter of the compound], and we'd talk to the other compound. We'd walk side by each with the guys in the other compound. Just keep walking around. Once in a while a guard would say, "Hey, bust it up down there." Walking around. Nobody was going anyplace. Just walking around.

Bomber copilot Frank Linc recalled several humorous episodes from his time at Stalag Luft III and XIII-D Nuremberg. For him, it was all about keeping a positive outlook.

Although life as a POW was harsh, we kept our spirits up by planning our future, making cooking utensils out of tin cans, walking, being buddies. I recall one time when we heard that more new POWs were to be added to our barracks, . . . I caught a large fly, tied a fine thread from my coat to its leg, and let it circle above my head like on a leash. As the new POWs entered our room, one of the men asked what I was doing. I replied that I was taking my fly for a walk. This guy looked around and asked, "How long has he been here?"

That evening, when we sat down for our barley soup, which had some worms that almost looked like barley, I placed about four worms from my soup beside my plate. One fellow asked me what I was doing, and I replied that I was saving the meat for later. "What kind of meat is it?" he asked. "Just worms," I replied. He wouldn't eat soup for two days, and as a result I had double rations. On the third day, he was hungry and ate the soup. *(laughing)*

Boredom could be punctuated by difficult, unwelcome moments, however. In the first months of 1945, bomber crewman Dick Brownlee was at XIII-D

To pass time, recalls bomber copilot Frank Linc, "everybody had their own thing to do." He filled his days at Luft III by creating detailed drawings of various subjects. Here, a view of his barracks in late 1944.

Nuremberg. The camp's proximity to the city brought potential danger when Allied planes bombed the urban area.

The most difficult thing was, we were right near Nuremberg, and the [U.S.] Eighth Air Force and the British would come over and bomb the town every once in a while. The British would drop these—at night they would come over and drop these huge bombs, and you could hear the explosion and see the—you could look out the window and see some of the flash. Then you'd hold onto the awning—the windows were closed anyway—and you'd, all of a sudden you'd feel the air jolt come in from that blast. From quite a distance away.

You know, when the Brits would come over at night, some people would get up and they'd move around. I guess the philosophy that some of us took, I took anyway, is if you're going to get it . . . *(trails off)*. So I never bothered to get out of the bed and tromp around like that.

The thing was, even though we knew—we kept saying—they [the Allies] *know* we're here [in this camp]. They're not going to . . . *(trails off)*. But the nervousness. . . . You'd find your hands quivering, like this. *(holds hand out flat, shakes slightly)* You'd try to stop the doggone thing, and it had nothing to do with, I don't know, with fear. *(pauses three seconds)* Oh, I suppose maybe.

The Geneva Convention articles permitted the Germans to assign enlisted prisoners to Arbeitskommandos, *or work details. Some POWs volunteered for this duty in the hopes of securing better conditions and more food. Men performed all varieties of work; some found these experiences to be an improvement on camp life. Enlisted man Arnold Sprong was a POW for nine months, most of it spent on a work detail in the small town of Adorf, in south-central Germany near the Czech border.*

The camp was in a U shape. On the one side of the U, the one leg of the U, were the two railroad gangs. These guys went out and repaired rail where our bombers had tore them up. The other side was the two factory gangs, one of which I was in, which went to work in town in a textile factory. Supposedly nonmilitary-involved textile factory.

The first thing they had us doing [though], they had gondolas of coal cars. The *Hofmeister,* the yardmaster, [was] a fellow that looked like a bulldog. He kind of picked on me because I was rather obstinate. He kept telling me I was not a good coal shoveler, and I didn't *want* to be a coal shoveler. *(chuckles)* So he would take me off to the side and take the shovel, and he would shovel a few scoops of coal and tell me, "This is how you're supposed to do it," and I'd go back to the old way that I was doing it, which wasn't very good, and he would just shake his head and walk away. He didn't . . . some of the other fellows worked a little bit harder, I guess.

Since I was not a good coal shoveler, the *Hofmeister* got rid of me. He sent me to the inside of the plant, which was fine with me. . . . [This] was a much easier job, and, not only that, this is winter in the lower mountains of Saxony, and it's cold. There was a spot inside where I could go and sit down next to a boiler of hot air. It was just . . . that's all the room was, a boiler and a wall on each side. I could go in there and sit and warm up a little bit.

In early 1945, Herb Kohnke was suffering in overcrowded conditions at XIII-C Hammelburg. One evening, the Germans announced an opportunity to get on a farm work detail. Herb found it was a good deal.

We were suspicious. But anything is better than nothing. And we had nothing.

[They said] we'd get something to eat every day. And we would have a building where it's warm, and we would have a bed. . . . Some of the fellows were skeptical. They were kind of reluctant in the beginning, but we tried to convince them that *anything* is better that what we've got. We don't have anything here. . . . The next morning we took a vote, and they all said okay, it sounds reasonable. Let's go.

The group was taken by train to Schweinfurt, eighty miles east of Frankfurt, then marched approximately eight miles to the village of Traustadt. The men were quartered in town and delivered daily to area farms. Herb, who understood German, was assigned to work on the Wiener family farm.

Mr. and Mrs. Wiener were just like my grandma and grandpa. Honest. It was great.

That Sunday when we went there, he [Mr. Wiener] introduced me to Mrs. Wiener, and then they had a Russian girl that was working there, and they had a Polish girl. One was Sascha, and the other one was Shimila. They were forced labor.

[That first day], we didn't even do any work. We just came down there to eat. We sat down, and we had boiled potatoes. We had creamed carrots. We had German ersatz imitation coffee. [My friend] Reed and I, we haven't had any solid foods. We were getting filled up, and we could have all we wanted. She had a great big bowl of potatoes, a great big bowl of carrots, creamed carrots.

They were so good to us. So when she got all done, we were talking. While we were eating, she was asking me questions: if I was *Deutsch,* if I was German. Yes. Were my grandma and grandpa German? Yes. They asked me where they came from. They come from Germany? Oh, yes, from Frankfurt. Everything started to get jelling. They started to be *real* nice to me then.

She came out of the kitchen with a great big kaffeekuchen, and it had apples on it. She came out, and she set that in front of me, and she told me, she said, "You eat all you want." I thought, Oh, my God! I was *so* full.

But I wasn't going to refuse it. She started cutting pieces off and giving it to me, and it was good. We had about two, three pieces. We got all done, and she said, "You take it back with you." She cut it up and gave it to me to take back. So then when I got back, I gave it to some of the other fellows that didn't get any of that. Just gave it out until it was gone.

Other prisoners recall their work details as difficult experiences. Raynold Carlson was an army infantryman captured at Salerno, Italy, in September 1943. He was on two separate work details in Germany, both farms.

We were in what used to be a pigpen. When I first came there, all they had was a plank there full of hay. That's what we slept on.

Well, [with] potatoes, you start in the morning. They tied rags around the neck and made a pouch. Here you'd have one of those big sacks full of potatoes. This is the way you had to carry them. Bend like this. *(like carrying bag on shoulder)* Every one of those potatoes, you had to pick that up and put that sack back on your shoulders. . . . We worked with, there was a couple of Polish girls, and then there was at least a half a dozen Russian girls. . . . There was one [German] bitch working there, too; she thought she was everything, but she was a real hag.

They sorted the potatoes. You put straw on the ground, put the potatoes on top, and then straw on top, and then about eight inches of dirt. You had to put that on top and on each side as we went. But then we used to smile when we saw the crops. These doggoned pigs would come, and they'd go right across the top, eating off the top. They would open it up, and the potatoes would freeze. *(laughs)* The animals were sabotaging, but you didn't care. You did your work, and that was it.

The Pacific: Hard Labor

For POWs throughout Asia, work experiences defined their daily lives. Men were assigned to hard labor in locations from Burma to China, the Philippines to Manchuria, building railroads, roads, and airfields and working on various agricultural projects.

After months at Cabanatuan, Glenn Oliver was selected for a detail at Nichols Field, on Luzon. The Japanese wanted a former American airfield expanded and made ready for use. The work was strenuous.

We were making a new runway. We dug it all by hand. Pick and shovel. We had two railroad tracks and . . . a string of like little dump cars. We had three men to a car, and two men would go down with the car full of dirt, and they would dump it. Then they'd bring the empty car back. It had a box on it that you had to fill that was probably five or six feet long and three and a half, maybe four feet wide at the bottom. The box was made so it tapered to the top with handles on each end so you could just pull it off. You'd tip the car over to dump the dirt out, then put the box back on.

The box was, it started out, I think it was two boards high, which would be probably about two feet. After Christmas [1942], they made new boxes. Another board on it. Made it a little bit higher, to carry more dirt.

We did about six loads in the morning and about five in the afternoon. It was about eleven loads a day, and some days we had a lot of derails. It was real difficult to rerail. It was real heavy. You had to dump it before you could get it back on.

The Japanese responded harshly when quotas weren't reached or rules were broken.

They would punish the whole track crew. You used to line up in groups of a hundred, four wide and twenty-five deep. We had to count off. It would be *(counts in Japanese)* . . . one, two, three, four, five. They'd make us open ranks and stand at attention. . . . Put our arms up there, straight up, you know, from the shoulder, and the soldiers would whip us with bamboo canes they'd get out of the blacksmith shop. Draw blood out through your clothing. Depending on where you were, sometimes you lucked out, because they'd be real energetic when they started out. If you're a big person, then you'd really get it. But if you're smaller stature or at the end of the session, they were getting tired and not so vigorous. I can remember two times I only got three stripes.

Rewards, such as they were, didn't come often.

[We got] days off usually once a month. And as a noncom you were supposed to get fifteen centavos a day, which would have been about seven and a half cents. The privates got ten centavos. Most times you'd get something out of the Japanese commissary.

Lots of time I'd work a whole month, and I'd get one Coke. Another time I got a handful of bananas. Philippine bananas are about as big as a man's finger. And there would be about five, seven bananas. You'd work a whole month to get that. One time I got peanuts. I got half a cup, half a canteen cup, of shelled peanuts. That was your whole month's wages.

Bataan March survivor Ken Porwoll got out of deadly Camp O'Donnell by being selected for a work detail. Over a four-month period in mid-1942, Ken worked on three details on the island of Luzon: at Batangas, Caluan, and Candelaria.

Men were being taken out on different details. The group I got on was a bridge-building detail. [Bridge building] was real hard physical work. Real hard. . . . [On one] we had to drive piles into the riverbed with big logs. There was a man operating a machine where a hundred guys go around and pulled on this rope and lifted this weight up above the pole and then let it go, and it would slowly drive this big log into the riverbank. . . . Everybody in synch; everybody counting in Japanese. This rope that everybody is pulling on, if you didn't get out of the way of that, it would snake, and it would rip your skin off.

Gerald Wakefield was captured on Corregidor and sent to Palawan Island in July 1942. His memory is of the work, the weather, and a permanent feeling of exhaustion.

We worked, sometimes seven days a week. On the airfields. Most of the work was airfield construction. . . . Everybody that could [went out on work details, every day]. They had a couple, three guys that cooked the rice; they stayed in. But the rest would go out.

We were building airfields. We cut down enough [trees] on one side of the road for one airfield and on the other side of the road for another airfield. We did it with a handsaw. And *everything* was by hand; it wasn't machines. Mixing cement, wheeling the cement—all of it with handwork.

And it was *hot*. They talk about how hot it is here [today, about ninety degrees Fahrenheit], well, hell, we worked in this stuff all the time. And it was humid, too.

I remember [sometimes we had] Sunday off. They didn't work us every Sunday, but we did work on Sunday many times. [On a day off] you

Abraham Sabbatini of the U.S. Army Air Corps (second from right), in the carpentry shop at Malaybalay prison camp, Philippines, 1942. Abe spent his childhood in Italy; skills gained there proved beneficial when he arrived at the camp.

During the summer when I used to go work on the farm, some of us used to have wood sandals with a canvas strap on top. So that's what I done—I spent all my time in the carpenter shop to make wood sandals for the POWs.

[I used] any wood the Japanese would give me. Some wood was maybe three-quarters of an inch, you know. When the POWs wanted a pair of shoes, I used to mark the foot, put the name on [the wood], and I used to make it. They would come back the next day and get them. For the strap, army canvas: double it over and put small nails in both sides.

had no way of doing anything, because you were locked up. *(laughs)* But with a day off, I slept if I could. I can't remember doing anything else.

Robert Heer served in the air corps. He was captured in May 1942 on the southern Philippine island of Mindanao. After some months at a prison camp at Malaybalay, also on Mindanao, in September 1942 he was transported to Formosa, where he worked as an agricultural laborer at several camps.

At Heito [we did] sugar plantation work. . . . This large field, probably about twenty-five acres, five acres square. They had Chinese coolies working with us. What they would do, they would dig down a meter, dig down into the earth a meter, and sift all the dirt a meter deep to get all the rocks out, because then when the rocks were off the field they had some good soil there they could plant sugarcane in. That was the purpose. And, of course, that was our job. That was the worst.

I remember when we first started working there, we had to carry these punkies between us. It was something like a . . . it's one guy on each end, and you had two handles, and you carry weight. It was a bamboo webbing in between, and we'd carry the rocks in that. We'd carry it by our side, a hand on the right-hand and left-hand side. The first three or four days, our wrists were so weak from carrying these things that eventually we just used pieces of cloth to tie around our wrist and loop around the handle of the punky so that our hands would be relieved from that. Well, we couldn't hardly hold a punky actually after about three days until the hands healed up again. But we got used to it.

They had this old narrow-gauge railroad track that went way down about a mile or mile and a quarter away from the camp, and it was flat country down there. They had the sugar plantation there. Sometimes we'd work pushing carts. They were made out of wood, these carts were, and were full of sugarcane stalks. We'd push them over toward the factory, and then there would be somebody to take them from us there and take them into the factory for processing. We liked this job because we could always break off a piece of a stalk of sugarcane and conceal it and take it home and eat it at night. It was sweet and like chewing gum almost, you might say.

Jim Whittaker was one of the tens of thousands of Allied prisoners of different nationalities assigned to the Burma-Thailand Railway detail. Beginning in late 1942, Jim worked on the Burma end of the project.

We spent three days at the Thanbyuzayat base camp. We got some idea of where we stood when we were met by a Japanese colonel, [Lt. Col. Yoshitada] Nagatomo, who stood on a box—they liked to dress up with their swords and their boots—and gave us a pep talk. We were "miserable remnants of a decadent race and should weep tears of joy that his Imperial Majesty was allowing us to work on the railroad and redeem ourselves." He advised us to work cheerfully and finished by saying, "no work, no food." The speech was translated to us.

We soon found his "no work, no food" was not an idle threat. Rations in the work camps were only furnished for the number of workers available, but because we were civilized, whatever came into camp was used to feed everybody, and the already inadequate ration would be further reduced.

The biggest challenge: working and surviving in the jungle camps.

The camps were very primitive, built in a jungle clearing and made of bamboo frames. There'd be a, we'd call it a guard hut; and two wooden posts with Japanese characters on them marked the entrance. The huts had no doors or windows and no lights or running water. There would be a bamboo sleeping platform about two feet above the dirt floor; the roof and low sides were made with atap, a kind of palm leaf. In the rainy season, the floors were all mud. There was never any running water, never any electric lights, no doors, windows; the huts were open sides.

To control camp hygiene . . . latrines were dug well away from the huts. The area around the latrines would be full of maggots; the blowflies would lay eggs, and you had to be very, very careful, especially in the dark, or you'd slip and fall easily on these maggots. There were thousands of them.

The first camp we went to was the 18 Kilo camp. . . . Our first job was moving dirt. The railroad was built almost entirely by hand. We started out with a quota—the Japanese assigned a quota. Where possible, the Japanese established a work quota as a means of measuring productivity.

We worked in teams of three. Teams of three would be given a chunkel—a kind of hoe with a large blade set at right angles to the shaft—a shovel, and baskets to move the dirt, which had to be dug and carried to or from the [railroad] right-of-way. If it was a fill, you'd dig it on the side and move it to the right-of-way; if it was a cut, you'd dig on the right-of-way and move it to the side. The quota was measured by a Japanese engineer using a heavy meter stick, which sometimes doubled as a club. Now, when they found that some of the Australians in better shape than us could complete this by early afternoon, they began to increase the quota. The quota, first 1.2 meters, was changed to 2 meters a man.

Stan Galbraith served with the army's 131st Field Artillery; he was captured in March 1942 on the island of Java. With a map of Thailand and Burma in front of him, Stan recalls his time in the jungle, on railroad construction.

Where I first actually worked on the railroad was here, *(points)* at Tarsau. The most stuff that I worked on up and down [the railroad] there was, you were shoveling muck. Making embankments with the old, what they called a chunkel. Piece of metal on bamboo, only not like a shovel—like a wide hoe. As far as the shovels were concerned, there wasn't—outside of an exception, you didn't *see* a decent shovel. Those chunkel, you pulled the mud out, but then a lot of times . . . you put them on a grain sack or something, and we'd carry them between men. On a bamboo pole. [We'd] do so many meters a day.

And clearing, doing that. Cutting teak, cut them, cut some of them down with the most *ungodly* saws. That's heavy stuff. And have to carry it out. At one point up along here *(points again at railroad line, on map)*, they'd used a few Asian elephants. If his handler doesn't want to push him, the elephant won't move. He won't lift too much. A lot of them, if it got too heavy, they just refused. They'd run in another, two Americans or captives. Instead of the elephant. *(chuckles)*

Stan worked on the infamous bridge over the River Kwai, made notorious through the film of the same name.

The first one [bridge], the bamboo one, I worked on that one when I first went up. Out in the river. They had you out there, and they had a pile driver. Steel or big heavy piece of lead or something, and they had the prisoners down in the water up to here. *(motions with hand to waist)* . . .

He [the Japanese supervisor] would count in unison in Japanese. Usually *ichi, ni, san,* and you'd pull on a rope and lift it up and then let it pile down. And you'd keep at that until you'd get the pilings down deep enough.

Working in the jungle, health problems were unavoidable.

On my fingers there, that was eaten down to the bone. That was from something that you got out in the jungle. It opened up like a petal, see? When it first got infected and after I came off the work details, I put it in hot water. I would boil a can and put my fingers in as much as I could.

An Englishman took a knife, and that deep one there *(points to scarred finger)*, . . . he got a lot of pus out of that one. But he didn't get the pocket [of infection], so five, six days later—I kept working, too—I put this in water, in hot water, as hot as I could stand. It opened up, like petals on a flower. I knew immediately when that burst open and I got that infection out—that felt better. Because one of the doctors had said they were going to cut my fingers off.

During more than a year and a half on the railroad construction details, navy pharmacist's mate Al Kopp treated injured, sick, and dying men from the jungle camps. Some men simply gave up the will to live.

If they're laying there thinking that's all she wrote, then that is all she wrote—they're going to die. If your mind goes, your body is right behind it. We had guys that would simply lay down and not eat anymore and die three days later. Can you imagine a guy dying in three days' time because he sort of willed it on himself?

We had a medical doctor [Dr. Cameron], an MD, well educated, a young guy. He was older than the rest of us, but he wasn't an old man. He was probably twenty-eight. . . . He told me, he said—and he was as smart as any guy I ever knew—he said, "This war's going to last ten years. And I'm not going to be around in ten years in this place." He flat told me that, and the next day or so, he told another guy that he wasn't going to be around until Thursday. . . . On Thursday or Friday, he was dead. That was real demoralizing. The guys all loved him. He had no medicines to treat them. What a terrible thing that was. When he just wouldn't eat anymore, he just lay there and died. He just gave up.

Several guys did that. I saw it. Some guys, you have to slap them into eating a spoonful of rice. One guy I gave it to one day, I sat there, and I gave him a spoonful of rice, and he just kept it in his cheek, and I gave him another one. He kept it in his cheek. He wouldn't swallow. I said, "Swallow that stuff." I kept putting it in there. Finally, I got quite a bit of gruely rice in him, and he blew it up into my face. I slapped him back and forth. Slapped him real hard. And, boy, did he get a spark. He looked up at me and said, "You son of a bitch. If I get out of here, I'm going to kill you." And he lived. And when did he die? Two years ago. All this time he lived. He was a tough son of a bitch.

I thought I was pretty good at preaching to the guys, about bucking them up. Really, it was the most I had to offer. It was psychological, I suppose. The thing is, if you can get their spirits up one way or another, if you can get them up a little bit and not let yourself down.

We had what we called "sick call" in the mornings. Still dark. They'd get them out of the huts, and the Japs would come in. Full bayonets, rifles. And we already had the sick call with the guys to say, "You can go out on the railroad today." Maybe say, "How do you feel?" Guys were *all* sick—even the orderlies were sick. But the guys that were half dead, they still made them walk there. I know two or three times, oh, more than that, I saw them take patients out, and they'd just have to lay there, they're sicker than a dog, and pound some rock. That was our sick call.

[Our doctor,] he did a couple of amputations that I helped him with, but the patients died. If you couldn't stop the ulcer, the patient is going to die. Because if you amputated, there wasn't enough nourishment in the guy to live. Simple amputation, like a leg. I personally did some, too. I did some toes. I took three toes off a guy that were full of ulcers.

You improvise tools. Guys brought in jackknives. Once in a while, they'd find another one. It couldn't be very big because the Japs would take it away from you. For instance, I did a lot of teeth extractions with a pair of pliers. Guys would hold them down. I did a full mouth on a guy one day. All his teeth, every one. All infected. He had a mouth like a pit.... He was so infected.... We couldn't pay any attention to [the possibility of infection] in the jungle, because the guy was screaming. So I pulled all his teeth with a pair of pliers. One at a time. He fainted along the way there somewhere, because the guy didn't have to hold him down anymore. Then it was kind of easy. I pulled the rest of them. You break half of them. There's no instrument to go in there after the broken root.

Even when the doctors did an amputation, they did it with a bread knife. Something they could cut with. You had no forceps there to stop the bleeders, even hardly enough to stop the bleeding. The guy lost so much blood, and of course you couldn't give him a blood transfusion because you had no facilities to do that. It was just a different experience. That's putting it very mildly.

In many Pacific camp locations, death was an everyday event. Men's hearts became hardened. After Bataan and Camp O'Donnell, Glenn Oliver ended up with thousands of others at Cabanatuan. His journal entry from the time is brief and almost banal: "September 26, 1942, arrived at Camp Number 1 Cabanatuan. Worked on grave digging and burial detail . . . about one month." Behind this simple description, though, are powerful memories Glenn can recall clearly more than sixty years later.

We usually buried anywhere between ten and twenty-five people a day.

Some days it would be more than others. But there was always eight, ten, twenty maybe, something like that.

We'd dig the grave in the morning . . . all in one long row when I was there. We used short-handled shovels, and we had to dig it one shovel-depth deep, and we piled the dirt up on the end. There wasn't room on the side. Oft times by the time you got down to the depth that you had to dig it, you'd be standing in two, three, four inches of fluids and water seeping in from adjacent graves.

Then in the afternoon, we'd go back over to the hospital and pick up the bodies. You'd have them out on galvanized sheet metal with a bamboo carry pole on each side, wired onto it. The bodies would be naked. Maybe someone stole the clothing. Nobody got buried in clothes or had any covering. Naked.

They'd hose them down, flush them off. A lot of them had running sores, gangrene. Wet beriberi, where their legs and thighs, scrotum swelled real large, sometimes so large the skin on the legs would split. I've seen them split from the knee to the ankle, and the flesh inside would look like a half-ripe watermelon, and then they'd get gangrene, and they either had to cut the leg off or they'd die. Most of them just died anyway.

And as soon as we got outside the hospital grounds, there onto the main road to go to the cemetery, they would let us stop, and we'd pull native grass, and we'd make twists of it and put them around the ankles and some on the crotch and some on the face. Keep the flies off the eyes and mouth. Under the arms there by the shoulders, so we wouldn't have to pick them up, touch their skin, to put them in the grave. A lot of time they'd have pellagra. . . . If you break the skin, the skin was just like . . . slimy underneath there. Real slick.

We'd put them in there [the grave]. A lot of them didn't have dog tags. Sometimes we'd have too many, and we'd have to double-deck them—lay down one layer and then lay another layer right on top of them and cover them up. You put the dirt on the grave and mounded it up. Then we would go back. Sometimes we had time to have a little service down at the graves. You got to the point where the only thing that bothered me was when a man from my company would be there. *(pauses three seconds)* [But if I didn't know them], that was different. Just another body.

Cabanatuan prisoner Harold Kurvers, too, speaks of a loss of compassion and a focus on self—but also of the guilt that accompanied these protective measures.

> [When I arrived at Cabanatuan in June 1942], I was in a building with a group of people that were not on the [Bataan] march. This guy by the name of Baker, he lay there in a fetal position all the time. I'd bring his rice to him. . . . I was able [to] go to the mess hall and get it. He wasn't, so I brought it back here. He'd push it away. He said, "We don't feed our *dogs* this."
>
> I tried to force him to eat, but he wouldn't. Instead of destroying it, I ate it. It's the guilt, thinking that, well, maybe I could have gotten him to eat. I fought to get him to eat, but he didn't want to eat. He died there.

Harold was amazed at the emotional response to another death he witnessed there.

> We went to view a body of a person that was caught trying to escape. His head's caved in, and his eye was gouged out. He was dead. [The Japanese] took us shack by shack to view that body and show us what was going to happen to us if we tried to escape. As we were going through there, I remember the guys saying, "Look. He's got a new pair of shoes. I wonder who's going to get those?" That's a strange thing to hear when you're viewing a body like that. Where's a man's heart? *(pauses three seconds)* It's gone.

3

Guards and Escape

PRISONERS CAME INTO frequent, daily contact with guards who patrolled the camps and inspected the individual barracks. For the POWs, once behind barbed wire in a permanent camp, this was the face of the enemy. Depending on location, experiences were drastically different.

From the German camps come accounts of guards, many in their forties and even fifties, with whom the POWs sometimes could converse and also barter for various goods. Former prisoners even displayed a certain empathy for particular guards, some of whom discussed their families, shared rumors about the war, and stopped for a cigarette on cold evenings. Treatment generally was consistent, and accounts of abuse are the rare exception.[1]

The situation in the Pacific was entirely different. Prisoners held by the Japanese uniformly described treatment by guards as erratic, brutal, and even sadistic, with physical punishment a common occurrence. Beatings were meted out for seemingly trivial infractions. More serious "crimes," like smuggling food into camp or stealing from one's captors, would bring more systematic punishment, even torture; here broken bones or even death could, and did, ensue.[2]

Allied POWs, products of western military training, were shocked by this physical abuse. But corporal punishment was commonplace in the Japanese Army: a senior officer could slap a junior officer, who in turn could hit a noncommissioned officer, who could beat a private. POWs, considered by their Japanese captors to have dishonored and shamed themselves by surrendering, were at the very bottom of this hierarchy. The guards, most simple enlisted men, took out their frustrations on the prisoners.[3]

FROM THE GERMAN CAMPS come numerous reports of escape and attempted escape. Idleness gave abundant time to think, plan, and dig. Mostly of European stock, Americans could visually blend in outside the prison camp; some men understood or even spoke German, increasing the chance of success. Importantly, the Geneva Convention offered a modicum of protection should an escapee be recaptured: "Escaped prisoners of war who are recaptured . . . shall be liable only to disciplinary punishment." For most of the war, official German policy was to respect this article. Still, films like *The Great Escape* (1963) notwithstanding, few men thought seriously about escaping and only a handful ever participated in an organized attempt. Most men were content to remain in camp.[4]

In spite of hard labor, abusive treatment, and near-starvation rations, there are but a handful of documented escape attempts from Japanese camps, the majority of them unsuccessful. Multiple factors worked against escape. The isolated location of many camps would have meant long journeys through unknown and inhospitable terrain—for sick and weakened men, nearly impossible. In addition, as historian Gavan Daws writes, "Any white captive was a prisoner not only in a Japanese camp, but in Asia. His skin was a prison uniform he could never take off." Tall Caucasians would find it impossible to blend in, and, because of Japanese threats, locals were far more likely to turn in fleeing POWs than assist them.[5]

But the most important factor explaining the paucity of escapes is more basic: life and death. The Japanese threatened to execute prisoners caught trying to escape—and on more than one occasion they carried out this threat. At times they did so publicly, to maximize the deterrent effect. To further reduce the possibility of escape, the Japanese instituted self-policing among the POWs. Thus, in some camps ten-man groups were formed, with remaining members threatened with punishment, even execution, if one or more escaped. In sum, Pacific prisoners were in for the duration, and they knew it.[6]

Guards in German Camps

Some POWs shared positive memories of their German guards, even empathized with them. Paratrooper Earle Bombardier provides one example, when he was on a work detail near Augsburg in late 1944 or early 1945, an instance where he believes his life was spared.

We had one young soldier that came in there. Not knowing his real name, we called him Africa because he had been in the Afrika Korps, in Rommel's force over in Africa, and he was wounded and sent back to Germany to the hospital. While he was recuperating, then they put him in there [at Augsburg] as a guard. He was only about eighteen years old. One of the finest people I've ever met.

He saved our lives. We were working on this air raid shelter, and right next to this thing was a, kind of a rooming house, and they had a little bar in there. We'd go in there and have our piece of bread in the morning and the afternoon, and . . . there was an old Dutch lady, who was a displaced person, that was kind of running this thing. Every once in a while after we got acquainted with her she'd tell us some of the things that were going on in the war. Finally, after quite a while, she got to trust us, so she told us she had a radio built into that bar and she was getting the BBC news.

So one day we went in there, and the guards always stayed outside. We told one of the fellows, okay, now you watch the window to see that the guard doesn't come in here without us knowing about it. This one fellow that was supposed to be guarding the window, he got to listening to the news there, and he got real interested and wasn't doing his job. All of a sudden the door opened, and here's this young soldier, and he could hear what was going on and everything, and he could see us there. He didn't say a word. He could have shot all of us right there and been justified in doing it. He just closed the door and walked away. And he never said a word about it.

Bob Knobel served in the air corps as flight engineer and gunner on a heavy bomber. Shot down over France, he arrived at Stalag Luft IV in July 1944. He has clear memories of the barracks guard.

Our guard for the room, his name was Schick. He was from Chicago. He'd had a meat market on some street in Chicago. He had gone back to Germany in 1936 to visit his family, and they put him in the German Army. He was forty-five years old.

He'd come in, and the guys would give him a cigarette. Of course, he'd stand back from the doors or the window so no one could see him smoking because he wasn't supposed to do that. He wasn't supposed to talk to us.

He'd tell us how the war was really going. In English. He'd read us the German newspaper, and he'd say, "A bunch of lies." He says, "This is the way it really is." He came in the early part of December [1944] and said, "You guys will probably be home by the first of the year." He came in on December 15 or 16 and said, "You're not going to make it by spring now. The dumb Germans just started an offensive [the Battle of the Bulge]."

Army enlisted man Arnold Sprong spent most of his nine months as a POW on a work detail in the small German town of Adorf. Returning to camp from the day's factory work, Arnold was carrying a loaf of bread he had acquired on the black market. He recalls that a guard saved him from possible punishment.

Underneath my overcoat I would wear this burlap sack with a rope on it—which a loaf of bread fit in there real nice—with a rope over the thing over my shoulder, and then my coat over the top. It's really kind of hard to see it because the coat was baggy.

Prisoners unloading potatoes under the watch of German guards at Stalag Luft I Barth, probably 1945. This photo shows the layers of barbed wire fencing and several of the many guard towers that ringed the camp.

We were dragging the cart back from the railroad station, and this one good guard, Karl was his name, big guy, but nice guy. He was *Volksturm* [home guard, made up of elderly men]. He mentioned to one of the fellows, who passed the word up to me, that they were going to have an inspection [when we got to camp]. They had suspicion that somebody was bringing extra food into the camp.

So I'm thinking, oh, my gosh! What am I going to do? I've got this loaf of bread hanging on me. So I took the loaf . . . now, we had loaves of bread on the cart, in bags. So I took my loaf of bread and put it on the cart. We got into camp. They inspected all of us. But it was a close call. I would have been caught had that guard not said something.

Contact with guards could lead to trading for goods. POWs were constantly short of food items like bread, which guards often could supply from outside the camp. But as the war dragged on and especially during the final year, the German economy was less and less able to meet consumer demand for many products. Some of these items were included in standard Red Cross parcels issued to prisoners, though, so guards and POWs each had something the other desired. The shortage of Red Cross–supplied parcels, especially during the last year of the war, often meant that two or more POWs had to share a single one. At Stalag II-A Neubrandenburg, army medic Dick Cartier and his buddy Joe were assigned a parcel. They divided up the goods, and Dick dealt with the Germans.

There was a carton of cigarettes [in the parcel]. Five packs [for each of us]. I didn't smoke. I got acquainted with a guard, and I would trade the cigarettes for bread, for a loaf of civilian bread. It cost thirty cigarettes for a loaf.

This guard would come around to the barracks after dark. He would have trading stock. He would tell the guy next to the door. So he would come and get me, and I'd go and talk to the German as much as I could, and he'd tell me what he had and how much he wanted for it.

I knew the German counting deal. I learned that. If he told me thirty-five cigarettes, I'd say, "*zu viel* [too much]." Sometimes we dickered, and sometimes he wouldn't dicker—he'd keep his price. So then I paid it.

One night he had a pound coffee can full of farina, and I paid thirty cigarettes for that. I said, "Joe, look what I did tonight. I got a pound coffee can full of farina. Boy, we're really going to eat for a while."

Cream of wheat and the bread was all he ever brought. Not a bad thing to get. And was that bread ever good. We kind of conserved that, one piece a day.

Yet these recollections tell only part of the story. As some prisoners found out, their German captors could at times be cruel, even sadistic, in their treatment of unarmed men. Wounded when he was captured in July 1943 in Sicily, paratrooper Ed Haider received some medical attention, including stitches on his back. He was recuperating in a German hospital facility in Italy when word came that all prisoners were to be moved.

[The Germans] came in and took us out of there. I was all in bandages and in my undershorts. The doctor said to me, "Just don't worry about it. They're going to take you to Germany now." And they took us down, and they loaded us on trucks. They wanted to get us to the train yard. But we didn't load on the trucks fast enough, so this [German] captain came, and he said [to the guard], "Use your rifle to get them on there!" Well, he wouldn't do it.

So the captain grabbed his rifle, and he started in with the butt, hammering us with that. The first guy he caught was me. He broke my incision open, and blood was running down my leg, and I went down on my knees. The next time the butt came, it cut me right in the forehead, and I went down on my face. I could see stars. Two guys picked me up. . . . Then we got on the trucks, and then we got to the train yard. And they put us in boxcars.

Stalag Luft IV was the second camp for ball turret gunner Les Schrenk—he began at Luft VI. Les recalls the trauma of the arrival in July 1944 at Luft IV. A train brought a large group of POWs to the nearest rail station; from there the journey continued on foot.[7]

That train took us to a town called Kiefheide, which was about three, three and half miles from the camp. . . . It was a hot July day, but yet they made me put my overcoat on. I don't know if they made everybody put their overcoat on, but for some reason they made me put my overcoat on. Then they shackled us in twos, so there was no chance of getting the overcoat off again. Arm in arm, two guys shackled together.

[We were] a large group. That was early morning. The first thing I remember was a redheaded German *Hauptmann,* captain, speak almost perfect English. He was strutting back and forth, telling us what a lucky day it was going to be for us. He says, "Today is your lucky day. You will not get only one Red Cross parcel; you are going to get two Red Cross parcels." Good heavens! I had never had a full Red Cross parcel all during the time I was [a POW]. I could hardly believe my ears. But sure enough, they gave us each two Red Cross parcels.

Then the next thing I heard was, "Fix bayonets," in German. They [the guards] all put the bayonet on. Then they released a whole bunch of vicious dogs and started chasing us down the road. Shackled. With overcoat on. July, hot July day.

Here come the dogs and bayonets. They're running us down the road, and this German *Hauptmann* is in a vehicle. He was shouting out orders, telling them that we were *Luftgangsters* [literally, air gangsters], that we murdered their women and children, and to shoot us. He kept on exciting them, telling them to shoot. . . . He's stirring up . . . he had red hair, and I can still remember it. His face was just brilliant red [from] being so excited.

I don't know why the order wasn't carried out, but if anybody tripped or fell they were jabbed with bayonets and kicked and every other thing until their partner either got them back up on their feet or in a good many cases they carried them. They carried their buddy.

They ran us through a woods, and if you glanced on either side, you could see machine gun nests pointed at us all the way along. So if we would have done anything wrong, we would have all been shot right there. And that lasted for about three and a half miles.

I was so desperate for food; I don't know how I ever did it. Most of the guys dropped both of their parcels. Just a few had one. I don't know . . . maybe I'm stubborn, but I managed to hang onto both of mine. My partner, he dropped both of his. The arm where I was shackled to my partner was just absolutely raw from . . . you can imagine, going down, and you're swinging your arms for three and a half miles, and you're not in synch with your partner. That was just eating into your flesh. And yet you were hanging onto a parcel.

Numerous prisoners from Stalag Luft IV recalled a brutal German guard, known by his nickname: Big Stoop. U.S. Army flight surgeon Major Leslie Caplan, a psychiatrist after the war and himself a prisoner at Stalag Luft IV after November 1944, described him as "about six feet, six inches tall, weight about 180 or 190 pounds, and . . . approximately fifty years old. His most outstanding characteristic was his large hands, which seemed out of proportion to those of a normal person." Three different POWs from the camp share memories of Big Stoop.[8]

Flight engineer and gunner Bob Knobel:

Every once in a while this Big Stoop, he would bring his goons in about, sometimes at two o'clock in the morning, and roust everyone out and dump all our beds out into the middle of the floor and then pour [food] that anyone had tried to keep onto a pile. Then they'd walk out.

LeRoy Shaw was shot down over France in May 1944.

The only one that ever abused anybody was a guy they had by the name of Big Stoop. He was there for all the roll calls and stuff. I saw him take one of the prisoners right off of the third bunk. He was sick; he had been throwing up and [had] dysentery all night long. And he took him with one hand, grabbed the shirt, and set him on the floor.

He also took my watch that day, too. I had my graduation watch, a Hamilton watch. He saw this watch on, and he came over and put one finger under that and threw it twenty feet over in the corner of the room. Disturbed me a little.

Earl Joswick was a gunner on a heavy bomber. He arrived at Luft IV in late July 1944.

Big Stoop, he was that type of fellow that he'd try to kick you around all the time. We went to interrogation there [when we arrived]. He kicked me from twice the length of this room [eight feet]. He kicked me [on my leg], and I had my busted-up leg and . . . I couldn't walk hardly.

I had a crucifix and a dog tag around my neck, and he saw that and started twisting it, [saying] "You swine" and cussing me up and down in German to beat the band and everything like that. When it broke, then he threw it on the floor.

In late April 1945, at the liberation of VII-A Moosburg, where Big Stoop had moved with the former Luft IV POWs, the newly freed men exacted their revenge: they killed him.[9]

Machine gunner Bill Hall has the last word here. The D-Day veteran reflected on the Germans with whom he came into contact as a POW during 1944–45.

I'll tell you, [the Germans were] a mixed bag. Most of our guards were World War I [veterans], old-timers that were guarding that camp. They were more humanitarian-like. We had a couple young guards. They were the wise guys. . . . I think it's a generation gap, if you will.

The one group, the worst part that we ran into, I don't know where they came from. I don't know what their backgrounds were, what their upbringing was. It must have been terrible. They must have recruited all the dregs they could, for certain drudgery positions.

We also ran into some German officers who were intelligent. High-ranking people. Civilized. And we ran into others that were certainly not. I think we had a good cross-picture of humanity. We had a real education. Certainly not out of the schoolbooks, but it was an education.

Guards in Japanese Camps

Captured on Guam island less than one month after Pearl Harbor, Marvin Roslansky spent more than three years as a prisoner at the Zentsuji camp, on the Japanese home island of Shikoku. His strongest memory of treatment from the guards is of how erratic it was.

The kind of treatment that we received from the guards, that was up to them. If they felt you were doing something wrong, they'd straighten you out. Either beat on you or whatever should be to show their power. They didn't need much excuse.

[They were] unpredictable. You would never know. You might get beat for doing nothing . . . even during your work periods. If you're working, they'd come up and club you. That didn't make any difference. You just keep on moving faster, faster. No apparent reason.

One time I can really tell you, the reason I was in the brig for a couple days [was] for smoking in the wrong place. You got beat for that, when you went in and when you went back out [of the brig].

[This guard we called] Club Fist, he evidently had been in the service in China. His hand was damaged. He would beat you for nothing. You didn't have to do too much wrong. They're unpredictable people. We had no idea what they might do.

Glenn Wohlferd in 1941, prior to shipping out to the Philippines. Captured on Corregidor, Glenn was at Cabanatuan by June 1942.

We stayed away from them [the Japanese] as much as we could. [At Cabanatuan,] there was three guys that tried to escape, and they caught them and brought them back, and they beheaded them in front of everybody.

Shot down in July 1944 over Chichi Jima island, Bill Connell endured nine months at Camp Ofuna, the naval interrogation center located near the Japanese city of Yokohama. For him, treatment from the youthful guards was both uncertain and brutal.

The guards at Ofuna were quite young. I would say they were sixteen and seventeen years of age. . . . And some of them were very mean. I mean, they were just downright *mean.* They had permission to do just about anything they wanted to us, other than injure us to the point, like break a bone or cut us to any degree. They could hit us with their fist or with the walking stick that they carried, or they could stick us with the bayonet on the rifle, but they just jabbed us enough to . . . barely break the skin. But they wouldn't penetrate your body. But they would hit us with the rifle butt as well. That was some of them.

About every ten days to two weeks, they would assemble us out there on this little parade ground we had. We had a Japanese hospital corpsman who was a chief petty officer. He didn't run the camp, but he was one of the more senior people. And all during this ten days the guards would keep track of any violation that we were guilty of, and they'd write it in a little book. . . . Of course, you had no way of knowing that you had committed an offense of any kind because half of the rules we didn't even know about.

[Say,] if you failed to acknowledge a guard, and you didn't address him properly. You couldn't wear your shoes in the barracks, so you had to take the shoes off. I made the mistake one day of stepping on the ground with my bare feet after I had taken my shoes off, and they just worked me over for about a half an hour because of that. So there was all kinds of little things, and you never were sure just what the hell was going on.

Then they would have us all assembled, and they would call your name out, and you'd have to go and stand in front of everybody, and then this chief petty officer would read off the offenses. . . . Then they would yell a term called *jetske,* meaning you assumed the position: you spread your legs apart, bent your knees, put your hands behind your back, and stick your chin out. He would tell the guards of what punishment that we were to receive, and they would then hit us with the closed hand. They didn't punch like we did. They used this part of their hand. *(holds hand out, palm forward and fingers clenched)* That's hard. And they would slap you with that. You'd get five or ten of those slaps, and you'd grit your teeth. They could knock you to the ground with just one blow they were so strong.

Then after they did that to you, then they would attack us with a club, a regular club, about the size of a baseball bat. It was about maybe an inch and a half, two inches in diameter. They would swat us across the buttocks and the thighs. They could lift you right off the ground. They could hit you that hard. And you'd get so many swats for that. Then they would call another guy out and do the same thing.

B-29 crew member Ray Toelle, burned on his hands and legs when he bailed out over Japan, distinctly remembers sadistic treatment from one of the guards at Ofuna naval interrogation center.

The first night I was there, this little guard came in, and he said, "Toelle, you die in the morning." He called me by Toelle. I thought, what the hell? How does he know my name? But he was a rough guy. I figured well . . . by that time I felt pretty bad, and I said . . . it didn't make any difference if I was going to make it or not in the morning because I was really hurting. My hands hurt so bad and stuff.

For some reason or other, I don't know, he was just a mean character.

If I wouldn't get up in the morning quick enough, he would kick me in the side. Or he'd make me stand up, and then he'd take his boots and rub them down my legs. He knew I was burned on my legs. He'd run his boots down from my knees to my ankles.

He wanted me . . . he wanted to pester me, I guess. I think what he was waiting for is to have me try to do something to him. But I didn't. I just stood there. When he'd go, I would go and lay down. That's all.

A couple times I didn't get up fast enough in the mornings when he'd come in. After that, I knew I had to get up. I always used to wake up early enough that I was waiting for him to open the door.

You *had* to [maintain your composure]. At least I knew enough . . . because you could tell. He was just waiting to do something to you. He always carried a rifle. He would swing that rifle at you and hit you wherever . . . your head or your back or wherever. So I didn't do anything. I had enough sense for that.

After his March 1942 capture on the west coast of Sumatra, Jim Whittaker and some other men were moved to Dutch barracks that had been taken over

Jim Whittaker (back row, second from left) with his Royal Corps of Signals unit in 1939 in England, prior to departure for the Far East. Jim served in Malaya and Singapore before his March 1942 capture by the Japanese.

by the Japanese to house prisoners. He immediately discovered there were new rules.

Walking in through the gate, I was surprised to see everybody standing at attention. The ones with hats were saluting, and the ones without were bowing. I couldn't figure out what it was all about until some poor unsuspecting guy walked about twenty yards ahead of the Jap, didn't see him; the Jap guard was taking us to the office in charge of the camp. He yelled out something and went over and started beating that poor kid about the head and face. We learned quickly that you had to salute or bow every time you saw these guys. And they would make a game of walking around the camp, trying to catch people not bowing.

Jim spent more than two years as a laborer on the Burma-Thailand Railway, enduring horrific conditions in a series of jungle camps. And while treatment of prisoners frequently was brutal, Jim recalls certain differences among the Japanese.

The Japanese engineers who supervised the work were, to a man, single-minded and interested only in finishing the railroad. Among the Japanese officers and men responsible for guarding us, we did sometimes run into one who tried to be reasonable, that was sympathetic.

On the job, if you did something wrong, the Japanese engineers would carry—we called it a beater stick—it was a club of some kind that they used to measure with. If you didn't move fast enough or if you didn't understand something, they'd be likely to take after you with this damn club. It's very hard to understand Japanese that's screamed at you. I don't think I ever heard Japanese spoken in a normal tone of voice—always screamed in short bursts, *(speaks Japanese phrase)* and this kind of stuff. You could quickly understand what they wanted when it's supplemented with a club of some kind.

Occasionally you'd run into one that would go easy on you and say they didn't like what they were doing. There was a Japanese lieutenant called Naito at the 30 Kilo camp; he spoke good English but was dangerous when drunk. One night he roamed around the hospital huts waving a pistol, actually shooting one of the Australian orderlies.

The Korean guards who came to the railroad were almost all vicious and sadistic. I have seen them taking pleasure in inflicting pain on prisoners and even animals. In a system that made them the bottom of the totem pole, they used every chance to take out their frustration on the prisoners. Some were just mean by nature, or they'd developed a way of being mean, these Koreans.

Jim remembers personal experiences.

The first time [I got beat up], we had come back from a working party, and the guard, probably Korean, was going around, and he was searching everybody. He put his hand in one of the guy's packs, and the guy had a piece of snake in there that he'd found in the jungle somewhere. He realized that it was what it was, and he got a hold of it. He jumped about three feet in the air, and everybody was laughing. These guys don't like to lose face, and to laugh at them was not very good. There were too many of us for him to beat, so he lined us up in two lines facing one another, had one side beat the other, going along to make sure you['re] doing it hard enough. Then he turned around and had the other side that had been getting the beating beat the ones that had been beating them.

The second time I got beat up was in Thailand, when I upset the guard in charge of a fifty-man light duty, men collecting firewood. I was late getting back from the noonday meal; I hadn't got out there on time. The Jap was waiting for me when I got out. . . . The Jap made me stand to attention while the whole party walked by and belted me twice across the head. A friend of mine used the flat of his hand to make a noise by hitting me on the shoulders. The Jap, or Korean, guard saw him and realized what had happened and hit him to demonstrate how hard I was supposed to be hit. Fifty guys then belted me across the face, twice. My head was ringing for a month.

Sunk off the submarine Tang *in October 1944, Floyd Caverly made his first stop as a prisoner on Formosa. At this stage, the Japanese guards weren't a serious problem; among his captors there was at least one who showed compassion.*

I remember one night one of the guards came in. He had some, oh, I'd call them popsicles. It was frozen sugarcane juice. It really wasn't sugar or anything like that. It was the juice out of sugarcane. He called it frozen candy. Now, he could speak a little bit of English, this guy could. He said, one of the things I remember was, "I am your Christian," he said. "I bring you some treat." So he gave us all one of these little icicles. We sucked on them.

But he was only there for that one shift that night, and he didn't dare get caught. He said, "I must not get observed talking to you. I will be severely punished." So he didn't talk to us too much.

But while a prisoner at Ofuna naval interrogation center, Floyd experienced human behavior of a completely different type.

They used to open up the [cell] doors at night. You'd be laying in there on your mat. Asleep, or half-asleep. And they would sneak in with a club, and then they would start beating you over the back, over your backside or your ribs if you were sleeping on your back. They'd hit you right across the stomach or across the pelvis with that damn club. That's what crippled my back today. I've got a crippled back today from dislocated vertebras that were cracked, there at Ofuna.

This was for no reason. This was sport. This was a lot of fun. You want to remember that these poor guards didn't have a thing for entertainment hardly. A few cards they would play or dice games. So they had . . . they would do anything. Beat you a little bit: this was funny to them. They'd run away, and you'd hear them laughing and giggling and telling one another about it. Let's say war is hell, and that was part of it.

Thoughts of Escape

Vern Kruse arrived at III-C Küstrin, located seventy-five miles east of Berlin, in September 1944. Asked whether he thought about trying to escape, he responded with a straightforward answer that summarizes the sentiments of the majority.

I wasn't thinking about [trying to escape]. I thought, that's putting my life in danger, and what in the world am I going to do to help the war? Our combat troops are way across Europe over there in France and Luxembourg, and I'm over here in [a prison camp] on the Polish border. What can I . . . how can I get there? Who can I trust on the outside?

There were guys that asked about it. There was a waiting list [to go out for an escape]. That waiting list was something that I wasn't interested in.

Captured at the Battle of the Bulge, in early 1945 Ernest Gall was sent on a work detail to the city of Zittau, forty miles east of Dresden. Escape just was not an option.

We had five guys that tried to take off from there [the work camp]. They thought they could get back to the American lines. Well, they were gone a couple days, and then they brought them back. And they left them lay in front of our barracks for two weeks, in the rain, in the snow, and everything.

They were dead, sure. They thought they could get back to the American lines, you know. But they never made it. They brought them back, and they left them there so no one else would get the idea to take off. I didn't know the guys. We had just been living together in that big barracks.

So we *thought* about it, but when we saw something like that, well, we changed our mind. 'Cause we knew what would happen if they ever caught us, you know.

Captured in Italy, Don Frederick remained a POW for seventeen months; most of this time was spent in Oflag 64, a camp for infantry officers located in Poland. Planning escape at this camp was an organized business.

Everybody had a job. I ended up . . . I started making escape maps. They [ranking prisoners] put me over in the big house [the main camp building], on the third floor. I think it had three floors in that thing. I got way up in the top there. I was making escape maps in a little room all by myself.

But actually to carry through with it, Don explains, that was something else.

Always *thought* about it. There again, I'm in Poland. *Where* am I in Poland? You didn't know. . . . I didn't know if I escaped if I should go north up to the Baltic Sea or if I should go back to Germany or should I head toward Russia? . . . Should we try and get on a train out of here? You've got to do something.

Nobody really knew what to do. You were isolated out there in this little burg. It was just . . . flat, like this *(moves hand back and forth on table)*. All they raised out there I think was potatoes.

Some of the guys, there were two or three of them there that made two or three attempts to escape. They got out all right, but they didn't last out there more than a few days. They were picked up. . . . It wasn't natural during the war over there to be out in the country with one or two guys, all alone. Suspicion. Everybody that made a move, you were stopped.

I didn't have any escape plans myself, but I did make some escape maps for the guys that wanted to get out.

Harold Van Every was a B-17 bomber pilot. He spent more than a year in POW camps, most of it at Luft III Sagan.

There were guys that escaped. . . . Your job is to try to escape. But I'm not one of them. *(laughs)* There's no point in trying to be a big hero when you know what's going to happen if they catch you. You're not going to go . . . well, you've got guys sitting up in a guard tower about every half a block all the way around the outside perimeter of this thing. You're not going to try to escape when they're sitting up there with machine guns and rifles and so forth. That's just dumb. *(chuckles)*

A few were involved in escape attempts. Shot down over the Adriatic on his very first mission, Dick Pfaffinger spent thirteen months as a POW. He was at Luft I, in far northern Germany; in his barracks there was a tunnel project.

I worked on it. I didn't like it. You were just in there so tight.

[I was tempted to try to escape] in the tunnel. You'd go down about five foot and dig through, and you've got to transfer all the dirt, and you've got to hide the dirt. Then you would realize that you're in something that . . . there's nothing holding it up. Instead of clay, it's sand. It could cave in. You made it [the tunnel] as small as possible so you didn't have so much stuff to get rid of.

Our barracks was in the center of the compound. The Germans figured there was absolutely no way anybody could tunnel out that far. But we were going with it. Didn't know for sure where we were at. We hit the guard tower post, big cedar post. So then we knew where we were at. We were all set. We were going to . . . two more days, we were going to be out.

We decided to work nights. We never worked nights before. They talked about it, and I said, God, I didn't like to do it because they had sounding detectors. In the daytime there was so much noise, everybody hollering and hooting. At night it was quiet. They went and worked, and the night before we were going to [go] . . . in the morning roll call in came all the guards and the dogs and sounded it, and that was the end of our six weeks of work. Anyway, it kept us busy, I guess.

There are stories of escape, too. Ball turret gunner Simon Velasquez's B-17 bomber was shot down on April 13, 1944, over south-central Germany. Simon was blown clear of the exploding plane and drifted to the ground in his parachute, landing in a wooded area. Germans were nearby and looking for him, but for a time he managed to escape being captured.

When I hit the ground, [I thought,] how to get away? I was pretty well banged up, and I knew I couldn't run, so the first thing, . . . I got it [my parachute] off, and then I started crawling away. I crawled probably a hundred yards away. There was a few bushes. I could hear people coming around, and I went in those bushes and crawled under there. To this day I don't know how they missed me, because I was there in plain sight. People were, I'd say, [fifteen, twenty feet away].

They didn't get me right away. So after they all went away from me, I knew where I was: I was on the German side of the Rhine River. I wanted to get to the French side of the Rhine River . . . so I could find the French underground.

Airmen had so-called escape kits and instructions to look for friendly forces.

Before you go on any mission, . . . they give you maps, they give you a compass, and they give you an escape kit, which is D bars and stuff to survive. . . . I had I think three D bars, which are chocolate bars. But they're more than chocolate bars: they're supplement[ed] with vitamins and that. You could last quite a while with just eating D bars. . . . And they give you money. Like German marks if you're going through Germany, or francs if you're through France. You get two thousand dollars' worth of all that money in your pocket.

They tell you, once you get into France, . . . the French underground has different signals how to recognize who they are. Like the French would have clothing that they wash, put it on their wash lines. Maybe [a] certain way the underwear is hung, their pants are hung. And a different day . . . they're all not the same day. They had different days. . . . They have a code.

Simon estimates that he eluded capture for about six or seven days.

I traveled mostly at night. Because an airman's uniform and that . . . *(trails off)*. I slept during the day. Slept during the day and steal what I could to eat during the day. Travel at night, and you have a compass. Basically you know where to go.

He noticed that he changed during this ordeal.

Like animal instincts take over because your mind gets so much sharper. Your hearing becomes so much sharper, and your eyesight. . . . You have that survival instinct, and you want to survive, and you can do a lot of things when . . . if your life depends on it.

Simon came to a river, perhaps the Rhine, and wanted to cross.

But I was . . . I couldn't swim. I was so well banged up, so I went and I stole a little canoe and started rowing. I got to about the middle of it, and I just couldn't row anymore, so the current brought me back to the German side, and that's where they caught me.

Simon was processed through an interrogation center and sent to XVII-B in Krems, Austria, where he remained until April 1945.

Lex Schoonover served in an intelligence and reconnaissance platoon of the 106th Infantry Division. His story of capture and escape begins near the Belgian-German border. On December 16, 1944, the first day of the Germans' Ardennes Offensive, Lex was behind the wheel of a jeep.

We got about halfway back to our unit when we were fired on from the gullies beside the road by Germans, and [we] decided to floor it to see if we could run the gamut. They were on either side of us, and [at] that point ahead of us we could see one of our two-and-half-ton trucks and an ambulance, and we thought that they were our lines and if we made them we'd be there. When we reached them we were surrounded by Germans and found that the drivers of both those vehicles had been shot and killed and those vehicles were a roadblock. At this point we were captured.

We were captured in the morning, probably about nine o'clock or nine-thirty, and the Germans were digging in on top of this hill where they marched us to. They placed us between themselves and our troops, and we were lying there in the snow . . . the entire day. They didn't take us back to be interrogated; we asked them to do that, and they ignored us because they were busy digging in. By this time [there] were eight of us. There were others that they had captured in the same manner.

We were moving around a little bit and kind of whispering to each other, and we decided that one of two things were going to happen, because our artillery was zeroing in on us: we decided that we could either freeze to death there or we'd be killed by the [American] artillery. So as dusk came we seemed to all understand each other, and we got up and started to run. The lieutenant who was with us was killed in this operation, because we would run, fall, turn, roll, do whatever. We were running down a hill. We got down into the shadows in the trees, and the first thing we did was take turns lying on top of each other to get body heat to try and get our frostbitten bodies to move.

I knew geographically where I was headed, and I was kind of the leader from that standpoint. But we had no ammunition, we had no guns, and we decided that if we were challenged by anyone we would be surrendering. The other thing we didn't know was the password to get through our own lines.

We followed the shadows. We went through the woods and stayed in the shadows and were concerned with any noise that we heard. . . . We were not challenged in getting through our own lines. How we did that, I don't know. But when we got there, we didn't know if our troops were still there. . . . We hid in the bushes there until we saw an American walking. Then we made contact.

I was a wreck. I mean, I was no good for guard duty, but they were putting me out on guard duty, and my nerves were shot. What I'd been through. I was a nervous wreck. I was frightened by anything.

Three days later Lex's unit was surrounded and he was taken prisoner—again. He spent the remainder of the war in IX-B Bad Orb.

Charles King was captured in North Africa in December 1942. After interrogation there, he was sent to a POW camp in northern Italy. It was operated by the Italians, then allies of the Germans, and housed mostly British troops. Conditions were basic but acceptable, and life settled into a routine—for a while.

Well, see, then Italy capitulated [on September 8, 1943]. That's when we didn't know what to do. We were afraid that the Germans would come in and take over [the prison camp]. So there were about . . . oh, I don't know how many, maybe twenty, twenty-five of us. We got together, and we decided that we were going to do something. That's when we took three bunks that we slept on, and we tied them together to make a ladder, and it was big enough to get over the wall. Then we had a blanket and folded it up to throw it over the . . . they had broken glass on top of the walls. . . . There were fourteen that got out that way.[10]

It was practically daylight because, you know, they had the lights on all the time. We didn't know where to go. We just took off. There was rounds that had been fired. I don't know whether they were shooting at us or not, but we heard that. We went probably, oh, maybe five or six hours before we ever stopped. Then we kind of wondered what we were going to do. We were getting . . . we were hungry.

That's when we met this little old Italian [who had been in America]; Tony DeMedici his name was. He took us to his place, and we slept in the barn. They fed us, well, what they had. It wasn't much. But we stayed there about two weeks. There was a couple three times that they thought they [the Germans] were close, and they told us [to] get out and hide someplace.

Well, see, then we got wondering what we were going to do, and we decided that . . . well, the one guy I was with, he didn't want to go, but then I found out about another guy, Gorshi, from Des Moines, and we got together, and he said he'd go. And that's when we decided we would try to get to [neutral] Switzerland. You know, that was the closest. But when we got to the Po River, there was no way we could even get across there. So then we headed back south [toward Allied forces, which had invaded mainland Italy on September 3, 1943].

The two men stayed together and traveled hundreds of miles.

Just the two of us. Well, then one time we had a British soldier. He caught up with us. . . . We were always on foot. And the same clothes we had in Africa. A light jacket. We froze. Our feet were froze. We were in the mountains. Sometimes we had to go clear up to, you know, where the snow was; you couldn't cross the big ravines. Days to go down and up. We'd go up and around.

We bummed food. They [the local people] were pretty good. We did stop at one monastery. This kid I was with was Catholic. They, oh, they treated us. They brought us all kinds of food. But we couldn't haul it all, you know.

We'd find a cave and get in it. Sometimes we had a fire but very seldom because we were afraid that it would attract attention. You know, the

Charles King (right) in January 1944, back in the United States after his successful escape from a POW camp in Italy.

Germans had a lot of outposts up in the mountains. In fact, a lot of times we ran into their wires they had strung up there.

We got down to the front lines [in December 1943]. We decided that if we were going to go through that we'd split up, because it would be easier for a guy to go by himself than the two of you together.

At night, Charles attempted to get through a German position.

There were quite a few Germans in there. . . . I remember I jumped in a, I think it was an ack-ack [anti-aircraft] gun pit. Well, I roused them, the Germans. And I was fired on. But I didn't even stop; I just kept going. I think I ran for . . . I don't know how far. I stopped a couple times, you know, and rested. And then it was, oh, probably around three in the morning, and I got halted by a British paratrooper patrol.

I hollered who I was, but they wouldn't believe me because I never had dog tags or anything. But they took me back to their headquarters. They found out that another American had come into another part of the front there, and that was my buddy. We got together the next day, and they took us over to an American unit. Air corps. That's where we got our heads shaved and showered and new clothes. We were really treated [well] . . . but still, we were put under military police. They weren't sure [who we were], and they weren't going to take any chances.

We were at Casablanca [Morocco] for about, I think it was probably two weeks, and they had a hospital ship. You know, they had a lot of casualties coming out of Italy, and when they had a shipload, that's when we went and came back to the States. It was over Christmas [1943] and New Year's [1944].

When we got back they took us to the Pentagon, and we were taken from there in an enclosed car and interrogated by five or six top-ranking officers. Separate—we were separated when we went in. I guess our stories jived, and they believed us.

Japanese camps offered a different reality, as Stan Galbraith explains. A prisoner first on Java and then in Singapore, Stan worked nearly two years on the Burma-Thailand Railway.

Everybody thought about it. Well, not *seriously*. I mean, now, where in the hell are we going to go? We're a white man in Asia. The Japs got the natives there, where there's a price on your head. Where you going to go? Not knowing the country.

There were prisoners that had . . . like English or Australian, that knew that country more from working up there or being out on plantations up there that tried it. I don't know of *any* that made it. And the few, the number that tried, mostly didn't. There were a few of them beheaded. . . . I knew I was stuck.

Douglas MacArthur was a prisoner on the Philippine island of Luzon, first at Cabanatuan and then at Clark Field.

I never talked about it, I guarantee you, because I knew there was no place I could go and have much of a chance to exist. You had nothing to go on: you had no rations to take with you; there's no way to take any food. It wasn't that easy to escape. You knew dang well if you went outside the perimeter, and got outside the perimeter, you wouldn't make it. If some Filipino didn't turn you in, the Japs would get you one way or the other.

Roll call of prisoners at Malaybalay prison camp on the island of Mindanao, Philippines, 1942. The treeless surroundings made any possibility of escape all the more remote.

Even wild escape plans came up against concrete reality. Bill Connell, the navy pilot shot down over Chichi Jima island in July 1944, spent many months at Ofuna naval interrogation center in Japan.

Escape? We *thought* about it because we weren't very far from a military airbase. We could see the airplanes taking off. There was a lot of talk about the possibility of trying to leave the camp and go over there and steal an airplane. But even then we got to thinking, where are we going to fly it to? Fly it to China? Fly it to Korea? Couldn't fly it across the Pacific. So there was no place to *fly* it to.

And escape into the Japanese countryside just made no sense.

At Ofuna we had an eight-foot wooden fence that went around the camp. There was one young guy, he was determined that he was going to escape. So at night he climbed over this fence. There's no problem with that: they had two-by-fours across it. He just climbed up and jumped over the fence. He was gone for two weeks.

Finally, he came back. We said, "What the hell? Why are you here?" He said, "I couldn't find anything to eat. You can't escape in this country." It's so populated. It's either rice paddies, and the rice paddies come right up to the houses, there's no front yard or nothing. And, he says, "Even at night, there's people out walking around. You can't move. I had to hide in bushes day and night. I never got more than a half a mile from this camp. I finally just came back." They worked him over, but they didn't do anything other than that.

Still, the Japanese sought to eliminate any chance of escape. Marine Irving Silverlieb, from January 1942 to June 1945 a prisoner in Japanese camps in China, recalls how the Japanese used ten-man groups, whose members were held accountable for each other.

If I screwed up or you screwed up or somebody screwed up, that person was punished but not as much. It was always group punishment. . . .

They had told us—we were in groups of tens—if one guy escaped, the rest of the guys would be shot. But we were in the middle of China. We were white. We were different in everything. Where could we go?

Punishment for attempted escape was no idle threat. After surviving the Bataan March and Camp O'Donnell, in summer 1942 Alf Larson was sent to Clark Field on Luzon. He was one of two hundred prisoners forced to repair the heavily damaged American airfield and get it ready for Japanese use. His captors placed Alf in charge of one of the work details. As a supervisor, he carried responsibility for the whereabouts of his men.

I was a staff sergeant at the time, so I was one of the higher-ranking noncoms in the camp. They put me in charge of two barracks, and all that meant was there was extra work because I had to assign the people their next day's duty. So that's what I had to do, besides going out myself.

I'll tell you, [being in charge,] you were supposed to know where they [the other prisoners] were and what they did and what they were thinking. Two instances of it here. I had two men escape from my platoon. I didn't know at the time that they were going to go. One man was married to a Filipino, and another one had a Filipino girlfriend.

The first one was a fellow by the name of Flannigan. He was from Florida, and he just turned up missing one day. He hadn't talked to anybody about going. Anyway, the Japanese hauled us out there and put me in front of them and made me the scapegoat of it [because I was in charge].

The Japanese meted out punishment.

The people that watch the movie *The Bridge on the River Kwai,* this little shack that they built, they built one of those out there. . . . Sheet metal, right in the middle of the compound. . . . It was such that you couldn't stand up. You couldn't stretch out. You had to be squatting the whole time.

And it was right out in the hot sun. It got hotter than heck in the daytime and colder than heck at night. The first time it was only two days, so I survived that, and I was able to walk back to my compound.

When another man escaped not long after, Alf believed the Japanese might kill him and the other Allied officers in charge of the detail.

Now the second man who escaped was a fellow by the name of Taylor, and he was the one that had a wife. He escaped while he was on a detail. When they came back in—because you counted off in the morning and you counted off at night—when they got back at night, they were one man short. They had the people there, they kept them all night out there, and they didn't know what was going to happen.

Here again, the next morning then they called our officers and myself out, and they marched us up to their headquarters. There were Captain Fleming and the medical officer and one other officer and myself. On the way up, Captain Fleming, who was in charge of our camp, he says, "Well, let's show them we can die like men." So we all expected to be killed. They treated us humanely up there, just questioned us pretty thoroughly. I guess they figured that we didn't know.

What they did again, they put me into this little shack. This time for *seven* days. I would have died there if it hadn't been for this one Japanese soldier. He'd always get the midnight shift. . . . Occasionally he'd let me have his canteen, and he'd also bring me a rice ball once in a while. If it hadn't been for him, I'm sure I would have died.

Gerald Wakefield was a prisoner on the Philippine island of Palawan from 1942 to 1944. When a man in his group of ten turned up missing, it nearly cost him his life.

They just didn't [ever talk about trying to escape]. They knew that we'd be shot if they did. It was no trouble: you could have got away easy enough, but you would have left all them people behind. We had one guy who watched his brother get shot; he was on a different detail. But that was someplace else.

Now one time we had a prisoner [in our section of ten] who got away. Street was his name. He snuck out to get some fruit, and he got lost. He just got lost. But for the Japanese, he had escaped. They were going to shoot the other nine of us. I was one of the ten.

They put us in jail at night. The day we were going to be shot, they found him. That's a hell of a feeling. We figured for sure we were going to get it, but they opened up the damn door the next day and let us go. If he had got away . . . *(trails off)*. That was the closest I've been to . . . *(trails off)*.

Relations Between Men

THROUGHOUT the Stalags and Luft Stalags, prisoners formed themselves into groups for both companionship and support. Generally comprising two to six men, these groups shared extra food, looked after each other during illness, and helped pass the endless days. Organization was sometimes by branch of service or home state, other times by religion or shared interests. Loners were few.

Many of these relationships became deep and lasting friendships. An army infantryman put it this way: "We spent *every* minute of *every* day together, for almost a year. With some guys, you get to *be* like brothers in a situation like that." There is tangible evidence that the bonds forged behind barbed wire proved long lasting: ex-POWs interviewed for this project were more than twice as likely to have remained in contact with men from their camp experiences than with men from their service units.

Yet not all was positive, for familiarity also bred contempt. Very close quarters, hunger, and an overabundance of free time could exacerbate personality and other differences and create friction. Still, perhaps surprisingly, physical altercations were rare. A notable exception: men caught stealing in the barracks, especially when it was food, could expect little mercy from their fellow prisoners.[1]

And food was a primary focus of everyday life, surfacing in conversations, dreams, notebooks. The Germans did provide food—poor quality bread, potatoes, and thin soups predominated—but there was a severe lack of meat and fresh vegetables, and amounts of food were barely sufficient and decreased as the war entered its final year. Minimal quantities meant a sharp focus on equal portion size, too. Hungry men paid very close attention to how food was divided, be it a loaf of bread, the evening meal, or the contents of a Red Cross parcel.[2]

This shortage of food sometimes allowed the darker side of human nature to surface. At certain camps, the strong preyed on the weak, and there are cases where the consequences proved deadly—men killed, and were killed, in attempts to steal food.

IN THE PACIFIC, too, the demands of life behind barbed wire led men to greatly rely on each other. There were closely knit tribes, with members providing the crucial assistance necessary to survive another day. Even more so than in Europe, loners were few—and loners that survived fewer still.[3]

The constant struggle to supplement inadequate rations consumed much of a tribe's time and energy. At first in most camps, in addition to rice the Japanese provided small quantities of vegetables, beans, even fish or the occasional portion of meat. As the war dragged on, however, these extras gradually disappeared and little other than rice was supplied; caloric intake, at the best of times less than half the daily average of a peacetime U.S. soldier, fell even further. In such circumstances, prisoners learned to eat anything they could find, including snakes, monkeys, insects, and frogs. Red Cross parcels, an important source of nutrition for Americans held in German camps, were rarely seen: the Japanese showed little interest in accepting and distributing extra food.[4]

Physically and even psychologically debilitated by the poor diet, prisoners craved food and conspired to get it in any way possible. As Japan's situation deteriorated, POWs received less food; as a result, men went to greater lengths to satisfy this urge. And as strong as friendships or as united as tribes might be, they didn't always stand up to starvation. "If the men were to survive, they had to live by their wits," writes Brian MacArthur in *Surviving the Sword*. "Thieves, racketeers, and black marketeers flourished in all the prison camps of the Far East, often at the expense of their fellow prisoners." Entrepreneurs prospered; the strong preyed on the weak. In the end, anything—and anyone—was fair game.[5]

Men in German Camps

After months in the hospital recovering from a gunshot wound, Dick Carroll, a bomber pilot, arrived at Luft I in December 1944. Friends were essential.

[Y]ou had trust and reliance. You knew the individuals. You knew what to expect of them, and you knew that you could get along real well with them. It was almost like having this blanket that a little kid runs around with. . . . It's that same security that you're looking for. I think all people need that. That's why the people that reacted not good . . . I think they were missing that security, and they were having troubles. We had one man that didn't react angrily; he just wouldn't talk to you very much.

Some [men] had a hard time keeping [a sense of optimism]. They would have to be rejuvenated every so often. My friend from Nebraska was real good on that. He'd take them for a walk around the circumference of the *Lager* and talk to them and encourage them to have faith that they'll make it. He was real good. Yes.

This was living life very close because you needed the warmth of the bodies next to each other to keep warm at night. So Hank was on one side of me and Wayne, from Nebraska, was on the other side. We were all six foot. Wayne was about six foot three, I was six foot one, and Hank was six foot. So we were all tall guys, and we got along real well. Actually, you're so close that when one turned almost everybody else had to turn at the same time to fit. . . . It was amazing during all of that time how well twenty-four men [in our room] that had to be literally shoulder to shoulder at all times managed to adjust to that living, without getting angry at one another.

There were two men that would flare out every so often, and you've got to expect it. You could predict that they would, and others . . . well, they would also aggravate some of the other POWs, too, but most would just ignore them . . . and so it wasn't a problem. Just a fact of life. It's pretty hard to expect you'd get twenty-four men that would adapt to everything impersonally and be adaptable and all of that.

Army enlisted man Bruce Brummond was shuffled between five camps during his four and a half months as a POW (December 1944–April 1945). One constant was friends.

We were more or less with the same group all the time. Ollie and Pete were two fellows. Ollie—his name was Todd Olson, we called him Ollie—he was from Evanston. Pete was, Peterson was from Minneapolis. Now Roach was there, and Soldo.

We just became friendly. We were more or less thrown together with the same group, and it just naturally evolved. When we got the Red Cross parcels, we'd get three or four of us and cook together. We'd take turns cooking. Take turns doing KP.

Recd Jan. 30-45

Luftpost
Par Avion

Kriegsgefangenenpost

Postkarte

GEPRÜFT 98

Taxe perçue

An

MR. HERMAN PETERSON

16.11.44-8

Gebührenfrei!

Absender:
Vor- und Zuname: 2ND. LT. DALE PETERSON
Gefangenennummer: 3418
Lager-Bezeichnung: Stalag-Luft-1
via Stalag Luft 3
Deutschland (Allemagne)

U.S. CENSOR 11338

Empfangsort: Nye
Straße: WISCONSIN
Land: U.S. of AMERIKA
Landesteil (Provinz usw.

Kriegsgefangenenlager

Datum: OCT. 15, 1944

DEAR DAD, I am still sweating out some mail. None yet and This is 11th of OCT. I wish you all a merry Christmas and A Happy New year. I hope you all are well back home. I am Feeling Fine. Love to all Dale

Kriegsgefangenenpost *(POW post): By terms of the Geneva Convention, POWs could use postcards to correspond with family and loved ones. Censorship—note the German stamp "*GEPRÜFT*"—meant the contents needed to remain generic. Dale Peterson wrote to his father, Herman, back in rural Nye, Wisconsin. Dale dated the card "Oct 15, 1944," yet the German post stamp is more than a month later (16.11.44, or November 16, 1944). Only ten weeks after this date, on January 30, 1945, would Mr. Peterson finally receive the card (see date in his hand, top of card).*

I think [having friends to share experiences with] was very important, because we would talk a lot about things at home and things we did before the war, things that we thought we were going to do after the war. Of course food was a big topic, and we'd talk about recipes and things that our mothers made and our wives made, those type of things.

Captured in Germany in October 1944, as a POW Bill Hall relied heavily on two close friends from his unit. He found out the value of this friendship at his first camp, XII-A Limburg.

I developed a severe case of dysentery. Terrible. I became—I went into a coma. And I had two good friends, Bill Shortell and Jim Jordan, who carried me over to the so-called camp hospital. It wasn't much better than the barracks we had. They had a British doctor, [but] . . . the only thing he had available to treat us with was Nestle powdered milk. That was to dry up our insides. So that's what he had.

I was in there probably I suppose a week. One morning I could hear a commotion outside the windows. I was [on the] second floor. And there was a group standing around a little podium. . . . Then I heard . . . "When you get on the train you'll have a little more to eat than you got here." I thought, my gosh, they're moving out! So I recognized Bill Shortell down there, and I yelled out the window, and I said, "Bill, are you guys going?" "Yes," he said, "We're moving out." I said, "Well, so am I." He said, "You can't go out." I said, "The heck I can't. Can you catch me?" So the two of them get under that window, and I jumped out of the window. I almost broke their arms. I jumped out of the window to get in that group to go.

I *absolutely* didn't want to be left there alone, [to leave] people that I knew. Because they were the ones that took care of me. I certainly didn't want to lose them. I knew nobody else. If they were going, I was going to go. So I made that trip in that train. Sicker than a dog.

Russ Gunvalson survived IX-B Bad Orb and then IX-A Ziegenhain. By the time the war ended, he was in tough shape. He talks about the value of having a friend.

You have to have somebody, a buddy that you can really trust and confide in, and knew he'd help you.

I can't think of any closer friend than I have in Hugh Kingery, my bunkmate. He lives in Birmingham, Alabama. He was with me in the marches, in the boxcars, in the prison camp [at Bad Orb], and with me all the way to Ziegenhain.

Like I go back to up in Ziegenhain, when we were getting so weak. I'd black out. I'd just kind of faint, and they'd take about six guys to roll you up to your bunk. And Hugh Kingery and I, when we got together at Ziegenhain, we said that . . . we'd take the top bunk, because heat rises and let's get up off that cold floor. So they'd roll me up there, and Hugh would come up, and we'd just lay together to keep warm. It's somebody that you looked out for, and he looked out for you. It was a buddy system. When you're alone, you're alone.

Some men were more withdrawn. Bomber pilot Lyle Pearson, from January to May 1945 a prisoner at Luft I, kept largely to himself.

Guys would get down pretty much, wondering what's going on and talking about their families back home. But you know, you kind of, I don't know, you didn't talk to one another about it so much. You sat and thought about it. I met a guy that I'd been in the old CCC camp with. But we didn't—and I saw him two or three times—we didn't even say anything to each other.

Communal washroom at Luft I. Everything in the camps was crowded, even washroom facilities. With cold water only, even in winter, they were often poorly maintained and not always accessible. This facility, at a camp for officers, was better than most.

Until one day we happened to be sitting, and they gave us some water to wash up, and we were right beside each other washing up, and then I said, "You're Swanson. You were in camp so and so, and you're from Minneapolis." And he said, "Yes, that's right." And so then we talked a little bit. But otherwise we just didn't have the, I suppose, the ambition to go out of our way to do anything.

But not all was positive. In close quarters, lacking all privacy, with hunger ever present, some POWs admit there were certain darker sides of camp life. During his months at Luft I, fighter pilot Bill Schleppegrell didn't have trouble making friends—not with everyone, though.

[There were some] you *wouldn't* want to be with. Everyone is different, and so there were some that you kind of buddied with and others that you wondered what they were doing. How they could possibly be. . . . Some of them were, I mean, they would tell stories of things that they did that were . . . *(trails off)*. We hear atrocities of what others have done to us, but when you realize that . . . *(trails off)*. I guess this spirit exists in every set of people.

Paratrooper Jack Ringgenberg was captured in January 1944 at the Anzio invasion. Passing through five camps before war's end, he came into contact with all types of men.

[Disagreements were caused by] bragging about something you knew was a bunch of bullshit.

Basically we all got along pretty good, but there would be a few people that all of us couldn't tolerate. They were bragging too much, or they knew too much. We had this one guy from California. He was in the air corps, and he was so full of hot air, and he would *never* shut up. You just get tired of listening to an individual like that. [There is] nothing you can do. Like some of the rooms we were in, there would be anywhere from twenty to thirty people.

Vern Kruse arrived in late 1944 at III-C Küstrin. He identifies a problem evidenced in many camps: theft.

There was a certain amount of stealing going on, sure. You had to fall out for roll call every morning. Somebody from another barracks, he might go in there. You can't watch the door on your building. [But] there wasn't that much. What was there to steal, outside of the food, which we only got maybe three Red Cross packages during the time that we were there? Other than that, only the clothes on our back. You didn't *have* anything. You *wore* what was yours. I mean, your bedding is yours. And that's just straw inside of a container.

Crowded barracks at Luft I, 1945. Prisoners pass time reading, writing, playing cards, or just standing around and talking. Such close quarters led to friction between some men.

After twice being captured during the Battle of the Bulge, Lex Schoonover finally made it to a permanent camp: badly overcrowded IX-B Bad Orb. Arriving in January 1945, he spent the remainder of the war there. At this camp, theft was rampant, and everything was a target.

If you heard somebody walking in the aisle [at night] between your bunks, you'd ask who they were. You didn't recognize the voice, they were there to steal something off you. You kept your shoes on, too. If you take them off they might steal them and trade them. . . . You wouldn't leave anything. If you left something, it would be stolen. . . . Anything of clothing that you might have taken off. Particularly shoes. I kept them [my shoes] on all the time. Otherwise, I may not have had them.

There wasn't much else that they could take. The only other time would be the time we got the Red Cross package. If we didn't eat it all and tried to save it, that might disappear. Or bread, if you were trying to save your bread.

If you had it on your person, then they couldn't take it. If you leave it unattended, it isn't going to be there.

Men in Japanese Camps

Burma-Thailand Railway prisoner Jim Whittaker.

Your main concern was for yourself, and surviving. But to do that you had to save whatever sympathy you had for yourself, or for your immediate friends.

Keeping a positive outlook and maintaining one's determination to survive presented a constant challenge.

To [mentally give up] would be fatal. If you didn't believe strongly that you were going to get out of it, if you didn't think positively, if you didn't try to accept what was thrown at you and handle it the best you could . . . *(trails off)*. You could tell by a guy—if he tried to keep clean, if he tried to be a soldier, didn't let himself go, if he tried to keep his beard cut off, generally the way they looked after themselves—you could almost tell. . . . If you lose respect for yourself, then you've had it.

It's very discouraging, of course, when you've worked all day in the rain, and you come in, and you've got watery rice for supper, and the wind is blowing the rain through the huts, and you're soaking wet, you can't get warm, and you know you've got to face the same thing the next day. . . . If you begin to feel sorry for yourself and don't have positive thoughts, you're gonna go. Most wanted to survive, but there were a few who just gave up. To be very sick and unable to face the miserable rice diet, that would make some people feel sorry for themselves, and that lessened the chance of making it. You had to have positive thoughts.

Jim firmly believes that an important factor in maintaining some positive outlook was having friends.

If you didn't have a friend, or a group of friends that would look after you, you were really in bad shape, because you were on your own. I believe it was absolutely essential to have a close friend, somebody to share things with and to look after you when you were sick. To be alone and have nobody to talk to about home and postwar plans would mean a miserable existence.

On the value of friends, Stan Galbraith agrees. He had a close friend, a man like himself, and they took care of each other throughout their ordeal: on Java, Singapore, and the Burma-Thailand Railway.

My closest one up there was Buster Spann. He was from Texas. . . . He was heavyset . . . about six foot. He and I were buddies, and he was about my age, which was a year older or so than some of the guys.

I didn't really know him until I met him in the Bicycle Camp [on Java], because he wasn't in D Battery with me. He drove a truck, and I drove truck. He liked to gamble. I liked to gamble, if I had any money. *(chuckles)* We'd . . . you might say we've been around the horn a little bit before.

We buddied up, and he and I, we carried all our equipment on a bamboo [pole]. . . . We had to march all the way from Ban Pong after the railroad there up to our first camp up at Tarsau, and we carried all our gear on a bamboo pole between the two of us. That means mosquito nets, food, everything. And neither one of us would give . . . we wouldn't trade anything for just a couple bananas.

You know, when a guy's down, like where we got in certain places . . . like along the River Kwai there. In the camp there like at Tarsau, where it was more or less something of a hospital, and you had a little more leeway because most of the guys were so sick, you could get some duck eggs or something from trade with the natives. He was in a position that he used to help me when I got up there. . . . He'd share. If he got, if he could get two eggs, I got one of them.

Howard Swanson agrees: it was crucial to have a few close friends.

It was kind of like a buddy system. You can't make friends with them all . . . but you can make close friends with a few of them. I think that's what happened. I think you *gotta* have friends. You can't be in a group like that without having friends. . . . You were going through the same damn thing. All together. You kind of share each other's misery.

Ski was a good friend of mine. Frank Glischinski. We never called him Frank. Always called him Ski. I met him at Cabanatuan. That's where I met him.

Prisoners doing exercises at Malaybalay camp, 1942. In the first months of captivity, conditions and food supply at this camp were markedly better than at other Philippine locations. Men had time and energy to engage in morale-boosting activities such as exercise. By October 1942, though, this anomaly was closed, and prisoners moved to labor detail camps, most in the Philippines.

Navy enlisted man Louis Bailen, held on Palawan Island, focuses on different aspects of friendship: conversation and the comfort men could offer one another.

[Y]ou'd sit on the bench there, and you could gab with just maybe three or four guys. That was it. Yes. You didn't go around to the army guys that you never knew. We ate together and talked. Just sat and talked. Yes, that's it. Brothers. Just a couple of marines and mostly navy.

One was named Herman Barger, and Bernard. He was army, though. Bernard was army. And Barger was navy. He was a boatswain's mate. I liked to talk to him because he was a gabby guy. He could rattle on and on and on. And he was a happy guy.

There was nothing you could help [each other] with. There's nothing you could help, because the guys I knew had ulcers on their leg that were three, four inches in diameter and circumference and deep that never healed. Never healed. So what could you do? You just looked at it and felt sorry. You were helpless. There was nothing you could do. You didn't really comfort each other. You just talked to them. Because you were all in the same boat.

Al Kopp was sunk off the USS Houston *in March 1942. In the first days after the sinking, the Japanese moved survivors to an old stone prison used by colonial officials. Al talks about how shared background led to the establishment of a friendship.*

[The cells] were about, maybe [twelve feet by twelve feet], and they put . . . they filled them all. Standing up. We couldn't lay down to sleep. We couldn't sit down because it was too crowded. So we had to do it in shifts, and of course the wounded ones had to sit and lay first. When your shift came around, you'd get to lay down. . . . I stood for an awful long time. I don't know. You just do it. You just hope and pray that you gotta get out of there or something.

We used to lay there. Here we were, three thousand miles from home and laying on a dingy, dirty, close area on a hard rock floor, a cobblestone floor. Half the guys are wounded. I was wounded. I had some shrapnel wounds, but they weren't serious.

I laid down with the guy next to me on the floor, and we're talking and talking, and he said, "Where are you from?" And I said, "I'm from North Dakota." "The hell you are!" I said, "Where are you from?" "*I'm* from North Dakota." I said, "What town?" And he said, "You never heard of it." And I said, "Try me." "Selfridge." I said, "Hell, I used to play basketball against you." Selfridge is only about forty miles from Raleigh. That's where I was born. He had graduated the same year I did. His name was Bigger. I remembered the name then. I knew him just barely on ship. He was in the fire division, and I was down below . . . but I wasn't a real close friend of his. Believe me, we got to *be* close.

Within prisoner communities, some men were treated as outcasts, as Alf Larson recalls. The Bataan March survivor was part of a work detail at Clark Field, Luzon. Upon arrival, the Japanese asked prisoners their mili-

tary occupation. Most men lied and said they were unskilled. But not all—some who had a skilled trade, such as aircraft mechanic, admitted to it. The Japanese had asked for a reason: the Army Air Corps had stationed P-40 Warhawk fighters at Clark Field prior to the surrender; some damaged versions remained, and the Japanese sought to make them airworthy.

There were some people that said, yes, I worked on the [P-40] airplane. [So] they actually worked on the P-40s that they had up there, that had been damaged, and they were trying to put back into shape. Of course, those people were exiled from anything in camp. Nobody had anything to do with them because they were working for the Japanese.

They were looked on as collaborators. Now whether that's actually true or not I don't know, but the ones that had said yes, we can do this [mechanic work], we sort of isolated them. Shunned them. . . . They had to live with us. It was pretty miserable with them. They eventually got together as a group and [moved to a separate area].

They felt they would get extra perks. And some of them actually *did* get extra perks. But when we were getting ready to abandon Clark Field, they were kept there [by the Japanese], because not only were they airplane mechanics but they were operators of machinery and things of that nature.

They all got executed. . . . We know they were executed because the Filipinos, when we got back to Manila after the war [awaiting evacuation back to the USA], . . . they told us that all the men that were there—they named them—they got shot.

Hunger in German Camps

Food at IX-B Bad Orb was always in short supply. Lex Schoonover remembers there being precious little to eat.

The only thing we got was a cup of soup and a sixth of a loaf of bread a day. That's what we lived on. And the brown bread was made out of part sawdust. It was a brown, dark brown bread. Hard, heavy bread. You know, when you're that hungry, it tastes pretty good. . . .

Conditions at the camp were among the worst. Thus, when extra food was available, its division was carefully monitored.

I can remember getting a Red Cross package, and we only got three in the whole time I was there. One of them had raisins . . . and we had to split them twelve ways. We made twelve piles of raisins. One, one, one, one, one and then two, two, two, two, two.

During March 1944–February 1945, Les Schrenk was at Luft VI and then Luft IV. Locations may have differed, but one feeling was constant.

I don't think anybody ever thought of women. It was *food*. Food became an obsession. Every time you'd dream of food, it was always something real rich: chocolate, sugar, butter. I mean, it was never potatoes or something like that. It was always something real rich. You would dream of the concoctions you were going to make after you were free again. Not only *dreamt* about it, but thought of it all during the day.

Hunger meant you ate what there was.

The thing that I couldn't stand . . . this came in metal cans, and I think it came from a place that maybe processed fish of some type, either cod-liver oil or something like that. Every piece of that fish was in that can, the head, the eyeballs, the fins, the scales. *Everything*. When you opened it up, it absolutely looked rotten. It *smelled* rotten. It *tasted* rotten. But that's all the food you had. I can remember taking a little bit of a bite, holding my nose, swallowing just as quick as I could.

Shot down over Germany on New Year's Day 1945, fighter pilot Bill Schleppegrell was at Luft I until the end of the war.

The food was, you know, it was really bad at that time. . . . [Hunger was] a *big* problem. We were hungry all the time. That's *all* we talked about.

[The Germans supplied] pretty regularly turnips, rutabagas, potatoes. Rarely did we get meat. It would be horse meat, I think. I'm sure it was because . . . there was a place we would send one person to get the food for the day, the commissary or whatever. He came back with a great big bone. Leg, with meat on it we had to carve off. It was cooked. But we knew it was a horse.

[We had a] cook. *(chuckles)* Didn't have much *to* cook. But there was a little kitchen area with a stove. Somehow we fashioned . . . not utensils, but pans out of some of the containers, out of tin. . . . We'd pool some of the stuff and made what they called *Kriegie* cakes, or *Kriegie* bars, and that was a real treat.

Many barracks were equipped with kitchen corners such as this one. Prisoners cooked anything and everything: items from Red Cross packages, food received from family, and bulk foods supplied by the Germans. Esteemed was the man who could create appetizing meals with few ingredients. For a year and a half at Luft III, Charles Woehrle managed to do just that.

I made a lot of things out of almost nothing. . . . For Christmas, I actually made a form with turkey legs and the turkey, because we had had cans of actual turkey meat, as a Christmas present, from America. Then I made a stuffing out of bread crumbs and mashed potatoes and put it inside, and then laid the turkey in this form, and the drumsticks were kind of like . . . they looked like egg beaters. I covered the whole thing with this dough that I made from millet seed and dried milk and potatoes and baked it. And it looked really quite like a real turkey. We had guys coming to our door wanting to see the bird.

Bob Knobel was a prisoner at Luft IV from July 1944 to February 1945. Here, too, food was scarce.

Our breakfast was a big kettle of hot water. It was like an oversized coffeepot, with hot water. That was what we got at breakfast, and from them at noon we got a water pail full of soup. So-called soup. Barley soup, kohlrabi soup, or dehydrated carrot soup. A lot of it would stir itself because of the bugs and stuff. *(laughs)* Then for supper, or for the evening, we got that same pail, got that full of boiled potatoes. That was what the Germans gave us.

Glen Naze, a prisoner at Luft IV during the same period, July 1944 to February 1945, recalls the community food preparation.

We had two American cooks, and [in the mess hall there were] big vats that they threw everything in. You'd go up there and get the pail of whatever it was.

We took the corned beef [from the] Red Cross parcels and gave it to the cook. He'd make a stew out of that. All these pound corned beefs—you might get three or four meals out of it, maybe more. I don't know how he did it. We had three thousand guys there, and we got fifteen hundred cans of corned beef. It went further if you gave it to him. So everybody would give it to him. The corned beef was all volunteered.

Hunger created desperate men and tense situations. The results, as numerous men related, could be ugly, even deadly. Captured in the first week of January 1945, army enlisted man Harold Brick spent six weeks at IX-B Bad Orb before being sent on a work detail. By this time, little but poor-quality bread was available at the camp. Here as at other camps, whole loaves were distributed; the prisoners, in groups, were responsible for slicing and distributing the portions. But these groups, as Harold explains, were not necessarily eight friends dividing up bread: they were eight hungry men who may or may not know each other or even like each other.

Initially the group that I was in, no one had any utensil to cut it. Break bread when you're hungry and you don't get it very even, that's a big problem. People get angry because, I mean, that's their lifeline. I mean, a crumb was worth a lot there.

I'll tell you how we got around that. Another guy and I, we took my canteen cup. We broke the handle off, and we found a rock, and we hammered it. Straightened it out, and we ground it down and put a little edge on it. We took, from my helmet, we took the band out of it. That was the handle. That's what we used for cutting the bread. . . . I've got that knife yet.

Being as how I had the knife, I was the slicer. . . . The thing of it is, someone had to do it. And I *wasn't* going to let that knife go to no one else. I wasn't going to give that to *anybody.*

After his capture in December 1944, Floyd Dahl spent the rest of the war at IV-B Mühlberg. Unscrupulous operators preyed on the unsuspecting.

One time we were real hungry for something more solid than the bread. . . . [A] group of Russians were in the camp also [in a separate compound]. We met a couple of Russians that had a can of Spam. So I talked Nash [his best friend, Ignacio Lopez] into trading some of his cigarettes along with some of mine, and we'd buy a can of Spam. We were so happy when we got this bargain. Bargained this down to where we could buy it.

Then we hurried back to our bunk. We opened up this can of Spam, and it was potato peelings. We had been taken: hook, line, and sinker. They put the top of one can in the bottom of another can, and they stuffed it full of potato peelings. So it was the right weight and everything. We never knew it until we opened it with a can opener. Oh, did we take off to see if we couldn't find those guys. Never did find them. [We were] angry! . . . We could have bought a couple, three loaves of bread.

Dick Pfaffinger was at Luft I. He relates an incident of theft—and the result.

I had to take care of it [the food we kept on a shelf]. The food started disappearing. I was watching all the time. I was up in the top bunk. All at once I saw a shadow, and I dove off that top bunk, and I hit this guy, and down we went. Of course, that woke everybody else up. Here he was just, "I'm so hungry," he said, "I can't stand it. I know you've got some food in there." I said, "What about the rest of us?"

The culprit was from their barracks.

He got roughed up a little. Everybody knew that I was in charge, so it was my duty to try to save the food, [make sure] that it didn't get away. . . . After we got done with him, we didn't have any more trouble, either.

When caught, not all thieves got off easy. Paratrooper Jack Ringgenberg relates an incident from one of the camps he was in.

There was one guy, prisoner, he was saving up his bread, and another guy stole it. So a bunch of friends of the guy that had the bread stolen took this guy and stuck his head down into a latrine. Later on [ten years after the war], I got a letter from the VA asking me about this situation,

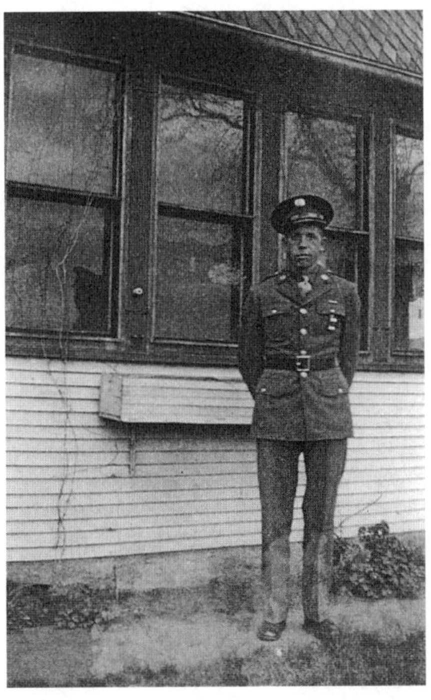

Ray Winter served with the army's 106th Infantry Division. Captured in December 1944 at the Battle of the Bulge, he spent hungry months on a work detail on the outskirts of Leipzig in spring 1945.

You took anything you got. If you found an onion laying in the horse manure, you picked it up and ate it. Anything edible. We'd take it back home, and then if we had a potato—and they had a lot of potatoes, you know, so you found them all over—then you'd take it back home, cook it up a little bit, and you'd have a bit extra to eat.

[By the end,] I was malnourished. I used to weigh about 180 pounds, like that, and when they liberated me I weighed 110 pounds. I lost about seventy pounds.

because I guess the guy that had his head stuck in the latrine was blind. Blinded by having his head exposed in, you know [the sewage]. It *had* happened.

[The VA] wrote and said this guy was suing these other soldiers. They wanted me to testify, and I just said leave me out of it. I don't want any part of it.

This consistent lack of food pushed men to take enormous risks to obtain it, as an example at IX-B Bad Orb illustrates. The camp's population swelled with men captured in December at the Battle of the Bulge, and the already insufficient food supply was stretched even further. Camp records document that on January 27, 1945, two American POWs named Lewandowski and Parks attempted to steal rations from the camp kitchen, with deadly consequences. Lex Schoonover and Harold Brick were prisoners at Bad Orb at the time.[6]

Harold Brick:

There was two guys. Somehow at night they got into the kitchen, and the

[German] guard caught them, and they hacked the guard with a meat cleaver.

The next day [January 28], we . . . were all lined up outside. The machine guns were pointed directly at us. In addition, they had some extra machine guns right on the ground level. We stood out there all day long. They told us why. They told us that we were going to stay there until such a time as those who had done it [stepped forward].

Lex Schoonover:

No one confessed, and we stood out there a whole afternoon, but as time wore on they decided they were going to shoot a man every fifteen minutes until they got it. And they did take some people away. Whether they shot them or not, I don't know.[7]

Harold Brick:

The two guys that did it, they finally were convinced that they should step forward. I think the chaplain had some input in it.

We were allowed to go inside [the barracks]. But we didn't have any food for that day. But that was the extent of it for us. The two guys who had done it, I have seen one of them. . . . What happened to the other one, I don't know.

Enlisted man Paul Peterson was processed through IV-B Mühlberg before being transported in early 1945 to a permanent camp at Görlitz, 110 miles southeast of Berlin. Then twenty years old, Paul witnessed the worst sides of human nature at VIII-A.

This was the second camp that I was in. We were moved there, the first Americans in that camp. When we got there, when we occupied this barracks that they had, next to us was another barracks that had been occupied by Serbs. Those people prepared food for us and brought it over to our barracks for us. It was a kind of rice and powdered milk and water, very nourishing and very tasty. We were hungry, and we were grateful for it.

But it turned out that two of our guys, while the Serbs were over serving us, were over looting the Serb barracks. I'm talking about our own guys. The Serbs caught them. There's no system of justice here; you're in an enemy prison camp.

They [the Serbs] were prisoners. So they brought them to us and said, "This is what happened. This is what your guys did." It was up to us to mete out justice. And the guys who were leading our group decided that we would hook these guys up with a belt on each wrist, announce to the barracks that these were the guys that ripped off the Serbs while they were over here feeding us, and it's your chance to come out and take a shot at them. These two guys were beaten to death. By Americans.

[This was] frightening. [But] there was no real alternative. These people needed some severe punishment for what they had done. I certainly felt that. I don't think anybody expected it would be quite as bitter as it was.

[The Germans were] blissfully unconcerned: "It's your problem."

Hunger in Japanese Camps

Harold Kurvers tries to find words for the kind of hunger he experienced while a prisoner of the Japanese.

You were hungry all the time. Even when you were full, you were hungry. There was something your system was crying for. Rice doesn't cut the mustard. Fills you up, but lacks something. You get filled up, but your body is craving something, whatever it is.

The Bataan March survivor spent two and a half years at Cabanatuan.

[There was] a lot of rice. At one time I think . . . Filipinos were allowed to send rice in to us, and we got an abundance of it. So you get built up to where you're pretty strong. But rice is all water, and if you get hit with dengue [fever] or malaria, then you're almost down to nothing in a few days again. If the fever is extended a couple of days, you go down.

There was a weed soup. Then we got *commode*—it was almost like a sweet potato—and things like corn. We got it when they [the Japanese] didn't want it. To cut that corn off the cob, you'd have to sharpen your knife. We soaked it and made hominy out of it. It had to be soaked for a couple of days it was so hard. *(chuckles)* All I can say is you'd have to sharpen your knife. And there was a *sinkomas,* another kind of a vegetable. Mostly weed soup. We'd get piles of it. It was moldy.

The amount of food declined as the war dragged on. Men struggled to get as much rice as possible, to obtain a few more grains.

You know the mess kit? When that started coming in, the bunches of rice, you could hear guys night and day, pounding. The mess kits were that deep *(holds fingers about an inch apart)*. Pound it out and make [it] hold more. It became almost like a bowl. It was that deep *(holds fingers closer to two inches apart)*. Real thin, the metal would be real thin. They pounded it out. Because they'd get it loaded up with rice.

From mid-1943, Stan Galbraith was at work camps in the Burma-Thailand jungle. The quality and quantity of food changed over time.

When we were still in Java, the rice was clean and we had other things. Beans, red beans and stuff. But . . . after Singapore, up along the river [in the jungle], a lot of it was spoiled rice. Gravel in it and some worms or maybe dead ones in it.

Of course, the Japs were getting . . . their troops were getting stretched out at that time, too [1944]. So they weren't going to give us the [good stuff]. . . . At first, you know, when we started getting that bad rice with worms, [we were] . . . a little fussy. That didn't last long. *(laughing)* Eat it or forget it! Naturally you wouldn't take a little pebble or something and break a tooth on it. But a little dead worm, a small one, that's just a little protein.

We learned watching some of the natives and that up there that there's a few greens that grew along that you could be safe, if you could get them before the natives. Cooking them, boiling them, and eating them. They did that.

Jim Whittaker also worked on the Burma-Thailand Railway. Like most Pacific POWs, Jim remembers a gnawing sense of hunger and the miserable rations that produced this feeling. There were few options to alleviate the situation.

I don't know what the calorie count was, but there was never enough food. Both in volume or quality, it was not enough to sustain the health of people engaged in heavy manual labor. We were *always* hungry. Food was always on everybody's mind. . . .

At best we got rice three times a day. And the Japanese worked on Japanese time. Japan time was a couple of hours ahead of local time, so the workday started in the predawn darkness. We would be given a mug of watery rice called pap, kind of porridgy stuff; there was no sugar or salt, and it was not very satisfying. You would drink that, and it would go right through and clean out the kidneys almost right away. That was breakfast.

The next meal would be out on the job. Cooked rice and watery soup would be carried from the camp, and we would be given a small pint-size mug of rice and a much smaller ladle of the soup. So you would eat that on the job; again, there's no drinking water, no tea or anything. The evening meal back in camp would be the same except the soup would include whatever meat was used to make the midday meal.

As for the evening meal, it would be the same small measure of rice, a small cup, about two-thirds the size of this—a small coffee mug size. Dry rice with a ladle of whatever had been used to make soup—it would be watery, whatever it was. . . .

And you would supplement this [ration] with whatever you could buy or find: eggs, or snake, whatever. . . . Anything thought edible was collected and eaten to supplement the issued rations. We would try to find edible food in the jungle; snakes were a great delicacy if you could catch one. The Australians taught us that there was something they called pigweed, a leafy green plant, that we could boil. Didn't taste very good, but we figured it was good for us.

Some [men] would have army-issue mess tins, others might use a hubcap, a tin plate, or even a container made from bamboo. There were never any tables or chairs: we ate squatting on the ground; back in camp, we might sit on our sleeping platform. Drinking water would be boiled on the job; in the cholera season, water would also be boiled to sterilize whatever was used to eat from.

The prison camps on Formosa held prisoners of different nationalities: Americans, British, Dutch—men captured throughout Southeast Asia. Robert Heer was there from late 1942 to the beginning of 1945. Constantly short of food, men used a variety of ways to acquire more.

Sometimes I'd work in the garden. You know, in the garden doing weeding and planting potatoes or digging potatoes up, bringing them into camp. Of course, whenever we had a chance, we'd steal the sweet potatoes.

Old aluminum canteens had this little round hole at the top. And when we were out in the garden weeding, whenever I saw a fingerling sweet potato about the size of your finger, I'd slip it inside my water bottle. By the time I got through in the day, that thing was full of little fingerling sweet potatoes. Then when I got in the camp at night, I'd take and fill it full of water and shake it until all . . . until I got no more dirt out. Then I'd fill it with water, and they had a fire there where you could . . . [it] was a fire for heating water for our baths. I put it in the fire and let it cook. When it was finished, I'd have sweet potato soup.

Stealing food carried the risk of being caught and punished by the Japanese.

We were caught stealing sweet potatoes just outside our barracks in the garden, and they took us out to the guardhouse, and they made us both get down on our knees. . . . Then they made us hold our hands straight up. And then whenever our hands would drop, the Japanese sergeant of the guard would come with a big kendo stick, and he beat us on the back with the kendo stick. Well, I didn't know it at the time, but he fractured two of my vertebrae. . . . Then afterwards they grabbed him [the other prisoner, Hook Johnson] by the hair and dragged him all around the front of the guardhouse. Then they threw us both in the guardhouse for three days with no food and just some water, and that was it.

As the war dragged on and went increasingly poorly for Japan, even the meager rations decreased.

When you get hungry, you'll eat almost anything. One time after we were moving up to Hokkaido [Japan, in 1945], they gave us some food. I ate my mess first, and one of the guys, he was eating his, and [he says], "Hey, did you see this?" I said, "Yes, I saw that." It was in my rice kit. He says, "Well, it's a grasshopper." *(chuckles)* And I said, "Oh my God, did I eat a grasshopper?" And I guess I did.

Shot down in July 1944, navy pilot Bill Connell spent much of the rest of the war at Camp Ofuna in Japan.

There was absolutely no talk of women or sex. It was food and survival. That's *all* we thought about.

We were allowed to walk around the compound as much as we wanted, and we would go in twos and threes, and we talked 95 percent of the time about food. *Food.* . . . We had people there [from all parts of the country], and we talked about how our mothers cooked different meals and all this. Food was primarily our main concern. Because we didn't have any.

The constant hunger often brought to the surface a negative side of human nature: trust was broken, the strong preyed on the weak, men did what they needed to survive. Robert Heer remembers the enormous strain on men and on their relationship with each other.

There were always some that were hungry, and they'd steal from their buddies . . . well, not from their buddies, but from anybody if they could get away with it. Like especially food. Well, that and cigarettes. Because cigarettes could buy food. . . .

They'd fight over rations sometimes. For example when . . . we had one guy, our squad leader down in Heito was a British lance corporal. He was a nice guy. He was one that always divided the rice up. I thought he did it fairly evenly. But sometimes some of the guys would say, hey, you gave him more than you gave me. It might have been maybe a half a teaspoon. Or maybe a teaspoon full of soup. Then that would start a fight. It was usually taken care of right then and there.

Harry Magnuson and Bob Michelsen, both B-29 crew members shot down in May 1945 over Tokyo, were held in a prison operated by the Kempeitai secret police. Cells were cramped. Bob remembers how the small amount of food, less even than that issued to standard POWs, was divided among the sixteen men.

I recall that we received one rice ball a day. . . . Always, to me, one rice ball and one cup of water each day. [T]hey would roll the rice balls in on the floor, through a little opening under the bars, and that would leave a few grains on the floor. The captain [Dick Mansfield, commander of Bob's B-29 and ranking officer in the cell] decided that those grains on the floor should go to whoever needs it the most, which was Bob Ring [from our crew], who had had the biggest wounds. So the captain would pick up each little grain and try to pass it down to Bob Ring, who most of the time was at the other end of the cell.

But as the starvation took hold . . . some of that food never got to him. So the captain ended that, after some effort to make it happen, *ordering* it should happen. . . . It didn't happen, so that ended.

Recalling the same event, Harry Magnuson remembers the animal instincts of the caged men.

At first everybody for himself as far as the food goes, the water goes, or *anything* goes. I mean we just—we were like cannibals. But then somebody realized, we realized, because when the rice balls came in, they come through a little chute . . . under the door, under where the bars are.

Maybe there's a big one. Maybe there's a little one. Maybe there's a big one. Maybe a little, little, little, little one. Every time one came through, if it was a big one, whoever was there would grab that one.

Well, we couldn't do that. What we had to decide to do is when those balls came in you move it around. And whatever falls for you, that's yours. Otherwise we were just, we would claw at each other. We'd kill ourselves. Because we were *so* hungry.

Bob Michelsen also describes how hunger worked on his mind.

I remember thinking about food a lot, and I began thinking about ice cream. And then I wanted a big chocolate bar, and I said, what the hell, why not put the chocolate bar on the ice cream? But I ended up saying the most important food to me would be green, anything green. I don't care what it is, grass, whatever; something green is what I wanted.

But even that left me after a little bit, and all of us were just there. And I think in the same condition, because I have talked to one or two other prisoners about this, and they said the same thing—their mind just refused to think about it, and they just *existed*. There was nothing else.

Ray Makepeace toiled as a stevedore at Port Area Manila (July 1942–July 1944); he later worked in Japan (August 1944–August 1945). He talks in stark terms of the relations between prisoners.

The strong fed on the weak. There was a lot of theft going on in the prison camps, and you know about this comradeship? Boy, in most cases the comradeship ceased to exist.

There was some theft there [at the Port Area, from the ships]. There wasn't much of it done from each other in Manila. More of that in Japan, yes. Because Japan was much, much more rugged. It was terrible. It was a case of survival of the fittest. And many of the stronger beat up the weaker. Beat the shit out of them. You bet your life.

When it got down to the bitter end there [in Japan], it was dog eat dog, and men stole from each other, which was bad. That's the worst thing you could do. You don't steal something. Man, that's his life. . . . Even [Howard] Swanson [fellow POW and close friend] one time almost tried to kill me, thinking I stole something from his Red Cross box, and actually what happened, there was some Mexicans, and we don't know which one, we know one of the three stole his box. That's a matter of life and death. . . .

Some guys could hoard their food. But then when they hoarded it, somebody'd steal it. So every time you lost some food like that, you became weakened. I'd eat it up as fast as I could.

Ray illustrates his point with an example from his time in Japan.

We got a bun for lunch, but nobody could even wait to get the bun. They'd eat it as soon as they get it. There was one guy that saved his bun. This guy, what he did, he put it in a canteen cup and then put water in, and it swelled up and made it look bigger, of course. He was sitting there feasting his eyes on it, trying to get warm.

The lights went out. The lights were probably out there for twelve or fifteen seconds probably. When the lights went on, the thing was gone. Somebody got it. How a guy could lose his meal there in almost like a flash, in front of your eyes.

The "Other"

SOME PRISONERS of the Germans faced additional stress and uncertainty because of who they were. Even though "a significant portion . . . were treated like any other POWs," American Jewish prisoners could never be certain they wouldn't be singled out and mistreated. Rumors circulated of Nazi atrocities against Jews in eastern Europe; thus, there was reason to fear. The selection in February 1945 of American Jewish and "Jewish looking" prisoners from IX-B Bad Orb and their transport to the Berga concentration camp is the most egregious example, but other documented accounts of American Jewish POWs being mistreated or segregated exist.[1]

Black POWs also faced uneven treatment by their German captors. African troops captured early in the war (mostly French colonial soldiers) at times were handled poorly, but this was the exception and not the rule. American black POWs, of whom there were but a handful, "often discovered that they were treated no differently from any other POW." "For much of the war period German and Italian treatment of colonial and black captives was probably conditioned by the knowledge that the Allies held large numbers of German and Italian prisoners," writes historian David Killingray. "Thus the needs of reciprocity overrode racial antipathy."[2]

Thousands of miles away, other captured U.S. military personnel endured a different kind of torment. Airmen, especially B-29 bomber crew members captured in Japan, faced interrogation and mistreatment as *hokaku beihei,* sometimes translated as "special prisoner." In part for the ferocious 1945 firebombing campaign on urban areas, the Japanese judged the B-29 men to have "violated the expected rules of engagement, and therefore [to have] forfeited any rights or privileges" of a regular POW. During the last months of the war, other airmen who had engaged in attacks on ground targets in Japan, for example carrier-based naval aviators, also were branded with this status.[3]

The military secret police, the Kempeitai, held a large number of these hokaku beihei in cells at their headquarters in Tokyo. Men were crammed into desperately small cells—nine men existed in the six foot by five foot cells; between sixteen and nineteen men in the eight by ten cells—and fed two or three small balls of rice per day. The prisoners were forbidden to speak and often not allowed to move; lice and vermin infested the cells. Trained interrogators routinely used different methods of brutal torture to extract information.[4]

Men captured outside Japan during the war's final year fared little better, as they often ended up in camps on the home islands—frequently after suffering severe mistreatment at the point of capture. There were solitary confinement cells at the Ofuna naval interrogation center at Yokohama, for example, and numerous accounts of torture and interrogation there by sadistic guards.

The "Other" in Germany

For nonwhite and Jewish POWs, there existed the legitimate concern of being singled out for mistreatment or worse. Mexican American airman Simon Velasquez was a prisoner at XVII-B Krems for a year after his bomber was shot down in April 1944. Simon believes he was discriminated against because he is Mexican.

Out of five thousand fliers that were in Stalag XVII, there were only five of Mexican descent. And we were treated different by the guards. Not by our fliers, because we were all one family. No matter who or what color I was, I was part of the family. [But the Germans] would come by, and they would see you and hit you by the kidneys with the butt of the rifle, or in the neck. And then they would start asking you a lot of questions, and then if you give them some smart answer, you'd go in solitary confinement for a week.

I think they were [picking on me], in a way. Because out of that whole five thousand, I think us Mexicans were in solitary confinement longer than anybody else. I was there quite a few times, for speaking back to the Germans.

Simon Velasquez's prison camp identity photo, taken upon his arrival at XVII-B Krems in May 1944.

The Germans knew I was of Mexican descent and . . . told me I had no business fighting with the Americans, because I was Mexican.

Shot down in the first week of March 1945, African American fighter pilot Harold Brown spent periods of time at two POW camps in southern Germany. He considers whether, as a prisoner, being black proved to be an advantage or a disadvantage.

I don't suppose I ever even thought of it in those terms. I know myself and George Isles [another African American fighter pilot and POW] used to joke, we said, "Hey, we're finally integrated, and we had to get shot down to become integrated." Because they [the Germans] treated everyone the same—put you right in the same damn compound, without regard to who you were. You were a flyer, a pilot, and everyone in those compounds were air crew men. We were all Allied forces, all in the same damn boat, all suffering the same way, day in and day out. . . . I couldn't detect any difference in the treatment.[5]

From his first camp at Nuremberg, Harold was in a large group force-marched south. Poorly supplied by the guards, the prisoners looked for opportunities to trade for food with civilians they encountered when passing through villages. Harold describes what happened when he knocked on one door.

This little old woman, she had to be in her eighties, she came to the door and [was] just sweet as she could be. All I knew was one thing: *"Haben*

Sie Brot [Do you have bread] for cigarettes?" *"Haben Sie Brot?" "Haben Sie . . . "* for whatever food you were begging for.

She came up to me, and the first thing, she looked at me so strangely. Curiously. That's when she touched me. Touched my face. Just as gently . . . and my hand. She was speaking, and she was saying words in German. Speaking. I didn't know what she was saying.

She was as friendly as you could be. I'm certain the questions that she was asking were things about me personally: "Who are you? What are you? Where are you from? Is that a color or is that dirt? Will it wipe off?" As she touched my face, she was probably saying these words. . . . I'm probably the first person of color that she had seen in her life.

Fellow African American fighter pilot Luther H. Smith, Jr., relates a different type of experience. Because of serious injuries sustained when he bailed out of his stricken plane, nearly all his seven months as a POW were spent in medical facilities. In one of these, in early 1945, he was approached by a German officer.

While I was still in the hospital . . . I was visited one day by a German SS major. He was a died-in-the-wool Nazi. He was in uniform.

He wanted to talk to me because most of the Germans wanted to talk about what I felt was going to happen to them when Germany was faced with surrender. What did I think the Allies were going to . . . *(trails off)*. Everybody in Germany was concerned about that. The best thing to do was to ask a prisoner, when he's the only American they had close to them. And I was using my German to tell them.

But this SS officer came in one day, and he was a pretty belligerent guy. He said—and he called me *schwarzer Amerikaner,* black American—he says, they've got you buffaloed . . . or something to that effect. In German. And I said, "What are you talking about?" He said, "You, *schwarzer Amerikaner,* you volunteered to fight for a country that lynches your people." I had never heard that before in my life. And I listened to his words. . . . It went through my mind when he said *you* volunteered to become a military airman, to be in the air force to fight for your country, and yet they lynch your people. And that hit me like a bomb. He was absolutely right: black people *were* being lynched in America.

I never thought about that. I'd *heard* about it. I was *aware* of lynchings and all that stuff, but it never crossed my mind that against that background, you still volunteered, which I did. I couldn't tell him, you're absolutely right. I said to him, *nein, nein, nein, nein,* you're all wrong. It was kind of like a standoff. I wasn't going to admit it. He was trying to say, you dummy—you haven't even got sense enough not to volunteer to fight for a country that lynches your people.[6]

So he left the room that day, and it just blew me out of my mind. I said, he's right. I never thought about it in that context. I wouldn't just volunteer to go out and do something with a group or nation that was against me. I'm trying to be an American. I'm trying to be the best I can. Of course, I volunteered because I thought it was the best thing I could possibly do. In World War II time, the 1940s, it *was* the best thing. It was the only real good, honorable thing that black people could actually do to be measured along with everybody else. . . . I'm glad that I did, and I've lived a rewarding life as a result.

After his capture in July 1944 in France, Arnold Sprong ended up at IV-B Mühlberg. He can clearly recall an incident from the autumn of that year.

One morning they woke us up about four or five o'clock in the morning. It was still dark. In fact, I had made a few new friends in the short time we were there in camp, and one happened to be Jewish. We fell out in the morning, and the first thing they asked was anybody who was Jew, take a step forward. [Along with some others] my friend did, and that's the last I ever heard of him.

Given Nazi racial policies and their actions to exterminate Europe's Jews, Jewish prisoners faced an entirely different situation. Several non-Jewish POWs recall specific incidents. At IX-B Bad Orb in late January 1945, army enlisted man Harold Brick witnessed both anti-Semitism and physical abuse.

The man of confidence [chief POW representative, selected by the prisoners], he was the guy that was really the American in charge of us [as] a whole. The Germans asked him to finger all the Jewish prisoners at Bad Orb. And he refused to do it, and that's when he got beat. . . . I physically saw him get hit over the head with a rifle butt, in view of anybody who happened to be close enough to see it. Not once but twice. I mean those kind of things. When you see that, that was . . . *(trails off)*.

When this American man of confidence, an army enlisted man named Hans Kasten, steadfastly refused to identify those POWs who were Jewish, the Germans then arbitrarily selected men who, in the words of one prisoner there, "looked Jewish." On February 8, 1945, 350 Americans from Bad Orb (Hans Kasten among them) were dispatched in boxcars to a concentration camp at Berga, Germany. Less than three months later, 20 percent of these men were dead, victims of overwork and abuse.[7]

After his capture in December 1944, army enlisted man Herb Kohnke was in a group sent by boxcar to XIII-C Hammelburg.

When we got there, all of us fellows that were on the train, they took us to one area there, and they lined us up four deep, and then an officer came along. [In our group] we had colored fellows, we had Jewish fellows. They [didn't have] signs on them saying they're Jews, but the black guys, they could pick them out. They just said, when they'd see a black, they'd say, you, you, you, you. Come out. *Raus.* We didn't know what they were going to do to them. We couldn't do anything about it.

So they asked for the Jews. *Juden,* come out. You know, there's some kids kind of reluctant about saying they were Jews. But these [German] officers, sometimes they'd look at some of these kids, and the profile of the fellow. Maybe he looked like a Jew, but they have him come out. They took all the Jewish fellows out.

We don't know what they did with them. They took them away from us, and that was the last we saw of them. And I had one of the buddies of mine, his name was Green, that was in that bunch. We never did find out what happened to him.

Marcus Hertz grew up in a Jewish family. He enlisted in the air corps in 1942 for a specific purpose.

I asked to go to Germany because of the publicity we had received here

Marcus Hertz in 1944, before being posted to a bomber unit in England. The Jewish air corps officer spent ten months as a POW of the Germans.

[in our synagogue] in St. Paul, Minnesota, on what was happening to the Jewish people in Germany and Poland. I'm thinking to myself, the sign is hanging out there, enlist in the air force and all of this stuff, and I'm here [in St. Paul], and they're being slaughtered by the trainload. *That's* where I want to go, [to Germany].

Navigator on a heavy bomber, Marcus was shot down in July 1944 and interned at Stalag Luft III. From the outset, he sensed his situation as different from the other POWs in the camp.

[Being Jewish made a difference], every damn day I was there. Every day I was a POW. . . . [My focus was] called survival. Very simple. *If* I survived. Every sentence starts with it. Every prayer starts with it.

I was not overcome with the confinement, because I had no alternative. Guys were trying to escape all the time. . . . I was told, and I believed it from the stories that we heard, don't try to escape—a Jewish flier identified by the Germans has no chance of survival. Don't do it. I never did. I was frightened. . . . Because I'm Jewish, I was pretty well off to sit out the war in a POW camp if I had to be on the ground. . . . You *bet*. You can say that and believe it, over and over.

Aaron Kuptsow was an air corps officer interned at Stalag Luft I, at Barth, Germany, beginning in December 1944. For him, Marcus Hertz's fears were realized.

After we got into Stalag I, I guess we had been there less than a month . . . this one day in formation, it had to be in January. We would be called out every morning for roll call, all of the POWs. And they would do a count just to make sure that nobody had gotten away. After the count was completed, they started to call out numbers. Each one of us had a [POW] number, like a four-digit number, instead of names. They said, "Stay here after the others are gone." And they dismissed the rest of them.

Then they gathered us into a group and told us, you know, they would escort us back to our barracks. Get our things together, because you're being moved. And so they did move us, to another section of the camp, where they had a locked barracks set up.

Once we got into that barracks, we started to check with other rooms. Found out that *everybody* in the barracks was Jewish. And so we did have a sort of a ghetto setup there, one big barracks in the far corner of the camp, which we found out later was right next to an ammunition dump. But that's where they kept us.

[Now] I don't think I was particularly worried because I didn't know too much about what was going on. But some of the others had ideas. . . . I started to hear others who, you know, started to complain and say, "This is not legal. We have to protest this to Geneva. We have to contact the American commanding officer of the camp to forward something to Geneva, the Geneva Convention for protest." . . . They contacted the [Allied] commanding officer of the whole camp, a Colonel Zemke. We did complain to him. This segregation, under the Geneva Convention, was not legal. The idea was to contact the Red Cross . . . to send a protest to the Red Cross about our being segregated.

The only problem was, people that were in the know said, well, you know, that could take a couple of months before it gets through channels and everything. Meanwhile, what can happen to us? We did find out later, within the last couple years, there had been an order written by the high command in Germany that we *were* to be sent to concentration camps, with the idea of being eliminated.

Japan's "Special Prisoners"

Bob Michelsen, the B-29 gunner who bailed out over Tokyo on May 25–26, 1945, endured brutal interrogation. After initial questioning he was taken to the Tokyo prison complex run by the Kempeitai secret police. Among strong memories one stands out: the individual human misery.

It was a horse stall. . . . But it had been converted to a, somewhat like a jail, with a floor raised up from the concrete and wooden bars and everything else. It measured about five feet wide by ten feet long, and there were *eighteen* of us in there. All Americans, all [B-29] aircrews.

Shorty [civilian Yasuo Kobayashi, the main Japanese interrogator] told us many, many times, "You're dead; it's only a question of when." And you have to believe it. . . . We had killed civilians. We had dropped bombs on civilians; we had killed in Tokyo maybe 100,000 people, burned to death. And they are not treating us like they treated other [POWs].

The daily life in the cell—now it varies with the longevity, with how long you've been in the cell. The first couple of weeks you're back and forth to interrogation, and those are rather drastic, so you're trying to recover from that a lot. Also you have dysentery so bad that you don't think that you can survive.

What you would call a toilet in that cell was a block of cement about three inches high, maybe thirty-six inches long and eighteen inches wide, with *one* hole. And that was your toilet. Underneath that hole was a box. The toilet is called a *benjo;* the box is the *benjo-soje.*

Once a day, a person from your cell has to go out and take the box, under guard of course, and empty it. It was in a moat or a river, a small river or a moat, and I did this a number of times until I was too weak to pick up this box. And then *two* of us would do it, and for that you get a little extra food, which was okay. But eventually two of us could not do it.

Your thoughts every day were of your family, and your friends, and my girlfriend at the time. But to be honest with you, you're starving, and you're hurting. And when I say starving, I don't just mean you're hungry. Your gums begin to bleed, and your legs are swelling up, and your beard is growing—it's full of shit anyway, because your beard is floating in that box of benjo-soje—and you're weak. You couldn't stand if you wanted to.

Your condition is such that you, you withdraw. Your mind will not even *think* about what is happening, and so you just withdraw from everything, and you try to become a blank. You're nothing. In your own mind, you do not dare think about anything. I think your mind is trying to save you, because you'd go nuts. So you just withdraw, and you exist, but beyond existence, there's nothing. . . . I mean, we aren't zombies by any means, but you can *not* just day after day after day after day sit there and think of nothing but your demise. So you think of nothing. What else can you think of?

Harry Magnuson was a prisoner in this same small cell.

No space at all. All we did was just sit there. Just sit there. Misery. . . . But it was so tight there, somebody had to sleep on that thing [the toilet] or

The Mansfield B-29 crew on Guam, May 1945, not long before their fatal mission over Japan. Airplane commander Dick Mansfield is standing, middle; Bob Michelsen is kneeling, second from left. Most members of the close-knit crew that survived ended up in the same cramped cell at Kempeitai headquarters in Tokyo.

sit on that thing all night. So we had to take turns. I think we just all got together and decided, that's the way it's going to be. So that worked out. *Somebody* had to sleep on that box, the benjo. So we'd all take turns.

But that damn light that was up in the ceiling, that was on all night long. Ooooh! It wasn't a bright light, but it was just enough. It was just glaring at you all the time, and when you're head and toe, head and toe . . . the floor was just solid with us. You couldn't move.

The stress of just sitting was punctuated by moments of terror.

[There was a] little window up on top. . . . You'd have to get up on somebody's shoulders to look out. But I could see B-29s flying by, going home or coming or whatever. Off in the distance. . . . And they would come at night. And they would come in the daytime. And they were really going at it.

The [air raid] sirens would go off, but they would never let us out [of the cells]. . . . We just figured, oh, God, here comes the sirens, here comes the bombs, and we're stuck in here. We can't get out of here. But that's what was going through our mind. "Hey! Let us out of here!" We were yelling at the guards.

It's kind of scary when you're stuck in there, and they won't let you out, and the bombs are dropping. [But] where would we go, anyway? There was no place. There was no place to hide. The bombs would just drop on us, and that would be it.

Navy pilot Bill Connell spent July 1944 through April 1945 at the Ofuna naval interrogation center; for the first two months he was in solitary.

When I walked through the gate, there was sort of the administrative building. There was an office, and they took me kind of through that building to the bathhouse. This guard had me strip, and they got me into a hot tub and gave me a bath. Then they gave me some old used Japanese work uniforms. It was a pair of like cotton trousers and a pullover top. I still was allowed to keep my shoes that I had on. I just had a flight suit. They allowed me to keep that. But it was dirty, and they had it washed. It got through being washed and was given back to me later on.

But then they took me from there, and they put me in a cell, and I was kept in solitary confinement for approximately sixty days. After I had been in confinement for about three weeks, they allowed me to go outside and sit on a bench. I could not *talk* to the other prisoners, but I could at least sit outside. As the prisoners would walk around this compound, they were talking to one another, but they in fact were talking to *me*. So as they would get within about twenty feet of me they would start saying who they were and what they were and so forth.

Even kept in cells by themselves, the prisoners at Ofuna found creative ways to pass information back and forth and to find out from new arrivals the war's progress. Floyd Caverly arrived at Ofuna in November 1944, a month after his submarine USS Tang *was sunk in the China Sea.*

We had what we called the underground telegraph. . . . You'd tell the guard, "Hey, I've got to go to the latrine." So he would take you up to the—it was the *benjo* in Japanese—he'd take you to the benjo, and while you're going up, you're talking to him. Sometimes it was something awfully stupid, and sometimes it was things you wanted some of your *buddies* [in other cells] to know and let them know who you were and where you were from.

Especially when they'd get a new pilot in. In would come a new prisoner, and we had quite a few B-29 pilots brought in there towards the last [months] because they began to hit the mainland pretty heavy with B-29s. Then we had a strike [air attack on Japan] in February [1945], an aircraft carrier strike . . . strafing runs and bombing runs and everything else off those carriers. Then they brought in some pilots that they had shot down.

We let them know who we were and what to expect from the Jap guards and what to tell the goon rebos [interrogators] when they come. Then when *they* went to the benjo they would tell us our troops are . . . now in the Bonin Islands, and things like this. We could just about tell how they were using the islands as stepping-stones. . . . Then when they started to work over Okinawa [in the months before the April invasion], that's when we began to get quite a bit of dope, because they were bringing in pilots then, too.

For Bill Connell, as for many of the men kept in solitary confinement, the challenge was dealing with being alone.

At first the days went by reasonably fast, but after you'd been in solitary confinement for about a week, and you're just sitting on the floor on what they call a tatami mat—you didn't have a chair to sit in, you sat on the floor—time began to drag, and so you had to start—at least I did—I started to think about different things to keep my mind active. Just thinking about things that I did when I was a kid, and thinking about my parents, and thinking about things I did in high school, thinking about flying. Anything I could concentrate on. That helped immensely.

Then I could do some calisthenics in the room—push-ups, sit-ups—which also helped. Basically [mental and physical gymnastics], that's exactly right. As long as you do that you keep the mental process functioning, and you don't go into depression, and you don't sit there and worry about what might happen. You don't have time. You're thinking about other things. You can't help but *think* about what's going to happen, but . . . *(trails off)*.

I was living day to day. I was optimistic in a way and pessimistic in another way. I was *optimistic* that I was surviving day to day, but I was very *pessimistic* as to how long I would be there.

B-29 crewman Bill Price barely survived a civilian lynch mob after bailing out over Nagoya. He was held there and interrogated by the Kempeitai for six days.

[The cell] had one small window at the top that I could see some tree branches, and that's all. And the only other thing I would see was eyes looking through at me through the steel door. The little slot in the steel door, they just opened that little slot in the back, and they'd roll a rice ball in to me and set this cup of water on the floor, and that was it.

Before [being captured], I weighed about a hundred and fifty pounds, and I was in not too bad a shape. But after they [the civilians] got through with me, I was pretty well torn up. I mean, my [flying] suit was torn; it was bloody; it was messed up by bowel movement. And no medical treatment whatsoever. Nobody came in to look to see how I was.

[I went] four months and ten days without a bath, a shave, or a haircut. Not even wash my hands. You can imagine what condition I was in. [When we were liberated], I was down to a hundred and four pounds with my clothes on. For what they were worth. . . . So I was just there. That's all. Just by myself.

They told me I was going to be [taken to Tokyo and] executed [as a war criminal]. Of course, that was a shock. But after he [the interrogator] left, I kind of thought, well, you know, this doesn't really make sense, because why should they take me to Tokyo to execute me when they could do it right here? So that gave me a little bit of . . . what should I say? Hope? Not much, but I'd say, hey, I'm around for another day or two.

Bill was transported to Tokyo and imprisoned at Camp Omori, a POW facility on the city's outskirts.

[I was] put in solitary confinement, in the Japanese guardhouse. That was my home then almost four months . . . four months of solitary confinement. Nobody to talk to. Nobody to see.

[The cell was] probably about eight by eight [feet], something like that. . . . They had a window on one side there, where I could see the sky. And there was nothing in that room. Nothing except me and a hole cut in the corner to relieve myself. The prisoners, the regular prisoners, emptied it from the outside once a week.

Once a day I would take my fingernail, and I would make a mark on the wall, trying to keep track of the days. . . . I just made the mark on the wall. It was just one more day.

The lack of human contact deeply affected Bill—during his time in prison camp but also for years after.

After a while, your mind starts playing tricks on you. You go through different moods. You find yourself crying sometimes. You find yourself doing strange things. You find yourself sometimes beating your head against the wall. Your fist, or something. You're losing your marbles, so to speak, or mind, if you want to put [it] plainly.

There's nobody to talk to, nobody to see. Day after day after day. Week after week. And, incidentally, it never leaves you, your entire life. You manage to live with it. You get moody sometimes. Thanks to treatment and to an understanding wife, bless her, . . . without her, I don't think I'd be alive today. Truthfully.

I mean, the beatings you can take, and everything else. Lack of food. But being alone with nobody to see, nobody to talk to, it affects you, mister, it sure does.

After nine months at Ofuna, in late April 1945 Bill Connell was in a group of eighteen "special prisoners" moved to Camp Omori.

When we arrived . . . they hadn't quite finished building the wall in this building they were going to put us in. When that was done, then the commandant came out, and he addressed us and told us that we were war criminals. We were going to be kept separate [from the other prisoners], and . . . if the Japanese lost the war, we would be executed. So then they just walked us over to this building and put us in there and walked away. We were there.

[Camp Omori] was an improvement in that we were able to go on work details. In other words, we were able to get *out* of the camp and get away from the confines of the camp. We were closer together because we didn't have individual cells [like we had at Ofuna]. We were just all together. So we were a little closer together in that respect. . . . [But] there was no animosity toward anybody. But like the crew . . . [of] the USS *Tang,* which was a submarine that was sunk, there were only ten survivors, and the ten of them, including the commanding officer, came to Ofuna, and they kind of hung out together because they were from the same ship.

I didn't know a soul. I just made friends. As a matter of fact, I made . . . one of the friends I really made was an enlisted man that had been shot down [close to Iwo Jima] the same day I was and was captured and was sent to Ofuna. So he and I kind of palled around together.

Now, [at] Omori we had work details. As a matter of fact, the eighteen of us would go out anywhere from a quarter of a mile to a half a mile from camp after a bombing raid and we would . . . what wasn't burned up, we would clean up. Because the roofs were made of slate. And we would pick up all the slate. Make piles out of it and collect all of the hardware, whatever, and make piles out of it. Then we would . . . we had like a pick, and we would turn over the ground and kind of plow it up and dig it up, and then we would plant vegetables, supposedly for the camp. We didn't get any of them, but we raised vegetables for the camp.

Then after we had done that for a while, then they had us go out on a real work detail. We were about two and a half to three miles from camp, and we were digging caves. We dug a big slit trench that was about twenty feet long, twenty-five feet long, about five feet wide, and when we got finished it was about eight feet deep.

The complex shaft and tunnel system they dug was likely meant for the defense of Japan in the expected invasion—which never came.

We . . . would go out in the morning. The eighteen of us would work. And we would work half a day, about three and a half, four hours. Then we would march back to camp, and then the B-29 crews, which was a lot of

Harry Magnuson (left) in 1944, prior to his deployment to the Pacific

those guys, they marched out, and they worked in the afternoons. [But] they never let us meet, no. They kept us apart.

At Camp Omori, the prisoners could witness the destructive incendiary raids by American B-29 Superfortress bombers. Bill vividly remembers one night.

Oh, [we could] *absolutely* [see and hear] the B-29s. I can remember one night—it was in May of 1945—that I had to get up and go to the bathroom. . . . And to go to the benjo, or the bathroom, we had to ask the guard for permission . . . and he gave us a little wooden chit. And we had to carry that in our hand, because we had to go out the front door [and] go all the way to the back of the building, where the benjos were. We had to have that ticket with us.

I had my little ticket in my hand, and I went out. And when I went out, I looked up, and of course the raids were going. As far as I could see to the south, using a panoramic view, and as far as I could see to the north, there was a *wall* of flame. It was at *least* three hundred feet high, and the whole city of Tokyo was on fire. It was like a firestorm. I could *feel* the heat of the fire. That's how close we were.

Another experience we went through: before the war was over, the U.S. Navy fleet was right off the coast of Japan, and the battleships were firing. You could *hear* the shells going overhead, and then when they would hit—they were landing, oh, probably three or four, five miles from us—the whole *ground* would shake. *(makes rumbling noises)*

It was a morale booster to know that our forces were that close to us. Of course, there was that fear of execution, but we were so happy that they were getting that close, and we knew that the war had to be over sometime.

In the war's final days, the group of about one hundred "special prisoners" being held by the Kempeitai were taken from their small, cramped cells and transported away. Harry Magnuson and Bob Michelsen both were in this group.

Harry Magnuson pulls back his memories from that day.

I can remember, we woke up in the morning and, lo and behold, rice balls. Almost as big as . . . like a softball. Maybe a little bigger than that. That started to come through the hole. We thought, oh, geez, what's this? Big, big ones. *Big* ones.

Something is happening. We got through eating that, and we got our water and then, all of a sudden, a whole bunch of shoes. See, we were barefooted. A whole pile of shoes came flying in the hall there. In piles. American shoes. So that's when we started to think, uh-oh. We must be, we're going to be pulled out of here. Perfect.

So they start. . . . I don't know if we went out in the hall and took a pair of shoes or they shoved the shoes through the hole. I can't remember. But we got the shoes. So we grabbed a pair of shoes. Whether they were big or small. . . . They had mold on them because they'd been sitting someplace. And they were stiff as a board. So we got that. When we got our shoes on . . . then as we came out, they blindfolded us.

Bob Michelsen continues:

For some reason, we [were] taken out of our cells and blindfolded, led outside into the sunlight, and told to get into the back of a truck. I believe there were three trucks. All who were in there—a hundred and some-odd—into trucks, and there were guards in the back of the truck, of course, and how long we were in the truck going somewhere I don't know. But we ended up on the shores of Tokyo Bay.

We were led out of the trucks, down to the shore, still blindfolded and with our hands tied behind our backs, kneeling on the shores of Tokyo Bay. And I thought, *(speaking slowly for emphasis)* this is the end. I thought, we are going to be decapitated here, and how am I going to survive? I thought, maybe if they are chopping the heads off, I could try to get underneath somebody that's already had their head cut off, and maybe they'll not notice me.

Now what are they going to do? *(agitated)* Now what's going to happen? I thought—I don't know about the rest of the guys, but I thought, this is where they're going to give it to us. Kill us. Our blindfolds came off, and we were untied and told to go into the ocean and clean up, wash. *(pauses five seconds)*

I don't know how long I was in the water, but I turned around and looked from where we had come on the shore, because we could hear noises back there. Three machine guns had been set up on the shore, and Shorty [Yasuo Kobayashi] was directing the machine guns. So I thought, well, we are going to be machine-gunned in the water or as we come out of the water. And I thought, geez, I can swim. If I can swim underwater, I might survive.

There was a terrific argument at the machine guns between Shorty and Junior [Kennichi Yanagizawa], the two interrogators. Shorty left *(pauses three seconds)* . . . and the machine guns were packed up and put in the fourth truck, and that truck drove away, leaving us there with Junior. And Junior said, "You're going to walk out on a causeway"—which we could now see, I think to the left—"and on the end of that causeway is a prisoner of war camp [Camp Omori]. That's where you're going." And he marched us out to that prisoner of war camp. Finally the gates opened, and we went into this camp. . . . That could have gone either way. But in retrospect, I realize now . . . I think it was Junior that saved our lives.

The ragtag group of Kempeitai prisoners was escorted into Camp Omori.

I don't know what the situation was, because when we entered the camp, we were at the parade ground, in the center of the camp, at attention. We were told to take all our clothes off and drop them on the ground and then proceed to a barracks, a building, and we were told stay in that building *(speaking slowly and deliberately)* and do not for any reason come out unless you are ordered to come out. . . . A Colonel Carmichael came in and said he was the senior aircrew member in this camp. He instructed us on how to act and what to do. . . . But basically he said, don't go outside, because you are in mortal danger if you go out. Because we were still war criminals, as opposed to a POW.

We were in a clubhouse now, in a mansion. We were so happy and overjoyed. . . . We could lie down, and we could talk, and everything else. This was much different, and we were very happy to be there at that moment. Some days later, we were allowed to cut our beards with a scissors and try to shave. But with only one razor for . . . one hundred people and with salt water, I gave up on it.

Harry Magnuson talks about his new surroundings—and himself.

[At Omori,] I just was kind of like a zombie. I just kind of followed everybody else. Never inquired, hey, what's going on? That sort of thing. I never was assertive. I never went out and tried to find out what was going on. I didn't do that. . . . You just stay inside this building, and that was it until the guards were gone [when the war ended].

Two weeks after the Kempeitai prisoners arrived at Camp Omori, the Japanese guards vanished. The war was over.

Forced Marches Across Germany

BEGINNING IN MID-1944, the Allies steadily drove German forces back to the country's prewar borders. In the west, U.S.–led forces pushed eastward from France; on the Eastern Front, the Soviet Red Army swept all before it. Especially in the east, numerous POW camps suddenly came within range of the fighting. As a result, during the last months of the European war, tens of thousands of Allied POWs were caught up in a large-scale human tragedy.[1]

Prisoners were concerned about their fate. Some worried Hitler might order the killing of all POWs as a final act of vengeance. Others believed the Germans would have to abandon the Stalags and Luft Stalags and advancing Red Army units would liberate them. But this possibility left many wondering about the treatment they might receive from the Russians—their reputation for violence and destruction was already well known. As 1944 drew to a close, rumors swirled through the camps.[2]

The German High Command (OKW) chose to prevent the liberation of POW camps by enemy forces. Instead, with the Geneva Convention as a rationale, OKW attempted "to conserve a large body of captured personnel who might still be of value as workers or bargaining-chips," issuing orders that prison camps were to be evacuated when "in imminent danger of being overrun." POWs were reduced to being chess pieces in a life-or-death endgame. With little if any warning or time to prepare, prisoners in a series of camps were turned out into the bitter winter cold.[3]

This decision to empty the camps created enormous difficulties. To begin with, no facilities existed that could accommodate the more than 100,000 prisoners ultimately evacuated: remaining camps already were filled to overflowing. Other factors further compounded the problem: the country's rapidly collapsing transportation network meant the men would be moved on foot. Yet many prisoners lacked adequate winter clothing, some even shoes, and were in a weakened state after their time in the camps. Also, Germany was in no position logistically to supply food and shelter for large groups of men on the move. And in a final, cruel turn of fate, the winter of 1944–45 was one of the coldest in decades.

What resulted was suffering on a grand scale, played out against the backdrop of Germany's *Götterdämmerung,* its final collapse and defeat. Long, straggling columns of prisoners were force-marched from one small town to the next, unsure of their destination for the night or where their next meal would come from—if indeed it came at all. Men were reduced to begging for food when they passed through villages, scavenging through fields and rubbish piles, or stealing whatever they could find. As for shelter, some nights there was a barn or other building; other times men were forced to sleep in fields, lacking any protection from the weather. Health quickly declined, and diarrhea and dysentery plagued many. Being on the roads presented another danger, too: marauding Allied fighter aircraft, searching for ground targets, on occasion strafed the pitiful figures, believing them to be Germans. It is estimated that between 2,500 and 3,500 prisoners died on forced marches from the camps; many others were little more than sickly skeletons upon their liberation.[4]

The weeks and months of forced marching gave a new definition to the importance of friends. Examples abound of small groups of men pulling together and helping each other survive another day, sharing food and blankets, or tending to those who were ill. Unfortunately, this was not always the case: on other marches, conditions devolved into "every man for himself," with prisoners displaying aggressive behavior toward each other and rampant theft of food and clothing becoming the norm.

Eighty-six Days to Nowhere

Located at Gross Tychow in Pomerania, approximately one hundred miles northeast of Berlin, Luft IV was opened in May 1944. By January 1945, it housed approximately 10,000 men, well above the stated capacity of 6,400.[5]

On the evening of February 6, 1945, with at least eight inches of snow on the ground and more falling, with temperatures below zero degrees, the Germans instructed the prisoners that the camp was to be evacuated—immediately. The Red Army was estimated to be only ten miles from the camp. Within twenty-fours hours, virtually the entire camp was on the road. Days of marching turned into weeks, and weeks into months. By the time the last prisoner was liberated, on May 2, 1945, this longest of all forced marches had covered nearly five hundred miles.[6]

With the announcement of impending departure, men searched frantically for ways to take along their meager possessions, especially food supplies. Lee Bedsted describes one rather ingenious solution.

> We made knapsacks out of shirts. Sewed the sleeve to the seam of the shirt and sewed the bottom of it together. When you sewed the sleeve to the seam, you had a sleeve loop there. So you put one arm through one of them and one arm through the other one. Then you tied it together in the front with a shoelace, and you could open the back up with buttons and stick stuff in there. I wish it had been my idea, but it wasn't. *(chuckles)* Somebody else suggested it, and we all jumped on it.

Glen Naze:

> [The Germans] used to tell us, we can't give you Red Cross packages anymore because your planes are bombing our trains and we can't transport . . . them to you. But it *wasn't* true. When we marched out, they had a [big] warehouse that was *filled* with Red Cross packages.
>
> They handed each one out. Of course, by that time, we were so weak we couldn't carry them. So along the way, a lot of that stuff you'd just throw away. Because they told us when we left that camp, you'll only be walking three days. . . . We were going to walk to another camp. Three days. . . . [Did I believe them?] Not really, but . . . *(laughing)* you *had* to believe them, really. But as soon as it got close to the three days, we knew that that was a farce.

Sam Nenadich was a gunner on a B-24 heavy bomber before his plane went down in flames in August 1944. He remembers a curious thing about the Red Cross parcel distribution.

There was a rumor a couple of days before, that we were going to move on. And as we left camp, we each got a Red Cross parcel. Everybody didn't want to carry the box. They were stuffing [items] inside their shirts, you know.

The funny thing they did, there's a strip about this wide *(holds fingers several inches apart)*, it had six or seven orange pills in there. And everybody was throwing them to the side. [It was] vitamin C. . . . I didn't really know what they were, but the Red Cross isn't going to put any *crappy* stuff in there. If they were in that Red Cross parcel, they were supposed to do some good.

[I picked up] every goddamn one of them. Never had a cold on that forced march. Sleeping in a ditch along the road, sometimes in a barn, or sometimes up against the barn. I took one a day. And I shared them with my two buddies, Phil and Bill.

B-24 gunner Sam Nenadich (right) in Wyoming in 1944, just prior to being sent to Europe. Within weeks, his plane would be shot down over Germany and he would be a POW.

Having left the camp, the men were headed westward. The Germans marched the columns of men as many as twenty miles per day to keep ahead of the rapidly advancing Red Army. Continued bitter cold and lack of food and shelter stretched men to the limit and beyond. Warren Claypool, who grew up on a farm in northern Minnesota, is certain that lessons he learned during his childhood were instrumental in helping him survive.

Being a northern boy, I know when I walked through that gate I had to keep my feet as dry as possible, and that you don't do in leather shoes. I also knew that if I ever took them off, I'd never get them back on again—I'd be walking barefoot, because there was swelling. I think my feet were froze completely for two or three days at a time. You got the shoes over them, you better leave them. . . . I'd unlace them and let the pressure off where I could and try to dry them on my feet.

The first time we got to lay down, we were told we could stay there the night. There was a foot of snow in the trees, and the mistake that was made, the group ahead of us had stopped there the night before, and it was a filthy place. Most of the time you just stopped and scraped the snow back and laid down.

Our dysentery was so bad we were passing blood. When you should have been resting, all you could do is get up. That was a *terrible* problem. . . . I do have to say this: I have to give my mother credit for helping that group of men. I was taught as a small kid if you had the runs, go to the woodstove and get a charcoal out of the ash pan. That will stop your runs. I had a pocket watch that was my dad's and the Germans hadn't taken from me because it was my own watch. I traded that to a German guard for a loaf of sawdust bread. We got next to a farmstead, and I got a chance to build a fire. I charred that loaf of bread until it was black all the way through, and I ate all I could and passed the rest out.

Les Schrenk has vivid memories of the pain of marching and of being exposed to the weather.

They mostly took back roads, sometimes even cutting across fields, muddy fields. The secondary roads, it was field rock about four to six inches in diameter alongside of each other. So it was a very rough surface. Every time your foot came down, especially if there was any ice or snow, your foot slipped either right, left, forward, or backward. When you walked very far, your feet were just absolutely killing you. Your feet, your ankles, your knees, the calves of your legs—it was horrible. . . .

I keep on using the word *march. March* is not the way to describe it. To me, a march, you're walking. We were so far gone, it was more like staggering. You could barely put one foot ahead of the other. You were that weak.

The worst was, I remember one day, the Germans got us up and started us marching immediately, before it was even light. It started sleeting. First rain, then [it] turned to sleet, then to snow. Of course, we had absolutely no protective clothing at all. We were wet right down to our skin, and talk about misery!

And then going to bed that way. That night we slept outside. When we woke up in the morning, the blankets were frozen just solid. We couldn't even get the blankets off the ground. We had to take our table knives and kind of pry it to try to get the blankets off the ground. They were frozen.

Some nights the Germans found shelter, but this, too, presented challenges.

Sometimes you would be out in the middle of nowhere. No barn, no nothing—just the middle of the countryside. They'd say, here's where we're going to be tonight. Other times they tried to hunt up some type of a shelter. Most of the time it was a barn.

We all preferred to be in the barn because, one thing, if it rained or sleeted or anything, you at least had a roof over your head. But it also had its drawbacks. You've all got dysentery, so you have to get up a number of times during the night. The Germans march you into this great big barn. *Wham,* goes the door shut. It's pitch black. There's more people in that barn than what the barn should hold. Say that you're either in the middle or the far end or even one of the sides. You have to get up during the night. You're literally crawling across a hundred people to get out. Now you come back in, and it's completely black. How do you find your place?

For many men, the difficult conditions made them thankful for a trusted companion. Lee Bedsted had a best friend on the march: the ball turret gunner from his crew, Melvin Gerhold. The men depended heavily on each other.

We were marching along, and he got to the point where he said, "I can't walk anymore." I said, "Climb on my back," and I carried him for a while. He was a big man. So we . . . that was the kind of thing that we shared. . . .

I had dysentery while we were marching. I would have to go to the ditch and relieve myself, and Mel always told me, "Don't you stay there! You get done what you have to do, and then you get back here!" So he kept goading me to keep going, no matter how bad it got. That was rough, because I was just passing mucous and blood. Then it somewhat abated, got a little better. Could get some food in. It got a little better. There was no medication. Didn't have any medication.

In contrast, on the march Bob Knobel remembers relying less on others and more on himself.

One waist gunner [from my crew] was in our group, but we weren't really . . . we were close, but not that close. . . . A lot of times you would be marching, and that guy couldn't keep up or wanted to go faster to get in with another; he knew somebody up ahead. And so you would just keep marching along. . . . I think you got—it didn't take very many days—you got to the point where you weren't concerned. Only, can I keep going? . . . I mean, you just say, keep walking; it will be over with. The day will go by, and we'll get someplace at night, and then we can sit down and relax. Yes, it was focus on just one day at a time. Not necessarily maybe the first four or five days, because I mean you're fresh and we're getting out of there and all that, but afterwards I think it became a situation of surviving.

You'd see guys faltering and dropping back, and you'd hope that they would be picked up by the wagon they had following. . . . You wondered what would happen [to them], but I don't think you dwelled on it because you keep going. Then you don't have to . . . *(trails off)*. You [hope you] won't be one of those that will drop out.

But above all it was the lack of food that dominated thoughts and conversations. With the economy in shambles by spring 1945, the Germans simply were unable to supply the wandering columns of prisoners crisscrossing the countryside. Men searched frantically for anything edible. A veteran of Stalag Luft VI, Merlyn Brandanger had arrived at Luft IV in June 1944. On the march, he says, scrounging for food meant you ate whatever you found.

It wasn't long before I came to the conclusion that it may be a long ordeal. The Red Cross parcel was gone, no food was being furnished, it was cold weather, I had no clothing other than that what I left with, and I was hungry.

It may have been five or six days before I realized that I had better start taking care of myself. When we stopped for the night, it would be in some farmer's barn or shed, or maybe just on the ground in the farmer's yard. I would start looking through the buildings as much as the guards would let me, and being raised on a farm I knew what to look for. If I were lucky I might find some potatoes, dehydrated sugar beets, kohlrabi, or even some eggs. Sometimes the local farmer or his wife might let us use an iron pot, so we would build a fire and boil some of these items. Otherwise we would eat them raw.

Warren Claypool relates a similar story: finding sufficient food became the daily trial.

[The challenge was] trying to sustain your body with something to eat, no matter even if it was wood. One thing that I managed to have, I managed to get a few potatoes in my pocket.

Usually they stopped us in a farmstead, and if you were sharp enough you could find their potato pit. The German guards, if you could give them a chunk of that when you cooked it up at night, why, they looked the other way. They weren't eating any better than we were, the poor guys.

When we made a camp and the Germans didn't give us anything, I managed to build a little fire under a tin can I had, and I boiled those potatoes, and I'd usually manage to try to get a hold of an onion to throw in with them. That was mighty good food. There was no water thrown away, either. It all went down. Such things as that.

One thing that helped me there: from the time I was small, I watched my dad throw his ax over his shoulder and head for the woods to cut timber. And then when he got [to] the hedge of the brush away from the house, he'd break a twig off, usually a basswood if he could, that had nice buds or a hazel brush or something that way, and he'd chew it all the time he was in the woods. So whenever I got near anything, I had that in my mouth, and I was chewing them. I didn't necessarily swallow it, but I got a lot of good out of them. To get something in your stomach. It was one thing that helped me sustain my strength.

Putting things in a larger perspective, Lee Bedsted reflects on his meaning of hunger.

We were never really hungry in the camp. We just, we knew we didn't get enough, but . . . on the march we were *starving*. I think once in a while we got a small piece of bread [from the Germans]. Nothing else. . . . I think I went from a hundred and eighty-five pounds to a little over a hundred. I was pretty rickety.

One night we came into a farmyard, and . . . they had just shoveled potatoes out of the potato bin and into the cooker. Sand, gravel, the whole works. But we munched out of it what we could. And it was hot.

One time we stopped at a farm, and I said to [my friend Mel], I said, "You know, there's some oats in this bin over here. I have no idea what we could do with that, but let's get some." . . . I said, "I think we could cook this oats." We built little fires out in the yard, and then we had a klim can; we used that for our cooking utensil. We'd wire a handle onto it, and we'd use that with a stick and try to hold it over the fire. . . . Well, the oats is full of hulls—it's not refined. We cooked it and we cooked it and we choked it down and, boy, it wasn't but a few minutes, and up it came again.

Some German civilians proved willing to barter.

Civilians, actually they had apparently seen enough of the evacuations and that, they knew that guys had cigarettes they would like to trade, and they would try to sell whatever they could to them. . . . You might be able to buy an egg or an onion. You know, when you're marching in a big group like that, there's an awful lot of competition to buy what they have. The first guy that got there and paid the price, why, he got it.

The forced marches represented just one aspect of the tidal wave of misery then flooding over Germany. Especially during the final weeks of the war, German civilian refugees clogged the roads, frantically fleeing the advancing Red Army. At times the POWs had a firsthand look at another mass of suffering human beings. For Les Schrenk, it was a chaotic sight.

We were just a long column, and there were a lot of long columns at that time, of Germans as well. . . . You can't imagine how many people were out on the roads. Civilians, people that had been displaced from their homes . . . every kind that you can imagine. German civilians pushing

Les Meader was among the several thousand airmen POWs evacuated in April 1945 from XVII-B, in Krems, Austria. Groups of 500 men trudged toward Braunau, on the Inn River. As on all forced marches, food was scarce. Les took a chance.

While we were in Braunau, we wanted something to eat. So we went to a farmhouse. I just knocked on the door and asked for bread. This woman . . . I suppose they were afraid. I'm *sure* they were afraid. I just asked for bread, and she'd just baked some. And I got a loaf of homemade bread. And if that wasn't like cake, I'll tell you.

baby carriages, pulling wagons, doing everything. Some of them were in much worse shape than we were.

I can remember meeting a column of Russians. They were walking barefooted in the snow. I'm sure that they were POWs. You would see them, but you would never get in contact with them.

Even as a POW in poor health, Rodney Shogren recalls feeling empathy for the human misery he encountered.

The civilians, they . . . weren't hostile. They were in bad shape, most of those people. The last few days that we marched, there was people walking as far as you could see in all directions. Getting out away from the Russians. They had everything on their back that they owned, or they were pushing a wheelbarrow, or they were pulling a four-wheel buggy with everything they owned. They were pulling them by hand.

A lot of these people were up in age. I mean sixty, sixty-five. They appeared to be, anyway. I felt sorry for those people. We were sick and in bad shape, too, but these were old people. They were civilians, leaving everything they owned. I don't know if they were Germans or if they were Polish. But they were all getting out of the way of the Russians.

Every Man for Himself

Seventy miles southeast of Berlin, in the city of Görlitz, was Stalag VIII-A. Opened in 1940, by early 1945 the camp housed at least 10,000 enlisted men of various nationalities. American POWs, some 1,800, had first been transferred there in January 1945. Conditions, never particularly good at Görlitz, declined even further. The evacuation of VIII-A began on February 10, 1945. Organized by compounds, the prisoners left in groups; the Americans who share their experiences here all departed the camp on February 14. In all, at least 1,400 U.S. prisoners left the camp at this time; some days later, the Germans split this group into two sections of about six to seven hundred men each.[7]

John Kline, Richard Ritchie, and Paul Peterson were all enlisted men serving with the army's 106th Infantry Division. They were among the thousands captured in December 1944 at the Battle of the Bulge. Kline and Ritchie, in the first section after the group was split, were on the road for more than fifty days, until their liberation by American forces in mid-April; Peterson and the other section endured more than thirty days of marching before being packed into boxcars and sent to the hopelessly overcrowded Stalag XI-B at Fallingbostel.

In contrast to Luft IV, these men were in poorer physical shape when they departed, malnourished and weak. As all three testify, this forced march rapidly devolved into small groups of men looking out only for themselves. Hunger and a severe shortage of food drove prisoners to theft and aggressive behavior, with scant regard for others.

John Kline passed through the camps at XII-A and IV-B before arriving at Görlitz on January 13, 1945. John describes how he managed to deal with the never-ending march and also how it affected him.

> You know, I think that you just slogged along. Now people have asked me this: how did you feel? You know, I think our feelings . . . I think we were numb. We just . . . we put our head down and put one foot in front of the other and just kept moving along. People said, how did you walk so far? I said, you just do it. You *have* to. They gave us a couple of old army blankets. Pull them over your head and try to keep warm. Just slog along. . . .

You're just trudging. You don't know what's going to happen next. There would be a bombing raid up ahead, so they'll stop you. Then you go off into the woods or go off into the grass.

Once you get into that mode, you're just putting your head down and just keeping going. You know you have to keep going because . . . you figure if you drop along the road, you're not going to live. You just keep trudging, trudging. I think your mind builds a block. . . . Hoping we wouldn't get bombed or strafed. Just hoping that the next town, they might give us some more food. Then getting up the next morning and say, well, we have to go to the next town. It was just automatic. We must have built into us a survival situation where the mind sort of goes dull but it says to you, you gotta stay alive. You *gotta* stay alive. So you just keep going, and you just keep going.

These conditions, but especially the lack of food, brought out the worst in men. John refers to his diary:

Diary entry for 2 March 1945: "The food supply is getting sparse. It's surprising how a man will act if he's hungry. George has a knack for begging and finding food, probably because he's so small and looks so feeble. I'm sure I also look awful, but he seems to get more handouts. And then the other night George had a loaf of bread and a can of salt in a burlap bag under his head. The next morning after awakening, the bread was gone. The other prisoners would cut your throat for something to eat. Like a bunch of starved rats. This is the great American soldier: nothing but a bunch of sneaky thieves. Your own buddy would turn you in to a guard if it would bring food as a reward."

John reflects on this passage.

We were in bad shape at that time. You were looking for anything you could eat. People were picking up stuff. I think there is a point where your spirit breaks down, and you do just about anything to get something to eat. That's about all I can [say to] explain it. But that did happen. It did happen.

I'll put it this way. You kept in groups of two, three, or four people. You didn't give a hoot about what was happening to anybody else. . . . It's like the buddy system, is what it is. Three or four buddies together, and if they stole food or found some food, they shared it between those three or four. They wouldn't share it with anybody else. That's the way it gets to be.

More than six weeks after leaving VIII-A, John was physically unable to keep up with the column, then still lurching slowly westward.

We were separated from the main column [on April 9,] right after we got out of Königslutter, because I couldn't walk anymore. They threw me on the *Krankenwagen,* and there were some other sick people. There was thirty-two of us in this so-called "sick group" that went on a separate route of its own.

We went straight east from Königslutter and [on April 12] ended up at [the city of] Helmstedt. As I recall, it was only two days before we got to Helmstedt. . . . I ended up in an infirmary. . . . I couldn't walk. They had to carry me into the infirmary.

The next day, April 13, American units entered Helmstedt and removed the men from the infirmary.

If the war had lasted two more weeks, I think I would have been dead.

Richard Ritchie was a medic with the 106th Infantry Division. He, too, arrived at VIII-A Görlitz in mid-January. As a medic, Richard was attuned to issues of health, but he also has strong memories of human behavior and what happens to people when there isn't enough food.

[We were] just more or less ambling along, not in a parade formation or anything like that. But so many abreast and people. . . . There were sick people. There were hungry people. There were cold people. . . .

[We slept] sometimes in barns and sometimes outside. . . . Of course, every morning you'd wake up, your feet were frostbitten or whatever, and you'd walk until you walked the frost out of them and that sort of thing.

They had guards up in front and then every so often a guard along the side of the troops. Then they had a mop-up crew with a couple dogs. Then following that was a sick wagon. . . .

A lot of guys had dysentery and diarrhea and that sort of thing. It weakens you. You're losing fluids, and you're not getting enough. I carried a bottle of halogen tablets with me. You could get a canteen full of water and put a halogen tablet in it, and it's supposed to kill all of the germs in it. It was something issued to me [as a medic]. So that was how I drank. *(chuckles)* But I got dysentery anyway, or diarrhea.

I remember going through some towns, and like little two-story buildings, people would be hanging out the window. Some of them would be ticked off at you, and others would be crying and knowing what conditions you were in and what you were being made to do and that sort of thing. They tended to be the older people who had gone through World War I, probably. . . .

On occasion, groups of guys would break away from the thing and go into where they had their vegetables along the fields buried in dirt mounds. Then [the guards] would let the dogs loose. Well, it got so plentiful doing that that pretty soon they started shooting into the crowd. Then they would move away, and there would be a couple guys laying there. But they would all get back in line.

We were approaching Braunschweig, getting close to the end of it [the march]. I saw these mounds along the roads. I didn't run right to the mounds; I just played like I passed out. The marching column kept on going, and the mop-up crew came along, and the next thing I knew they whacked me in the back of the head with a rifle butt, and it evidently knocked me cold. But they left me laying there. They expected the sick wagon to pick me up. I guess the whole crowd went by, and the sick wagon went by, and there I was, all alone. I went over to the dirt pile, and I dug out carrots, and I ate carrots until they were running out of my ears. *(laughs)*

Army medic Richard Ritchie. He recalls that prisoners were close to starvation on the forced march from VIII-A Görlitz: men would eat nearly anything.

I'd find dead rats and animals of all kinds . . . you know, small rodents of some kind in their knapsacks, which they planned on using as food. People would be downing potato peels, and an apple core—that was a prize. . . . I picked up apple cores that had been eaten before and cleaned them off, and I picked up potato peels when I had the chance. But a sugar beet I didn't have much. . . . They were too sweet. They were too watery. They didn't have very good taste to them, but I ate them. Yes. Anything.

Within days, advancing U.S. forces found Richard and other men in his column.

Paul Peterson is the final 106th Infantry Division soldier to share his experience of the forced march from VIII-A. Paul's memories are consistent with those of John Kline: it was every man for himself, and survival meant banding together with others.

> We formed up little groups as prisoners. . . . In order to protect ourselves, there was a group of seven of us. There were a lot of groups like this that worked together. Within the group you had a job. We had two guys whose job it was to trade stuff. We had two guys who did nothing but try to get off the road and grab stuff to eat and get back in before they let the dogs loose at the end of the column. And there were two guys whose job it was to divide the spoils among the members of the group. I was the seventh guy; I was the *Dolmetscher* [interpreter]. I could speak a little German. . . .
>
> In this one place we were going along, there was a little narrow sidewalk, and we were in the street. We had told our people in the group how to beg for stuff: *"Brot, Brot, Brot. Bitte, bitte, Brot."* [Bread, please, bread.] This guy was walking along, and this little old lady was hobbling. She had been to the market with her bag that she was carrying. He went into this *"Brot, Brot, Brot"* business, and he looked down, and in that bag was a loaf of bread. I mean, a big round loaf of bread. Not the kind of stuff we'd been eating. He looked and said, *"Bitte, bitte, Brot."* She looked around to see where the guards were. And she opened the bag. And he put his hand in and grabbed that loaf and pulled it up, and between his thumb and the bread was her ration book. And he looked at us, the rest of us: what am I going to do here? He could have taken it. He let go. He let it go back in there. She would have been in trouble if he had taken it. But he kept the bread. And we divided it in seven parts, complaining bitterly about the eyesight of the guys who were supposed to be dividing it up.

The group owned a bar of soap, a remnant of a Red Cross parcel divided up some time earlier.

> [T]he German population didn't have any real soap. They had ersatz stuff, worse than Lava soap. So I got one of these trader guys to go rap on the windows in the towns. Head into town, rap on the windows, haus-

frau comes, you wave the soap and say, *"Seife, Seife für Brot."* [Soap, soap for bread.] So she'd run and get you a hunk of bread, and the idea was to grab the bread, keep the soap, and get back in line. The line was too long, and there were not that many guards.

That worked about three times with the *"Seife,"* grab the bread, keep the soap, get back in line. The last time, *"Seife, Seife für Brot,"* she grabbed the soap and closed the window. That was the end of that one. *(laughs)* Well, it worked for a while.

After we'd gone as far as Eisenach, pretty far west, they turned us back to Erfurt and then north to a little town called Duderstadt. There's a brick factory there. We were housed in this brick factory. They were trying to decide what to do with us, I'm sure.

By that time, my guy that I was walking with was Bert Doane, from Sioux Falls, South Dakota. I had liberated a blanket somewhere. It was just an awful German ersatz blanket. Made with wood chips, I think. We slept in that. We stayed on the main deck in this brick factory because it was close to the latrine. Neither of us were in very good condition by that time, toward the end of the march. One morning I woke up, and Bert didn't.

You know, everyone was sick. Nobody knew *how* sick, because we all looked the same. Everybody had lost weight. He just didn't make it. Buried in a mass grave. They took his clothes, boots. He was finally dead.

We were [at Duderstadt] for a little while. Then we were transported by train from there to Stalag XI-B Fallingbostel. Huge camp. Our compound was the American and British compound. There was a French compound. There was a Russian compound. I don't know how many others there were. It had been there a while. There were a lot of Russian prisoners. A lot of Russian prisoners died in that camp. It was just warehouses of corpses.

British troops liberated Fallingbostel on April 16, 1945. By then, Paul was in the Lazarett *(camp hospital), suffering from jaundice and dysentery; he had lost some eighty pounds.*

Liberation and Odyssey

Stalag III-C was located some three and a half miles northeast of the Oder river town of Küstrin. Opened in June 1940, this camp for enlisted men ini-

tially housed French, Belgian, and British POWs; Soviet prisoners came after mid-1941. Americans arrived first in late 1944, but already more than 2,000 were in III-C by the end of January 1945. By that time, the camp was bursting at the seams, with a population of at least 38,000 prisoners.[8]

With Soviet forces fast approaching, the Germans made ready to evacuate the camp; this began early on January 31, 1945. The Germans instructed the POWs to quickly pack their few belongings and march out the front gate.

Bill Hall:

It was early in the morning. The Germans came through the camp and told us *"Raus! Raus!"* The Russians were coming, and we had to evacuate the camp immediately. Some of us had kind of wooden boards that we were dragging that we used as a kind of a sled, and we put some of our meager possessions on those. We all lined up on the road outside the camp and began to march.

Here, the similarity to other forced marches abruptly ends. Shortly after the long column moved out on the road toward Küstrin, it was fired upon by Red Army troops, who apparently believed the men to be Germans. When the gunfire erupted, there was instant chaos and panic. Vern Kruse shares his perspective on the Russian attack.

The road went through a hedgerow. You could see the buildings on the other side. . . . We also had a staff car or two, with the camp commander in it and the Germans that we knew. They had just got through the hedgerow and all of a sudden . . . *aka-boom! Prrrrrrrrt!* All the machine guns went off. First they killed all of the Germans that were in those first cars.

The Russians. Yes, they were waiting. The Russians had their tanks on the other side of this hedgerow. Seventy-five millimeter [guns]. Then they opened up on the troops with machine guns. . . . As soon as they opened up . . . the ones on my left side went *that* way *(motions left)*, and the ones on my right side went *that* way *(motions right)*. We hit the dirt. I had been walking shoulder to shoulder with my buddy, Jerry Jerome. Here's Jerry—he went off *that* side of the road *(motions left)*. I went off to *this* side *(motions right)*. They were shooting machine guns and artillery but mostly machine guns. All of these tanks up there. Guys were dropping on the road. . . . Some got hit.

Sam Alle was in the column, too.

All of a sudden, *bang, bang, bang!* The first thing I did was head for the ditch [at the side of the road]. I didn't know where it was coming from. After a while, I couldn't hear any noise. I looked up, and I couldn't see anybody. [Other guys] started to pop up, too. Being a medic, I looked for wounded. I found two dead people. I don't know who they were. . . . There wasn't hardly anybody there. Just a few of us like me that came out of the ditch. I saw the Russians coming. . . . I got up, and there was a guy standing there. I said, "Americanski."

The soldier motioned Sam and the others to head toward the Russian lines.

It was like a . . . farm, with all big buildings in there. I first went there, and there was still shells going around, so I hid in one of those pits in the garage, where they raised the cars up. I sat there; me and two other guys sat down there for about an hour or so. Guys were populating those buildings; there must have been about five hundred altogether. I think

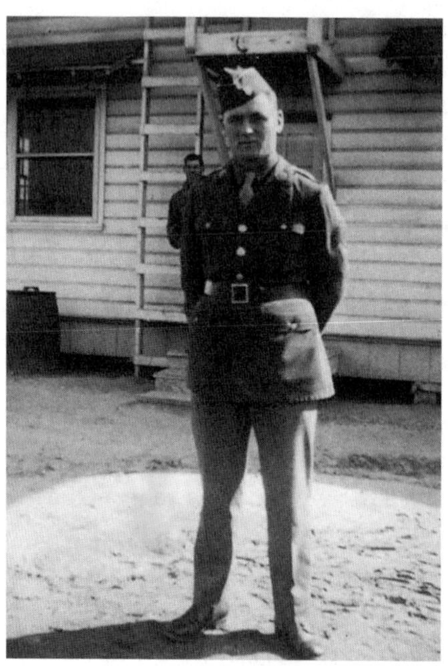

Alvin Schmidt was further back in the marching column, away from the gunfire and confusion up front. Because of his position, he experienced the events quite differently.

The first group were about a mile down the road when they met up with the Russians and they opened fire. We lost a few POWs, but I never did find [out] how many. We returned to our barracks, and the Germans left. We stayed there until about midnight, when the word came [from the Soviets] to get into groups of eight and leave the camp.

all the rest of them went back to camp. Then we got together—there was thirteen of us from my room—and we stuck together.

Bill Hall was in a group of about twenty men that formed spontaneously from the chaos of battle. After encountering some German combat troops, who told them to leave the area and head back to camp, the men decided instead to head the other direction—into the town of Küstrin.

We decided we'd go back up the road and maybe we could go across the field or something. We didn't go very far, maybe a block, and the Russians opened up on us again. Instead of going in the camp, we . . . rushed into Küstrin. We thought, boy, we're going to make it. The Russians are coming. . . . We're going to surrender to them. We're going home.

There were twenty of us running in there. The vast majority of the people didn't. They either stayed in the camp or waited for the Russians to come. . . . We're looking around for a place to safely stay. There was a shed in back of a building. The building wasn't big enough; we could hardly keep the door closed. So we had to find somewhere else.

There was an old grizzled German with a Mauser rifle standing at the door, and he told us, "March, march!" He was going to march us back toward the camp. As we were marching down the road back toward the camp . . . a German lady came out of her house across the street and spoke, screaming German at this old guy, . . . we got the impression [she was saying], let those people alone. So he threw up his hands and walked away, and she motioned for us to get behind her house into a shed.

Vern Kruse had run off the road when the first shells hit. Fleeing, he became a target.

I was running next to somebody else; he was bouncing against my [left] shoulder. He was close enough that our backpacks were hitting each other.

I'm running back and away from them, back in the direction of our POW camp. Because there's a patch of woods back there with a little house in it. It wasn't much bigger than my garage. Anyway, whoever was shooting at us had me and this guy picked out for a target. Here's two of those guys that they could shoot at. I hear this *crrraa*AACK*!* The shell went just over our heads and blew up ahead of us. It made a noise like *wham* BANG. Then they knew . . . they were a tad too high; they shot over us. They must have lowered that gun just a little and fired again.

The next shell came down, and it hit the ground right *there! (motions with hand to lower left)* Right between us. A seventy-five millimeter. It blew me for about twenty feet. The explosion cleared the snow off the ground in about a forty-foot circle. What it did to this other guy, I didn't know. My ears were ringing, and I was down on the ground in the snow. As soon as they fired that shell, they figured they got us. I figured, it's safe now to run because they were still picking off guys around there, shooting at them.

So I went to this patch of woods with that little house in it. I thought, maybe Jerry is over there. He wasn't there. They had a dugout basement where I could go down. A bunch of GIs were in there. [A bit later] I came back upstairs, and the shooting had stopped.

Bill Hall and his group followed the German woman's advice and went to the shedlike building.

There were other GIs in there, so there were probably sixty, seventy of us. We all went in that little building, and we could hear all this firefighting starting out there. The Russians were approaching that camp. We were in the middle of a firefight between the Russians and the Germans. . . . All that first night, aircraft strafed the area. Just screaming all night long. Bombs dropping. And you could hear tanks going up and down the road. That went on for four or five days.

The German lady had a son, probably a fifteen-year-old son. [The third day,] he knocked on the door, and he had four loaves of bread. She was giving us this bread. We thanked him very much, and he left. We never saw him or the woman again.

Wehrmacht soldiers found the hiding prisoners.

[T]hey ordered us out of the building. So we came out, and the house that the woman had lived in, the roof was gone; part of the wall was gone. There were dead horses on her lawn. There was part of a Russian tank with the turret blown off up the field here, and it looked like an arm and a shoulder or something laying in the road.

The Germans had successfully repelled the Russians. So they had taken over the town and recaptured us. . . . The following morning they just lined us up along the fence. I remember a redheaded German guard came along and told us to follow him. So he marched us out of town, down the road.

With several hundred other recaptured men, Bill Hall endured a march of more than one hundred miles to III-A Luckenwalde. He spent the rest of the war in that camp.

After emerging from the dugout basement, Vern Kruse approached some Red Army soldiers standing nearby.

I went over [to the Russians] to see if they would go and get my buddy there, who looks like he's badly hurt. They said, no, you go. Go. Pointing. The Russians, it was a woman tank commander . . . they told us GIs to move on. It ended up that pretty soon we got up to fourteen of us POWs. . . . From there on, I was on the trip of my lifetime with thirteen other ex-POWs. These guys were all from my barracks building because we were in that first group. Some in my own first bunch, my first barracks, like Jerry Jerome, I never saw him again, until later on. He went back to the camp.

Sam Alle, Vern Kruse, and Alvin Schmidt were among a small number of ex-prisoners from III-C who embarked on epic treks to freedom. After nearly two months and more than a thousand miles of travel through war-torn Eastern Europe, they arrived at the Black Sea port of Odessa. For all these men, though, returning to the west proved difficult, as Soviet authorities in Poland refused permission for aircraft to land and evacuate the ex-POWs. The only exit route approved by the Soviets was by ship, through Odessa—thus the long journeys by foot, rail, and other means. Disagreement and mutual suspicion existed between U.S., British, and Russian officials on the question of repatriation—and, ironically, war's end actually compounded such problems.[9]

For the former III-C prisoners, unaware of the governmental wrangling, this situation meant an unforgettable journey across Poland and through the Soviet Union, encounters with soldiers and village folk, and firsthand experiences with a completely foreign world. Vern Kruse and Sam Alle were in the group of fourteen. Away from the fighting and free from the POW camp, a very big question remained: where to go now?

Sam Alle:

The Russians made [the decision] *for* us. They told us to go *that* way [east, toward their lines], and we went through. They didn't bother us. We just walked on by our own. [The first place we stopped was] some vacant building.

Vern Kruse remembers just heading away from the fighting.

We were on our own until we got to this place where we stayed for roughly a week, trying to recuperate. There was some food there. It took us all day to get there. My records [diary] say it was twenty-eight to thirty kilometers or so. . . . It was starting to get late, and we had to find someplace to hole up for the night. It was pretty good refuge. It was this horse farm and resort that they ran. People went there for recreation, for riding horses. I think the Russians had shot the two ladies that lived there. . . . [The corpses] remained out there in the pigpen, and the pigs were nibbling on them.

The men found food at the farm, but this location was not a safe haven. Vern reads his diary entry from February 2, 1945, just two days after the group arrived:

"Being bombed, shelled, and strafed all day by the Germans. Shells have hit the house I'm in, and I've been shaking like a leaf all day. . . . One building burned down, but GIs escaped to others. We had a good hot cup of coffee before bed, and it sure made us feel good after sweating out the strafing all day."

Vern recalls the cities and town the men passed through. Scars of war—of years of war—were everywhere.

Some of these towns were just obliterated. Take a big city like Warsaw. Oh, my gosh! . . . Warsaw—there was so much rubble there. . . . People walking around between rubble. The bridges—there was a number of railroad bridges and road bridges for cars—they were bombed out. . . . No tall buildings left. Everything is crumbled down. A spire would be sticking up [out] of a church. That's the way it was. I can remember it quite well.

Little towns. Very few people. They're all poor. All the women, they had babushkas on and [were] wrapped in . . . some kind of a blanket. They didn't have much in the way of clothes. A lot of the men had their legs shot off. . . . They would be sitting on these little wooden platforms with the wheels on the bottom. They'd have to push themselves with their hands. You find a lot of those people at the train depots. They would be begging from civilians or soldiers, for whatever was available. Even from the POWs. Although *we* would almost be begging for stuff.

Some of these people had something to sell. Say, if I had an undershirt and I could get six eggs or something like that for that, I might do that. Somebody else had something else, maybe an extra pair of socks. They'd go and trade that for whatever was available. It might be some vegetable. But mostly it was eggs. It was into winter, so there was a limited amount of the things that they could be selling outside.

You scrounge for *everything*. You don't go in any store and buy anything, not there in Poland and Russia. You wouldn't steal, but there were plenty of bombed-out houses, and you'd find things in there.

Sam Alle talks about the people the men encountered on their travels.

I rode in boxcars a lot of time with Polish people that were going home.... A lot of Polish civilians ... that had been slave laborers in Germany. They were going home. They didn't know where—if they had a home or not.

You get in that boxcar, so crowded you couldn't all sit at one time, you had to sit and some stand. ... I mean, they share everything with you. They had nothing, but they would give you half of nothing. ... Some old lady came out. She broke off her loaf of bread. Others would share. And they had gone through a lot more than *we* ever did.

I remember that one boxcar, I swear, they were singing something in Polish, and I swore I was singing with them. And I don't know a word of Polish. *(chuckles)* But I just loved the people.

After being directed by the Soviet troops to leave the prison camp at III-C in groups of eight, Alvin Schmidt and a number of others remained in the general area for a few days before moving on.

After about a week we started [east] for Poland. We decided to split up in pairs, as it was easier to find food. ... When [my buddy and I] got to Poland, we stayed with an elderly couple for about a week. They had plenty of food but needed firewood and were afraid of the Russians, so we gathered up quite a pile for them. Very nice people. We left there and headed for Warsaw ... and after many days of stealing bicycles and one time two horses and once in a while [riding] on a tram, we got to Warsaw.

Drawing from Vern Kruse's diary, 1945. Vern picked up this old date book—from 1942—and used it to record daily events on the trek through Poland and the Soviet Union.

There was a camp that was set up for Polish who had no place to go, and they let us stay there. . . .

One day as we were walking the streets, we came upon a group of Russians that rounded up a bunch of Polish men and women to help build a bridge that had been blown up. Well, when the Russians saw us, they made us join the group at gunpoint. When the guards were not looking too close, we made a run for it. They shot at us, and one bullet hit the heel of my shoe, but we dived into a bombed-out building and got away.

It was tough going. . . . As we got farther, we could get on boxcars, and that is how we got to Odessa. . . . On the way to there, we were so hungry I traded my pants to a Russian lady for roasted chicken. . . .

Vern Kruse, too, has distinct memories of the Russian soldiers.

We did not trust them because most of them were drunk. We went into one town, and here was a real nice-looking young Polish girl laying alongside the road. . . . I think she might have been raped; her dress had been pulled up. You're just in a country that you don't know what's going on with the Russians around anyway, because they were half plowed. Where this girl was on the ground . . . we had just gone past that. Went down the road to the town we could see up ahead. Here were some Russians. They were sitting on the fence on the right side of the road. They were shooting the farm animals there with their pistols. They were *shooting* them. I thought that was so wasteful.

We had moved into one of the houses—it was like a two-story farmhouse—and the Russians came along. They wanted it, so we got kicked out. This was, of course, in the real cold weather. So there was a little shanty outside that used to keep the horses dry in the rain. That's the only cover we had outside. So we slept there. We didn't freeze anymore, but we were pretty cold that night. They didn't let us in that building. . . . You're not going to try to start a fight with Russians that are trigger-happy.

We're all unarmed; we didn't have a thing. Not that we probably couldn't have picked up something. But we were unarmed. We were POWs, and that's all that we were. . . . We did not have—we were men without a country. You're wandering out in the middle of Europe, and you're nobody, really.

To help with identification, Vern made an American flag patch and sewed it onto his shirt. He is wearing the shirt, one of his proudest possessions, as we talk.

Every time that we came across some Russians that were wondering who we were and stuff—they had guns; we're not afraid, but we're concerned—and I would show them, American. *(points to patch)* I would say, "American." They understood that. I was the only guy that had that, so I always made sure that I was up there talking to whoever had stopped us.

Other Russians, though, made a more positive impression on young Vern Kruse. He shares another diary entry, this from February 20, 1945:

"Went to the train station and caught one two hours after we got there. We rode in crowded boxcar all day. Got too stuffy for me, so I moved out and rode with the Russians in their day coach. They gave me cigarettes and tobacco, and I had a good time with them. They asked me to stay with them overnight, as they had a good warm bunk for me. I slept with the Russians."

They were a happy bunch in there, very happy bunch. They were all wounded . . . all full of bandages, but they were a happy-go-lucky bunch of guys, and they treated me real fine in there. *(laughing)* I really don't know [how we] communicated, but we did. We did. Yes, they were very good. These guys weren't drunk. Some of them were under medication, and they were . . . going to the hospitals back behind the lines.

By the end of March, many of the former III-C prisoners had arrived in Odessa. Through the confusion of war, there were many different sorts of soldiers in the teeming port city, some ex-POWs, others there for reasons not always clear. As groups were assembled, ships transported them via Istanbul to ports in Allied-occupied Italy.

Alvin Schmidt:

We were in Odessa three or four days, and then we were put on an English boat that took us up to Naples, Italy. There we were taken to several army headquarters to get our records up to date, etcetera. After several days, they decided I was not in shape to rejoin the 90th [Infantry Division], still fighting in Germany. They put me and others on a plane, and after stops, plane changes, etcetera, we arrived in New York City the day the war ended in Germany [May 8, 1945].

Vern Kruse:

We got on board ship. Different nationalities were on there; we had quite a bunch by the time we shipped out of there. We had quite a few Americans that went on board.

On March 25, 1945, Vern's ship docked in Naples. There Vern found his best friend, Jerry Jerome, whom he hadn't seen since the day III-C was evacuated, two months earlier.

Here, two months later now, I ran into Jerry Jerome in Naples. That was quite a reunion.

He also went down to Odessa. He got there before I did . . . and hopped on board a ship. That ship went down to Africa, and . . . then he came back across the Mediterranean to Naples. And here I ran into him again. *(with emotion)* The first time since we parted back there near the POW camp. . . . It was kind of weird—here it is hundreds of miles apart, and we bump into each other again.

Reunited: Vern Kruse (second from right) and Jerry Jerome (right), best friends from III-C Küstrin, enjoy a relaxing moment in Minneapolis, 1945. The bonds forged in prison camp lasted a lifetime.

7

Hellships and Slave Labor

SEA TRANSPORT DETAILS are perhaps the least-known aspect of the Pacific POW experience, even though more than 126,000 POWs were transported and more than 21,000 died en route. By the prisoners, and in the literature on the subject, these transports are most often referred to by a singular name: hellships.[1]

From the war's beginning, the Japanese had moved prisoners from point of capture or collection camps to where labor was required—to Burma and Thailand, Manchuria, Formosa, and various points in between. Early journeys were often short, inter-island trips. By 1944, however, most lasted weeks, as the Japanese sent increasing numbers of POWs to Japan to fill the labor void in their domestic economy.

A level of danger from Allied submarines had always existed, but this risk multiplied as the war went on and the Allies gained control of the seas. By early 1944, U.S. and British submarines regularly patrolled the western Pacific and South China Sea, main shipping lanes used by the Japanese. From mid-1944, carrier-based aircraft increased the risk of attack.[2]

The risk to the prisoner transports was great, as the Japanese did not identify these ships as carrying POWs. Recognizing this danger, the International Red Cross had worked for an accord governing the safety of any and all POWs being transported, but in neither Europe nor the Pacific did the belligerent powers ever come to an agreement. As a result, in the Pacific, Japanese ships continued to sail and submarines and aircraft continued to sink them. Indeed, more than 19,000 of the POWs who perished on hellships were killed by this so-called friendly fire. The web becomes more tangled: by 1944, U.S. intelligence often knew the names of Japanese ships carrying prisoners; picking these ships out of a convoy would have been nearly impossible, however, and so orders were issued to submarine commanders to attack the convoys. And so men died.[3]

Many Pacific POWs describe the hellship transport as the absolute worst period of their incarceration. The time spent on these ships indeed resembled time in hell. Temperatures in the holds regularly rose above one hundred degrees. Packed in so tightly they often were unable to sit, prisoners received almost no food and, maddeningly, far too little water. A lack of sanitary facilities meant men literally lived in sewage. Submarines attacked convoys, and the sounds of nearby ships exploding at times led to near panic as men feared their ship was next. Time aboard a hellship was the ultimate test of a man's will to maintain sanity; survival, as one prisoner described it, demanded that he simply shut down his senses and crawl inside himself.[4]

Surviving a hellship journey and disembarking in Japan initiated yet another chapter in men's lives as POWs. On the docks, contingents of prisoners were split into groups, varying in size from a few dozen to a few hundred, and transported to locations where labor was required—in this respect, a system similar to the Japanese practice since 1942. But unlike the Pacific islands and South Asia, where in almost all cases the military administered the camps, in Japan most camps operated in union with private industry. Japanese companies—including well-known concerns such as Hitachi Shipbuilding, Kawasaki Heavy Industries, and Mitsubishi Industries—contracted for and made extensive use of POW labor. Camps usually were attached to an industrial concern, such as a steelworks or a mining operation; additional prisoners worked as stevedores or on various construction projects.[5]

Conditions in Japan steadily deteriorated in the war's final year. The work often was grueling and, as with mining, very dangerous. Camp guards on the whole proved no better than those at other locations. Unheated, poorly insulated barracks combined with inadequate clothing to accentuate the cold. By early 1945, food rations were being reduced to absolute minimum levels: imports essentially stopped as submarines continued to take their toll; domestically, a severe labor shortage and destroyed transport network further reduced what food was available. Japanese civilians suffered; POWs even more so. Friendship and trust were tested as never before—with some unfortunate yet predictable results.

Finally, prisoners across Japan repeatedly were told that if, or when, an Allied invasion took place, they all would be executed. Men were forced to live with this Sword of Damocles hanging over their heads: if the Allies ultimately were victorious, they likely would not live to see it. What a psychological burden to endure, day after day after day.[6]

Alf Larson spent nearly two years on a work detail at Clark Field on Luzon. In August 1944, the Japanese moved the two hundred–man crew to Manila; after a brief stop at Bilibid Prison, Alf and many others were part of a group of 1,135 prisoners placed on board the Noto Maru, *a freighter headed to Japan.*

Just a freighter was all it was. We were all crammed into this forward small hold. All in one hold.

Up a gangplank and down a rope ladder. All went down one rope ladder. I was more or less fortunate because I wasn't the last group to get on, but I wasn't the first group by any means. The first groups, they were shoved back as far in the hold as they could get, and the air there was . . . it just wasn't.

It was a dark, dingy hole. The only light was through the hatch that we came down. I don't know what it was before, but it stunk in there. It probably was from shipping horses and stuff before.

You could sit squatted down. Pull your knees up, and then the man ahead of you, he had his back against your pulled-up knees, and your back was against the other guy's knees.

Our bathroom consisted of one big wooden tub right down below the hatch, and the Japanese would lower it down and bring it up, and they weren't too fussy about when they brought it up, either.

The only time we got on deck was [when the ship stopped at] Formosa. After we left the Philippines, they brought us up on deck one time and hosed us down. They'd have a group of us go up and get washed and then go back down, and the other group would come up. That's the only time we were on deck until we arrived in Japan.

There was very little talking in there. The only time there was any noise on the trip from Formosa to Moji was when we were attacked, by submarines. . . . There were submarines out there . . . but we didn't know that until after we got going. . . . We could hear the thuds, and the people that were navy people said, that's depth charges. But all of a sudden there was a big explosion, and the hatch was open, and we could see this light from whatever. So we figured that somebody hit an oil tanker. You never heard such a roar in your life. And the Japanese, they mounted a machine gun up there and closed the hatch.

I would say that most of the consensus of opinion was, hit us! Hit us! Get us out of this. Just get us *out*. We probably figured we would die, but it couldn't be any worse than what it was. We just . . . in fact, I would say *everybody* was praying that they hit us. *(with emphasis)* Hit us! If the Lord's willing, I'll survive; if not. . . .

Alf talks frankly about how he got through.

You just ignore everything. You just . . . you take . . . everything is out of your mind. Just make your mind a blank. I don't know [how] you do that. It's not easy, I'll tell you. When I got to Japan, I knew my name, rank, and my serial number. That's it. I turned everything off.

After their capture in May 1942 on Corregidor, Ray Makepeace and Howard Swanson spent mid-1942 through July 1944 as stevedores at Port Area Manila. Then came the word: all the men working there were to be transported to Japan. The ship was the Nissyo Maru, *a 6,510-ton passenger-cargo auxiliary. The Japanese attempted to pack more than 1,600 men into the rear hold, estimated to be sixty feet square.*

Ray Makepeace:

I remember, I thought, shit, I don't want to get on this thing, because it was hotter than hell and guys were passing out from the heat and the humidity. We were just too crowded. They tried to get everybody . . . they tried to get sixteen or seventeen hundred guys in the back hold.

It came to cursing, screaming, and fighting among the men. "The psychological pressure," recalls one survivor, "was incredible."[7]

I remember going down there, and I thought, I gotta get out of this place. I had to take a crap anyway. So I told the Japanese, in Japanese, I had to go to the *benjo* [toilet]. On my way through the hold, I saw some men who were already in little cubicles, and, geez, they were crowded in there like sardines. There were guys passing out from the heat. I remember one guy came up. He says, "Have you got a razor?" I said, "What the hell, you want a shave now?" He says, "I want to cut my wrist." That's what he said. So I got away from that guy.

When it proved physically impossible to cram the men into one hold, the

Japanese shifted about half to a forward hold. Still, conditions remained cramped. And then the ship sat a full week in Manila Bay, baking in the July sun, compounding the problems.

Howard Swanson:

We were loaded aboard that thing. . . . It was just *full* of people. Full of men. . . . And that journey . . . it took us about three weeks. Because what happened: . . . the ship went out and parked in Manila Bay. In the bay, just sits, *sits* in that damn bay, and the sun beating down. Little water. Guys with the shits.

That ship just *sat* there—this is what made it so miserable. It was so hot and miserable and stinky and crap and piss and everything else. Puke. Whatever you can think of. Guys *died* in the hold, and they just threw them overboard. That was the most miserable part of the whole damn prison life. That was just *miserable.*

Guys went goofy in the holds. One guy, they had these kind of fins that stick out from the bulkhead, you know, in the hold. I remember him *banging* his head on that, trying to kill himself.

There was a constant noise, constant moaning, groaning. Continued throughout the night. Hell, you can't sleep. You get snatches of sleep. Cramped conditions. Guys getting in fights because . . . I don't know. You might get stepped on or something. Some guy has to take a leak or take a crap and can't make it quite to the can, craps on somebody. It's pretty awful. . . . That was the *worst.*

Ray Makepeace:

We were in the rear hold. . . . We had seven hundred plus in there, they said. But I *know* there was more than seven hundred. So three hundred men could sit down, but four hundred had to stand up. We shifted every hour. . . .

[W]e had men crapping out because they didn't get any water. They said they gave us water, but it probably—if you did get water—it would probably have been a tablespoon a day, you know, and these bodies perspiring, and the humidity down there. . . . And the men were, some of them were licking the condensation on the side of the ship.

Men become violently ill, and then they vomited and shit and everything else. All mixed in the bottom of the ship. . . . The bowel movements were moving around in the hold down there. I sat in shit, five inches of shit there, for about fifteen days, I guess. It was slimy with shit. And vomit. . . . It couldn't have been worse. . . .

If your bowels gotta move, then you'd just go in that tub. And to get over to that tub, you took your life in your hands because you had to go over bodies of slippery, slimy men. They were mad, pissed off, insane.

This human misery drove men over the edge.

It was [really a dog-eat-dog attitude down there]. Any buddy-buddy shit, that went over the side when we boarded that ship. It was every man for himself, believe me.

Oh, there was a *lot* of fighting going on. Man, they were just trying to kill each other, it's what it was. They were murderers. In other words, there was no quarter. If you get the guys holding one guy back, he gets pissed off. He'd poke him. We had one hell of a time. Then the Japanese are going to throw grenades down there and machine-gun us if we didn't get quiet. They got some kind of order down there finally.

Then there was no water. That's the bad part. We suffered for lack of water. . . . The water was the hard thing to go through there.

You better [have someone to depend on], because there was some killing going on in there. . . . Well, there were guys that would kill a man, and then they'd suck his blood. There was no water.

An old guy, I always remember his name, Renkin, . . . an ornery old bastard, and I often worked with him [at Port Area] on details, and working on loading and unloading ships. Never liked him. He didn't like me. [But] he happened to be close to me, and he said, "Makepeace, you and I never got along." He said, "But it's a matter of life and death. I'll tell you what we do. You and I are going to buddy up here. You sit, and I'll guard you for an hour, and then we just change positions." I'd stand, and he'd sit down with his knees pulled up.

Howard Swanson:

They gave us food. They gave us some rice. And you can't swallow. Now, you can do without food much longer than you can do without water. I thought to myself—I really believed this—if I *ever* get out of here, I'm always going to have a canteen full of water with me. Wherever I go, I'm going to have water. You can't imagine . . . thirst is terrible.

The conditions on the Nissyo Maru *reduced Howard's world to himself—nothing and no one else.*

> [You depended] on *yourself*—the only person that you can depend on. Now it's down to you. Of course, there were other prisoners on the ship that weren't in our camp, too. The majority of them were from other camps. You didn't know them.
>
> I don't know how [you keep your sanity]. I guess you just keep it some way. Some guys lost it. . . . And that's why when we got back, we didn't like to talk about it. People wouldn't *believe* us, some of the things that happened. That trip. That trip. *(pauses five seconds)* I think something happens to a person's mind. It shuts down feelings and shuts down even physical movement. It shuts down a lot of . . . something within a person. *(pauses three seconds)* Can you understand what I'm trying to say?

Nissyo Maru *finally sailed on July 18, bound for Takao, Formosa, and joined a convoy that became thirteen ships. American submarines, prowling the waters, finally attacked the convoy. Three ships were hit, and when smoke from a burning tanker blew through the* Nissyo Maru*'s holds, "hysteria broke out . . . and men scrambled for the hatch, thinking they had been torpedoed."*[8]

Ray Makepeace:

> [S]hips on both sides of us took torpedoes. Then [the Japanese] started dropping depth charges, and this is when the men panicked. The Japanese, they surrounded over the top there. They had machine guns and grenades ready to throw down [into the hold] because we think the ship is going to go down. . . . [Men] panicked. They howled like dogs. . . . I just said, this is it. The last chapter in my life. I don't know. You say, the hell with it.
>
> In our hold we had a priest, Father Riley. . . . This priest got up there, and I don't know how he did it, but he got the men to dead silence, and then he had them say the rosary. That was in our hold. That quieted them down. That saved our lives.

On July 27, Nissyo Maru *arrived in Takao. She sailed the next day for Moji, Japan, arriving on August 3.*

Ray Makepeace:

[After the stop] at Takao . . . it didn't get any better. Men were still dying. They were still howling like wolves. . . . I can't say how we survived. I really don't know. . . . How could people be this cruel to people? Like the Japanese were to us. Life didn't mean a damn thing. These guys had all gone through combat experience. They were good people on the ships, and here they were a little quivering, skinny piece of meat. Not even talking sensibly. Losing their mind. Screaming. Hollering. Wanting to kill somebody. You can't describe it.

Howard Swanson:

When we got out of there [in Moji], it had rained. God, that was it. I just got scoops of water in my hands and drank.

Harold Kurvers survived both Bataan and Camp O'Donnell before spending more than two years at Cabanatuan. In December 1944 in Manila, he was among the 1,619 POWs loaded onto the Oryoku Maru, *a 7,362-ton passenger-cargo ship. Also on board were more than 3,000 Japanese: troops and civilians being evacuated from the Philippines. The ship set sail on December 14. Survivors described the situation: "The heat, thirst, and lack of oxygen drove men mad. There were deaths from suffocation and deaths from being trampled. As on a few other hellships, men turned into vampires." Within the first twenty-four hours, about fifty prisoners were dead. Harold minces no words regarding what the men encountered in the holds.*[9]

Terrible. [We were] packed. Just *packed.* Shoulder to shoulder, belly to back. Standing up. . . . We were in a smaller hold, a smaller group of people. We were shoulder to shoulder and just screaming, hollering, wild. *(pauses three seconds)* Maybe I was doing it, too. I don't know.

I was in the smallest group, and our hatch cover wasn't completely pulled [closed], so we were getting some air. But the forward and after holds were just packed. Nothing. They were the ones that went berserk. . . . They went mad that very first night. Guys were cutting throats, sucking blood.

On the night of December 14, U.S. Navy planes launched from the aircraft carrier Hornet *twice bombed the* Oryoku Maru; *heavily damaged, the ship was anchored about three hundred yards off Olongapo Point, Luzon, and the Japanese passengers were discharged.*

[Did I have a sense of fear?] I don't know if it was fear. I can remember on the first bombing [of this ship]. Come to think of it, we had enough room, because I remember being on my knees and asking God to get it over with, kill me. I got on my knees and begged. This is hard to believe, but when you're thinking that way, fear is gone. You want to die. Fear is gone; it's all over then. But through the bombing, I didn't care.

But the next raid, again, the fear is back again. It's the truth. I didn't go to that again, the prayer to get me out of that. The fear was there. I don't know what I did. *(pauses three seconds)* It's a helluva thing to go through.

On the morning of December 15, the Japanese forced all prisoners over the side of the ship, with instructions to get to shore.

We were in the hold of the ship. We knew it was on fire. We knew it was sinking. The feeling was there—you knew it was going down. The guys started going up the ladder, to get topside. It was a rope ladder, and this Jap started shooting those guys. They dropped back in the hold, and [the Japanese] pulled the ladder out. We were at a loss. What in the hell is going to happen now?

And then a ladder comes down. We think [at the time] it's the Japanese, but I [learned later it was an American]. He was in another hold. They were able to get out. Some of them got out—in fact, some of them got out the side of the ship: there was a hole blown in the side, and some of them went out through that. He heard us screaming, and he looked down there, and he saw us down there and saw that ladder there, and he dropped the ladder. Anybody that could walk got out of [the hold].

For me, I looked over the side, and, oh, God, it was terrible. . . . I looked down, and it looked about eight miles down. *(chuckles)* . . . I don't know; it was a pretty high ship. [I picked up some empty canteens there on the deck, thinking they would float.] I put them on, through my belt. I took the cap off, unscrewed it, and put that chain [around my belt], and then screwed the cap back on the canteen. And I had one on either side. Then I looked for the debris of the ship, and that's when I jumped for that. Flailed away.

There was a chaplain that was going out, trying to help some of the other guys that were in the water. There was one off in the distance, a lifeboat; I could see them. They were rowing to shore, but they probably weren't strong enough to keep it going as fast as they should have. From shore, [the Japanese] machine-gunned them. They shot at them. And you could see that they were pulling toward shore, not toward the sea.

Survivors, totaling only about 1,300 of the original 1,619, were collected together on shore. For five days, the Japanese held the men in a tennis court fenced off with wire; food wasn't issued until the third day, and in spite of the heat, no water was issued at all.

These men then endured weeks on board several more ships as well as additional bombings by U.S. aircraft. When the final transport ship, the Brazil Maru, *docked on January 29 at Moji, Japan, Harold was one of just 450 still alive: 1,169 men had not survived the journey from Manila that had begun some six weeks before.*

Perhaps the greatest fear for prisoners being transported on hellships, particularly in 1944–45, was the danger that the unmarked ships would be torpedoed and sunk by American submarines active in the area. John Morrett and Onnie Clem were among 750 American prisoners packed into the hold of the Shinyo Maru *when the 2,634-ton transport sailed on September 7, 1944, from Zamboanga, southern Luzon, in a convoy of seven ships bound for Japan. The journey was a short one: late that afternoon, two torpedoes from the American submarine* Paddle *tore into the side of the ship.*

John Morrett:

There was this terrific explosion, and the hold was filled with flying debris and dust, a lot of dust. And some figures just groping around.

The partition [between holds] was blown away, and I went forward into the next hold and climbed up on a lot of gear and got up on deck. There were several of the Japanese guards that were near the hatch covers, and they must have been hit by the hatch covers at the time of the explosion because they were just splattered out on the deck.

Onnie Clem was among the hundreds literally scrambling for their lives as seawater poured into the hold.

It was filling up right quick. I saw that, and I thought, well, I've got to get out of here or I'm going to drown in this ship. There was such a mob trying to get out that hatch that I saw no way that I could possibly do it, and I decided I'm going to just put an end to this and suck in a bunch of seawater, and it's all over for me. I had my eyes closed. And I started to take a big gulp of seawater, and there was air. My head was above water. So I thought, well, I'll see what I can do.

I managed to get in the mob that was floating up toward this hatch cover. The hold was filling up with water, and you'd work your way up [the ladder]. Have to pull somebody out of the way. It was dog eat dog. You'd go up a little bit, and somebody'd get a hold of your belt or back and pull you back under. Just [a] constant fight among everybody to get out.

John Morrett was on deck.

The forward end of the ship was going down slowly in the water. There was debris from the deck of the ship beginning to float on the water, on the ocean there. Off in the distance, I could see land. I estimated it about three miles. And I felt certain that I didn't have the strength to swim that distance, but if I could just get a hold of some of that debris, I could stay afloat. My mind was racing, believe me.

I jumped overboard. I know I slid partway down the side of the deck of the ship. Got in the water. At that time, there were Japanese guards shooting the Americans. I could see some of the guards still up on deck, firing at the prisoners. There was a little enlisted man near me, and I said, "Hold onto this"—there were five two-by-fours—and then he was shot, and I couldn't drag him. So I got away from him and scissor-kicked my way from the ship as fast as I could.

Then all of a sudden the ship. . . . I saw it go right up on end and down in the water. There was a sort of a crinkling sound as it went down into the water.

Onnie Clem managed to fight his way up onto the deck of the sinking ship.

By that time the ship was really . . . starting to slide down. I could look over to shore, and you could see the outline of palm trees. I had one of those loincloths on, and I said, you better get rid of anything that might be a drag, and I pulled that loincloth off and dove over the side of the ship, on the shore side.

The other ships in the convoy had put out lifeboats. There had been a whole bunch of Jap soldiers on the ship, on the *Shinyo Maru*. These other ships in the convoy lowered lifeboats, and they were picking up the Jap soldiers and at the same time they were executing any Americans that were in the water. They'd either shoot them, or some of the officers were standing up in the front of the damn boat, and they'd pull up and take a whack at the American's head with their sabers. They were just killing a lot of people. I knew that I was going to have to get out of there, so I was swimming as hard as I could.

I could feel those spurts of water around me. It was Jap bullets hitting in the water around me where they were shooting at me. All of a sudden my right arm quit working. I couldn't move it. I looked at it, and, hell, there was blood pouring out of it near the shoulder. I'd been hit. So I was left swimming dog paddle, with one arm. I finally was able to work my way to shore.

John Morrett also made the long swim to shore.

It may have taken an hour [to reach the shore]. I don't know. Then as we approached the shore, we could see machine gun bursts over around us, and then we heard this hissing sound and jumped into the underbrush, and here were three Filipinos. They apparently had seen the whole incident. They motioned for us to follow them. We began walking down this little path, and then by that time it really was starting to get dark. There were these Filipinos along the path who began to give us food along the way.

We must have walked for maybe an hour. My mind was so filled with what had happened that I just can't begin to put any time into things. But anyhow, we walked some distance. We came to a . . . it was dark . . . and we came to a little shack, and there was a sergeant in charge of the guerillas there with, I would say, maybe four or five guerillas and then maybe by this time six or seven Americans. Then others began to be collected there as kind of a collecting point.

Just eighty-two prisoners survived the sinking of the Shinyo Maru. *Cared for on land by Filipinos, on September 29 they all were evacuated to safety by an American submarine.*

The eighty-two Shinyo Maru *prisoners survived in part because the ship was sunk so close to shore. Should a ship be sunk on the high seas, however, the chance of rescue would be near nil. For Glenn Oliver, this scenario would be reality.*

On October 11, 1944, Glenn and nearly 1,800 other prisoners from camps across Luzon were herded aboard the Arisan Maru, *a 6,886-ton cargo ship. After leaving Manila, the ship anchored several days off Palawan Island before returning to the city on October 20. The next day,* Arisan Maru *was part of a seventeen-ship convoy that left Manila, bound for Formosa. On October 23–24, however, American submarines torpedoed and sank nine of the convoy's ships—including the* Arisan Maru. *Most men left the ship quickly after it was hit; Glenn, however, remained on deck as long as possible.*

When the ship got to the point that the railing was only five or six feet above water, I went over the side. Went over the side and lowered myself into the water and swam a couple hundred feet away and turned around and watched the ship sink. . . . [The ocean was] big, sloping waves.

It was getting almost time for the sun to set, and you could see men still on the ship. Some were hanging onto the rails. Some were sitting down. As the ship sank . . . the more it sank the more vertical it got, until it was almost entirely vertical. There was probably fifteen, twenty feet of the bow still sticking out of the water. Then it just plunged out of sight. Shortly after that, a big geyser of water and air and debris came up like a waterspout.

I had two canteens. They were about half full of air, some buoyancy. . . . I was just going to paddle around, and then I bumped into some planks that came up from the ship. . . . I got about three long planks, piled them one on top of each other, and a couple of short boards. I found a couple of kegs that had Japanese rice straw rope on them. I undid the knots and took the rope underneath my gun belt, and I kept getting bumped around with debris.

Then I got violently sick. I had diarrhea, and I vomited. I had eaten some half-cooked rice, and I suppose I ate too much and drank too much water. When I got through, I was pretty well cleaned out. I was pretty weak. So I put my chest up on top of the planks and hung my arms over the side, and I must have . . . I don't know what happened. I don't remember anything. . . . [I evidently] passed out. I don't know. . . .

The next thing I knew it was daylight, and I looked around, and there wasn't anybody in sight, and I couldn't hear anybody. As far as I knew, I was the only one there. So I started to fix these planks: tie them together with this rope so I could sit on it so I would be more out of the water. Up until then I was in the water, and I was getting cold and water-soaked.

I can't remember [if I was optimistic or pessimistic at this point]. I suppose I was doing what's normal—trying to survive. Try to extend your life as long as you can. You struggle to survive. Make it today, and see what happens tomorrow.

The next morning—I had assembled my planks and was sitting on them, but they weren't enough support; I was still immersed in water up to my waist, but at least I could sit up. This [Japanese] destroyer . . . it bore down on me. They were going very slowly. It was headed directly for me.

I had a short board, like for a paddle. So when it bumped me with the bow, I pushed real hard against the boat with my short board, and I went away from the destroyer probably at about a forty-five degree angle. That's where the destroyer, which is quite long, saw me, and finally there was what looked like navy men [standing] in formation. . . . They were all in a line on the deck. Heck, they were only twenty-five, thirty feet from me. They saw me. One of them, he was the last one in line, he was sucking on an orange. He threw it at me. They went down a ways and made a real hard turn to port, to the left, and steamed out of sight.

The following day, another survivor found Glenn.

Then shortly after that, somebody hollered at me. That was Phil Brodsky; asked if he could come over. I said, "Sure. Come on ahead." We put his plank, added it to the two or three that I had, and sat there the rest of the day. Saving our strength and not knowing what to do.

That night the wind started to come up, and the waves are getting bigger, and my rice rope was coming all apart. Planks were going to come apart. So we were going to split the planks. Each one take half of them and see what happened. Just about that time, I looked over my left shoulder, and I spotted four life rafts. They were waterlogged, tied together in a string. They were about five, six inches thick, three-quarter-inch flooring top and bottom. They . . . were large enough so you could lay down on it, which was a lot easier than trying to sit on the plank.

When I woke up the next morning, both my canteens were gone. They had torn loose during the night or whatever. No water. Still had the gun belt and the rope, [the] Japanese rice rope. But no canteens; they were gone.

We were either going to live or die. There wasn't anything we could do to help ourselves much. I tried to catch fish with a small knife blade, without success.

One thing Brodsky and I said, we agreed not to discourage each other. We'd both read horror stories and stuff like that [about cannibalism on rafts]. We both agreed, no matter what, nothing like that would happen.

[One] morning when I woke up, I found a dead fish laying between Brodsky and myself. Probably three inches long. I showed it to him. I said, "We'll share it." I took and bit off what I considered about half of its body. The head end; I figured that was desirable. I chewed it up slowly and swallowed it and gave him the other half. The next night . . . another little fish committed suicide, and he got the head end.

At least we shared; I could have taken it all myself. Anyway, another thing I did: when we were tying the rafts together on top of each other, there was a piece of gauze snagged into the rope. I pulled that loose and rolled it up into a ball, about the size of a pea, I guess, something like that. I put it in my mouth. As a Boy Scout we used to learn to take a pebble and keep it in your mouth because it would promote saliva. Worked for me: my mouth and lips were in a lot better shape than his.

On October 28, four days after the sinking, a Japanese vessel hauled the two men from the water.

Brodsky . . . saw smoke on the horizon. . . . Finally it got where he could see the hull. He had a white shirt with long sleeves. He stood up and waved that white shirt back and forth. They steamed up to where we were and slowly stopped. I lay on the life raft there. I was too weak to get up. I was almost beyond the point where I was thinking. I figure [I would have lasted] maybe one more day, if that. I was just about done in.

Glenn Oliver was one of only nine survivors of America's largest loss of life in a single sea disaster. But while saved from death in the water, Glenn yet had far to go on his POW odyssey. He was taken to Formosa, where he spent until late January 1945 at a work camp. This camp was then closed and the prisoners transferred to Japan. On a hellship.[10]

Slave Labor in Japan

Surviving a hellship journey meant a new chapter in men's captivity experience. Now in Japan, they were used as slave labor in a wide variety of jobs. Bob Heer arrived from Formosa in March 1945 on the Taiko Maru. *A group of the prisoners were put onto a train.*

The train was a regular passenger train, but they kept the windows covered. They took us all the way up through [the island of] Honshu. It took us a hell of a time to get up there. But anyway, when we went through Tokyo, we looked out the window. One of the guys had the slit open, and I'd look out the window, and all these people . . . we were going through the railroad depot there in Tokyo, and everybody was running and screaming. A big [American] bombing mission was on. We were lucky actually to get out of there before they came over.

Bob was sent to a camp in Hakodate, a small seaside town on the southern tip of the island of Hokkaido.

We got there, God, in the middle of March, I guess. And we worked as stevedores. I think we first started out at unloading coal in one little place there where we'd meet. . . . We had these big scoop shovels. It was in the wintertime, and they always had a fire going there for us because the guards would build the fires to keep warm.

But anyways, one day they had one of these—it was a tank car, but it didn't have a top; it just had sides—and that thing was full of mackerel, freshly caught. So what we did is, we went over to the water faucet and cleaned off our shovels. Cleaned the coal dust off our shovels, and we were frying those mackerel, and the guards didn't seem to mind. As a matter of fact, I think we fried a couple of them, of mackerel, for them. That was a real good day for us.

In June 1945, when the main camp was closed, Bob was in a group transferred to a mine-working detail at Akabira, in central Hokkaido.

We were working at the mines up in Akabira. . . . Usually we'd have to walk to the mine. Then we'd have to get down to the bottom of the mine, and there were just a lot of things we had to do. We were drilling through slate to get to the coal, and it was very dusty. . . . We worked ten and twelve hours a day.

But anyway, we'd work the face of this wall, which was pure slate. It was about six feet high, the wall was, and about six feet wide, maybe a little wider. And we'd drill four holes across the top a meter deep, a little over three feet. Three across the center and four across the bottom.

Then the Japanese worker there . . . we'd blow those out with an air hose, and then he'd put the dynamite in there with the wires on them, and they'd be sticking out the holes at our end. Then they'd pack those with sand. They'd pack each hole with sand, then put all the wires together, and then they'd run that wire up around a little place where he'd detonate it. That's where we'd go so that we wouldn't be in the area where the rocks would be flying. Then we'd have to go up and clean up that mess, and that was our day's work.

There was this [Japanese civilian], he was in his early fifties, and he was always talking under his breath about, telling us about *(speaking Japanese)*. He was trying to tell us that the [American] B-29s were causing a hell of a lot of damage in Tokyo and other places. He also mentioned one time, he says, "Maybe soon war be over. Maybe soon war be over." But he did it very quietly, so the Japanese guards wouldn't hear him. But he was one guy that really encouraged us. To feel that the war was coming to a close.

Other prisoners also have clear memories of the arrival of American air power. After a late 1944 hellship journey from the Philippines, through June 1945 Abraham Sabbatini was part of a group of 150 POW laborers at a factory in Yokkaichi that produced acid for batteries. Abe recalls the B-29s.

I remember [when] the first American plane came over. . . . We were going out [to work], it was early in the morning, and the siren blew, for air raid. So the Japanese sent us back to the barracks. And then in nighttime, they came over around seven o'clock at night; they came to bomb Nagoya [across Ise Bay]. The planes came over, one plane after the other, until about three or four o'clock in the morning.

Abraham Sabbatini at Camp Number 7, Toyama, Japan, summer 1945. Prisoners laboring in the Toyama scrap iron factory were photographed for identification purposes. More than three years as a POW are etched into Abe's face.

Oh, yes, we could see Nagoya being bombed. We could see a lot of explosions and a lot of anti-aircraft [guns]. We were worried that they would bomb us, because our barracks didn't have no red cross on it or nothing. We were afraid that sometime, by mistake, that we would be bombed.

Thousands of Allied prisoners were used as slave labor in coal mines. The work was uniformly dangerous and difficult. Harold Kurvers, for example, labored at the infamous Mitsui Company mine at Omuta, known as Fukuoka Camp 17; Douglas MacArthur, who arrived in Japan in September 1944, worked in a mine in central Honshu; Irving Silverlieb finished the war at a mine in Utashinai, on the northern island of Hokkaido. Ray Makepeace and Howard Swanson worked in a lead mine owned and operated by the Mitsui Company, too. The two men arrived together in August 1944, part of the Nissyo Maru*'s human cargo. There was a train from the port of Moji to the small town of Kamioka, in central Honshu.*

Ray describes the camp at Kamioka.

[At] Kamioka, we lived in a barracks-type [building]. We slept on a mat—that thing was infested with lice and fleas—and we slept on a platform. Let's see . . . I think there was sixteen men in each one of these units. One room berthed sixteen guys. Each man had his space; it was twenty-eight inches. There was a lower bunk and upper bunk on both sides. In the middle there was a little square box that had sand in it. Every great once in a while they'd give us a handful of charcoal, and that was our heat.

See, there was no heat in those barracks. The only heat we had in there was, when we came in from the mine there was a hot room, because when you come in from the mine you walked down the mountain through the snow. It was colder than hell, and you're wet. I think they gave us a half an hour, and the guys would sit there up to that stove, and their legs would swell up as big as their thighs. That was beriberi, you know.

You woke up, I think, five forty-five, six o'clock every morning. Then you had to have your bed arranged, and you had to stand at attention until they came through and inspected you. You had to have your blouse buttoned up, all the buttons, and you better not be missing any buttons, too. And we had no needles or thread, so they'd work you over for that. *(chuckles)*

It was underground work, six days per week.

Ray Makepeace:

Actually, we were all issued little hard hats, you know, [like] they wear in the mines, and a little lamp which operated off of the same stuff that you use for welding: carbide. And we were just issued enough to last about four hours, but you always, in your mines, you worked in groups of maybe six, eight, or ten, so all of us didn't use our lamps at the same time, or we'd be in the dark. Terrible dark in a mine. It's dangerous walking around, too. There are chutes you could go down if you're in the dark.

So we had to go down. It was, I think, three hundred steps down. When you go up the side of the mountain, into an entrance up there. Just like a cave entrance, and then down you go. Then we, our group, each time that we went down, we'd meet in a little room there. There were electric lights in it. Kind of dim.

Then the bosses in the mine would call how many men they needed. They called them *holes,* the same as we'd call them. Then they'd call off . . . like I was always in *san* hole. *San* is "number three" in Japanese.

Howard explains how the prisoners loaded blasted rocks small and large into ore cars. And they endured abuse from Japanese overseers.

We had to fill these carts, cars. . . . They ran along this rail, narrow-gauge tracks. These carts, some of them were pretty well beat-up, and the wheels were out of line. It was hard to push those things, especially if you load them up with rock. We half loaded, about three-quarters loaded this car, and this mine guard came along and saw this, and the word they used was *bakayaro;* that means "fool." Like, you damn fool. *"Bakayaro!"* He motioned to us to fill the car. We knew what he was talking about, so we did.

We loaded the next one, and the third one we figured we wouldn't load so high because they were hard to push. And he caught us again. I tried to explain to him that it was hard to push, so he beat me with that club that he had. And you have to stand and *take* it. If you flinch, you duck . . . *don't* duck. That's the *worst* thing you can do. Just take it until they finish. . . . It ain't easy [to stand and take it].

At that time, most of the Japanese were pretty mean. But there were some *good* ones, too. There are differences. And it is the *individual* that you dislike. I think a lot of the prisoners . . . felt that way to a certain ex-

Marvin Roslansky of the U.S. Marine Corps, picture taken by the Japanese in June 1942 at Zentsuji on Shikoku. Captured in December 1941 on Guam, Marvin spent the rest of the war as a prisoner at Zentsuji. Toward the end of the war, he did stevedore work in the rail yards of the nearby city of Takamatsu.

They would bring supplies in on freight cars, and we would haul it to different destinations. . . . Everything was done manually. The rice was in burlap. Most of it was in regular straw-made bags they made. . . . You'd walk up planks until you got to your destination and drop your bag down. The heaviest was a hundred kilo.

One time I fell off the planks, and my shoulder got so bad I couldn't carry any longer. But I was only off about two days. Had to be back up there. . . . [If you] stayed back, your ration was cut, too.

tent, too. They're all bastards, you know. But you can't carry that. You just *can't.*

Slave labor, meager rations, and a cold, snowy winter claimed victims from men weakened by three years as prisoners.

Ray Makepeace:

There were quite a few [that died at Kamioka]. We burned them all. When they died, we'd just take them [to] . . . about a hundred and fifty yards from camp, there was a, I guess you'd call it a crematorium. We put the guys on a tray, and of course no clothes on. You always saved the clothes.

They always showed that they'd had an autopsy, all split from the breastbone down to their belly, and the cause of death is always pneumonia, heart attack, something like that. Never hunger. The guys starved to death or got worked to death. Exhaustion. We did have this Dr. Jackson; he did the autopsies.

It's kind of sad, you know, taking a guy down there, and just terrible. You had to put him in there, and they had to have their knees up so they could burn them. He's like a chicken; you tied the wings and legs together. *(pauses three seconds)* That was the way it was. And then of course you go back to camp, and it [the corpse] was burning, and you could smell it.

Starvation meant a constant, intense search for any bit of additional food. And when someone found a way to get extra food, a crucial decision had to be made: Do I share? And if so, with whom?

Howard Swanson:

In the mine they had, I believe they had two eight-hour shifts. Then, see, I worked at that Kamioka special detail. At that place we worked *twelve* hours.

Yet Howard volunteered to get on this detail because there was an opportunity to steal food at that location.

Because that's when we robbed the Japanese warehouse. Yes, that was a bonus. Because I *did* steal food, and I cooked it up there, at this place. I volunteered for it so that I could do this.

Howard and others on the special detail shared the food, but only with best buddies. For Howard, this meant fellow marine Glischinski, who was in poor health—and no one else.

I was stronger. That extra food like that. And Glischinski didn't know where the hell I was getting that food and . . . I couldn't *tell* him. I didn't want to tell . . . *none* of us [on the special detail] wanted to tell anybody. We had to keep that tight.

In September 1944, Alf Larson debarked the hellship Noto Maru *in Moji. At the port, the POWs were loaded onto a train heading north. Alf was in a group that ended up at a new camp, Nomachi, near the city of Takaoka, on the west coast of Honshu.*

There were two barrack buildings. Then there was a kitchen compound and toilet facilities. Also there was this big hot tub. I don't know if it had been used by Japanese soldiers before or not. When we got there, we were issued two blankets and this big thing, brick—we called it a brick—with straw, to be used as a pillow. And the mattresses . . . there were just two tiers of lower and upper, with these tatami mattresses.

[The Japanese] weren't too bad. As long as you didn't give them any trouble, they didn't give you any trouble. The camp commander, we called him the One-Armed Bandit because he had lost his arm over in Manchuria. . . . The only thing about him, in the wintertime, he'd get roaring drunk, and he'd come into the barracks, and he'd say, "Fire up the stove. I'll get you wood tomorrow morning." . . . We burned up the wood, of course, because he made us. But we never got any replacement for it, so we were cold for a couple of days. Lieutenant Sense, our American commander, went back [after the war] and testified for him, not against him.

Alf became a machinist.

They came through [the barracks] and asked if anybody could run a lathe, and I could, and so I said, yes, I can. So that's how I got [the job]. That's the only job I had in Japan. And all we did was make wheels for these trundle cars that the other prisoners in the smelter used to haul the ore into the furnace.

At Alf's last detail, Clark Field in the Philippines, those men who had volunteered for certain jobs were treated as outcasts.

[But here] nobody accused us of anything. In fact, the people that were there knew me from Clark Field, and they knew that I kept a pretty tight, fair ship. We got [no preferential treatment] other than the fact we could go eat at the barracks. But the other guys, they ate at their jobs at noon over there, too.

Alf and another American POW operated lathes in a machine shop with Japanese civilian workers. They had a Japanese civilian supervisor.

He would come to the camp and get us and walk us to the compound—about I'd say half a mile, maybe not quite that far—and then he stayed at the compound because he worked there. But once you got to the machine shop, he went off to his job, and the others were doing their work, and they left you alone.

At the machine shop, there were several Japanese working in other areas. . . . You were working on your own; . . . you're just there doing your work, and that's it. [The Japanese,] they're doing theirs. There's no intermingling.... But the two Americans, myself and this other fellow [Floyd Wade], were the only ones that ran the lathes.

We tried to sabotage a little bit: like, we'd make the axles a little bit larger. But we didn't want to make them too bad because we knew that if we did . . . the other guys [might be blamed for sabotage].

Glenn Oliver debarked in Moji in early February 1945, having survived the Bataan March, several camps and work details in the Philippines, and the sinking of the Arisan Maru. *But his ordeal as a POW of the Japanese still was not over.*

Three other men and I were part of group of forty that were to work for the Kami-Gumi stevedoring company.... It's [in Wakayama, on the] outskirts of Osaka. It was down on the waterfront, and they had a bunch of warehouses down there. We worked on the pumper, to pump the sump pump underneath the building.

[We worked with] a bunch of the longshoremen . . . Japanese civilians. They had the free run of everything. They [the guards] would march us in there in the morning and turn us over to them, and then they'd take off. There would be no guards around that I remember. They [the civilians] would divide the men into different work groups, and off we'd go.... The Japanese civilians, the ones working there, were pretty lenient. I mean, they didn't bother us.

Some days we'd be unloading railroad cars of steel, where they stamped out metal for shells. Other times it would be defective shells [or] empty shell casings. Maybe they had been already fired and salvaged and sent back to be reprocessed or something. Or it would be black . . . like sand. Some of the guys knew what it was. It's a metallic partially processed metal, before they'd smelt it. And we'd unload railroad cars of that. Usually that was wheeled and dumped into barges that would be parked underneath a ramp where we'd run out there with the container on wheels and dump it into the barge.

[I focused on] just the daily living—something to eat—and I buddied up with two other men, and we shared our food. . . . It was so cold—if you had water in the room it would freeze at night. Most everybody buddied up with another person. You take four of your blankets—each person had four blankets. We'd put four down underneath us, and then we'd have four to put on top of us. Then if you had any extra outer clothing, you'd pile that on top.

Three months after arriving in Japan, Glenn was transferred to a new detail.

On 20 May 1945, I was in a detail of two hundred men that went by train to Maibara [on Lake Biwa], between Osaka and Tokyo, to a new work camp. . . . We were digging a canal, extending it to the water. The bottom I suppose was about maybe five feet across . . . and then sloped up both sides. We had to haul the dirt up and pile it up on each side. Used that for one of the walkways on top. . . . They had four big electric water pumps there where they pumped the water back into Lake Biwa. The idea was they wanted to drain this bay, I think so they could plant rice there.

Sometimes . . . when we started there, there would be a little ice on the top of the water, and you had to get down in the water there, maybe halfway between your knees and your waist. And of course there was mud. You're digging with a shovel. One guy would dig, and you had two men with a woven basket, and you threw the mud in that basket. When it was loaded up, then they'd crawl out of the canal and dump it and come back, and you refilled it.

We caught frogs when we were planting rice, and we'd smash them with rocks at lunchtime. We had a piece of galvanized tin to cook them on. . . . It was just a little green frog, three inches long, something like that. We'd just bang them together, two rocks together on one, and crush them. Then we'd fry them up that way. Didn't clean them or anything. Ate the whole thing.

Ken Porwoll debarked in Japan early, in October 1943, after a journey on the hellship Taga Maru. *He worked the next twenty-two months, until war's end, as a stevedore at Rinko Coal Yard in Niigata, a city located on the west coast of Honshu.*

They had Chinese prisoners of war in the holds of the ship to load, to shovel the coal into the cargo nets. The cargo net then was lifted and dropped into a barge and emptied while an elevator poked the bucket nose down into the barge and picked the coal up and brought it up to the elevated track. But we were to handle the coal from the elevator, and either put it on the ground in piles to be later shoveled into coal cars or to drop it directly into the coal cars as you pushed it around the track.

I was pushing a coal car. And the wheels were rigid so that whenever you had to go around a corner, you had to push extra hard to get that sucker around the corner. Just really something.

In the wintertime they would allow us . . . they had steel baskets about eighteen inches high, with holes around it. And you put the coal in there and start a fire, and then you go there and get warm. Of course it's soft coal, and so . . . sometimes soot would string from your nostrils, hang down, or from your eyelids. . . . But it was warm. At the end of the day, you were just a mess. Just a mess.

[We worked] every day of the week. We were to have one day a month off to wash our clothes and to do whatever toiletries needed to be done. I don't remember having any facilities to wash clothes, or mirrors or anything to shave by, or a razor. You weren't supposed to have a razor, anything sharp.

Military guards, they took you to the camp and guarded you there, and then they brought you back to the work site and guarded you there, too. But the civilian guard was hired by whoever you were working for, was there to see that you got the work done. And they all carried clubs. It got to the point they were called "vitamin sticks," because if you thought you couldn't work any more or harder, and then they start laying this club on you, you found energy. You found you could move again.

We walked about three miles to work, [through] part of the town. And at one point the schoolkids would gather, the boys particularly, and they got to throwing rocks. So we said, everybody get a rock and peg at these kids and be sure you hit them. If you don't, you're going to be blamed for it anyway. So you're not going to be scot-free if you don't throw a rock and you think you're going to get by with it. We're all going to swear that everybody in the column threw a rock. And we only had to do it once, and those kids went running and screaming. *(chuckles)* And they never showed up again.

Ken survived various difficult moments during forty-plus months as a prisoner, yet one incident in Niigata affected him more than any other.

The second year, they took us to their public bathhouse for a bath. It's a big tub, about [twelve by twenty feet], about three foot deep or more. And there the women were vying for jobs that day that the Americans were bathing. [How do I know?] Because they're all lined up along the wall, tittering and tee-heeing. *(chuckles)* What the hell? I want to take a bath, and I'm not going to let them deter me from it.

And my first bath, I cried. I absolutely cried. Because I am dreaming of this hot tub, and I'm dreaming— . . . my head was terrible; I just itched, itched, itched—and I can just feel getting down in that tub and washing my head and my hair, and I'm going to feel so much better. What a wonderful day it's going to be.

You got a thousand gallons of water or something in there. And *heated*. So I get in there and I'm . . . the only thing I can think of is warm water, and *washed*. I get in there, and I go down under the water, and I'm scrubbing and scrubbing my head, and I come up and *aahhhh!* Then all the damn gook on top of the water sticks to my hair, and I'm worse off than I was before I went under the water. . . . I'm in the third group to get in this tub. [They weren't changing the water.] Heaven's sake.

And I think that's the only time I ever cried in prison camp. I just about couldn't take that. I just had a terrible time getting over that.

8

Liberation

WAR'S END IN EUROPE: in separate ceremonies on May 7 and 9, 1945, Germany's leaders placed their signatures on the surrender document. For most POWs, though, the end had come days or even weeks before the actual surrender, as advancing Allied units liberated camps and forced-march columns.[1]

Liberation produced a wide range of emotional responses, from celebration and exhaustion to uncertainty and disorientation to anger and a desire for retribution. And there were instances of violence and lawlessness, directed both at former captors as well as at civilians in nearby towns and villages. Rightly or wrongly, scores were settled. Thoughts quickly turned to the future, though: immediate concerns like eating a meal and getting rid of lice, and distant ones such as notifying loved ones and returning home.[2]

Evacuation from the prison camps at times proved problematic, however. In addition to the logistical difficulties associated with transporting tens of thousands of men through a smashed country, disagreements arose between Great Britain, the United States, and the Soviet Union on the thorny matter of repatriation. The Soviets insisted that all its captured nationals be returned to them—most especially those men who had switched sides and fought for the Germans and then surrendered to the Americans or British.

As the United States and Britain were loath to return thousands of men to virtually certain death, Soviet leader Joseph Stalin effectively used ex-POWs as pawns in a diplomatic chess game. At camps liberated by the Russians, and now in their agreed zone of occupation, evacuation of British and American prisoners was held up until Soviet repatriation demands were met. This standoff continued even after V-E Day. Ultimately, hundreds and perhaps thousands of former prisoners, tired of waiting, took matters into their own hands and struck out in the direction of Allied lines.[3]

WAR'S END IN THE PACIFIC: with planning under way for a November 1945 invasion of Japan, events in early August brought the war to a sudden end. American atomic strikes on Hiroshima and Nagasaki and the Soviet declaration of war convinced Japan's leaders to capitulate.[4]

For prisoners in Pacific POW camps, the news of Japan's surrender came entirely unexpectedly. It was clear to many men that Japanese fortunes were on the wane, especially during 1945, but few if any foresaw the abrupt end to the war: most assumed Japan would fight to the bitter end. The war's conclusion meant one thing: they would survive. Many had ceased believing they would see the peace—after all, the Japanese had repeatedly proclaimed that in case of an Allied invasion of the home islands, all prisoners would be executed. From one day to the next, then, this death sentence was lifted. Men were left numb, speechless, scarcely able to believe what they heard. The contrast to European camps could hardly be more pronounced.[5]

While the Japanese agreed to surrender terms on August 14, the actual document was signed only on September 2, 1945. By agreement, POWs were not to be repatriated and evacuated until the surrender became official. During the days between, airlifts of food and medicine into camps helped to alleviate the worst shortages. Pacific POWs were uniformly in poor physical condition, regardless of camp location; the final year, especially, had taken its toll on their health.[6]

In the camps, most Japanese guard personnel melted away in the final days, with only minimal staff remaining; typically the most abusive guards were among the departed. While the vast majority of men remained in camps pending evacuation, there exist accounts of retribution by some prisoners against their former captors. As in Europe, here, too, scores were settled.[7]

EVACUATION FROM THE CAMPS represented merely a first step on the road back. Officially, ex-POWs everywhere received a new name—Recovered Allied Military Personnel (RAMP)—but men cared little about the acronym as long as they were heading home. In Japan, recovery teams brought RAMPs by train or truck to Yokohama, where the army met immediate health needs: hot baths, new clothes, food, basic physical exams, telegrams home. Most men then traveled by ship or plane to the Philippines, to a sprawling tent camp in Manila. From this central processing facility, transport stateside was organized. In Germany, most RAMPs were processed through field hospitals and then trucked or flown to a central facility, known as Camp Lucky Strike, located near the French coast. Care matched that provided for Pacific RAMPs: basic amenities and physical recovery.[8]

Both in Manila and at Lucky Strike, the military paid scant attention to the psychological impacts of captivity and physical abuse, starvation diets and slave labor, hellships and forced marches. From today's perspective, this approach may seem difficult to understand—but it was a different era. The syndrome which came to be known as post-traumatic stress disorder, or PTSD, had not been identified as such in 1945. John Glusman, whose father was a navy physician and Pacific POW, writes, "The experience of POWs . . . was utterly new to stateside psychoanalysts. Systematic, quantitative studies on the psychological effects of captivity, on the threat of imminent death, and on starvation were rare." The ex-POWs would need to make their own way in the postwar world.[9]

Europe

Located in southern Bavaria, VII-A Moosburg by April was filled with tens of thousands of POWs, many marched there after other camps were abandoned. Units of the American Third Army approached the town of Moosburg in the last days of April. Prisoners could hear the sound of battle; Kelly Martinson remembers the anticipation.[10]

The night before, the Americans were firing over our camp into the town of Moosburg. *(makes whistling noise)* Could hear it go over us. It was just one by one. *(whistles again)* Just whistling. All night long. Over the camp.

Then the next day, we saw thirteen or fourteen tanks come over the hills in different places. I think it was right about noon the P-51s [Mustang fighter aircraft] came over our camp, and one guy did the slow roll, so close you could see him. I'd say he was within a couple hundred feet, if not closer. *(chuckles)* That was beautiful. . . . It's just something that you . . . it's so vivid in my memory: those airplanes came over, and I saw the tanks all around.

Captured in December 1944 at the Battle of the Bulge, Ernest Gall was in a small work detail camp located in the former Czechoslovakia by late April. Ernest recalls liberation in the first days of May—by soldiers of the Soviet Red Army.

The Germans just disappeared that night, and the next day the Russians came in. They came into camp. . . . We were so glad to see them [the Soviets] that we could have hugged them.

They went out to get food. They found a hay wagon from someplace, like the farmers had, and they went and they got that filled up with bread in town. I don't know how far they had to go into town or anything, but

In a Lend Lease American Jeep, some of the first Red Army soldiers roll into Luft I, May 2, 1945. Many U.S. prisoners fashioned handmade armbands with "American" written in Cyrillic letters to ensure the Soviets could distinguish them from Germans.

they came into camp with that bread, and they fed us. *(chuckles)* They had plenty of rotgut, too, and they tried to stuff us with that. We couldn't. Boy, vodka: that would have been the end right there. *(laughs)*

Aaron Kuptsow was at Luft I, in the Baltic town of Barth. The Germans abandoned the camp on April 29; the Soviets arrived three days later.

When the Russians came in, they came in at night. That was very exciting: [the] most exciting evening I think up to that point in my life I ever had. But they came in on the road right outside the camp, and we were all lined up near the barbed wire there watching them come through. The ones who came in the beginning were Asian-looking Russians. I don't know whether they were Mongolians or just where they were from. But a very rough looking bunch of soldiers, on horses. To me it looked like they were eight feet high, the horses they were on. . . . They were shooting in the air and singing and everything.

Then there were horse and wagons, and on the wagons there were some women. Apparently the Russian troops always traveled with women. Anyhow, as they would advance they would stop, and the women would get out these little ocarinas or the harmonicas and things like that, and the bottles of vodka would pop up from the bottom of the wagon, and everybody started to drink and sing. They were having a good old time. That certainly got us in the proper mood. But it was very exciting. We were all so happy to see them.

Red Army units also liberated III-A Luckenwalde. Bill Hall, the III-C Küstrin prisoner sent here after his recapture, has clear images from that day.[11]

[E]arly in the morning, we heard this big rumble, and here came three or four Russian tanks right through the gate. Didn't open it; just right through the gate. Just knocked it right down: wall, fence, and all. And driving one of them out, at least in the turret, was a woman. And she was standing up and waving, and she stopped, and we all climbed on that tank, on the treads, and she gave us halves of cigars. The worst thing I've ever had in my life. *(chuckles)* We lit that, and I couldn't breathe for a month.

And then vodka. Pour it out in a tin cup. She gave us vodka. It was like drinking gasoline. I've never had any liquor during all that time. And it was the *worst* tasting stuff. Apparently they loved that. And this Russian woman, in full combat [gear]. Then behind her came more tanks and more trucks and more troops. And they just took over the camp.

Fighter pilot Harold Brown was liberated from VII-A Moosburg.

You have thousands of guys that are hollering and screaming. The war is over with. Jubilation. Celebration, big time.

Another Moosburg prisoner, Marcus Hertz, remembers the rumors. Then it happened.

We went to sleep about ten or eleven o'clock, and the following morning the word went fast: they're Americans, and they're close, and they're coming. And the next thing you know, about ten o'clock in the morning, through the barbed wire fence came a tank. A GI gray-green tank with a white star on it, and a guy standing up out of the turret said, "Any Americans in here? Any Americans?" Boy, did we find him fast!

Oh, jubilation. I'm telling you, since [we were force-marched out of Luft III on January 27] . . . we hadn't slept in a bed, hadn't had a cooked meal, hadn't had a toilet. . . . And here comes an American through the fence. "Any Americans here?" Boy, they climbed on that tank just like bugs.

About two or three o'clock in the afternoon [of April 29], a Red Cross support wagon came through the hole in the fence. . . . And then the following day, the Red Cross truck came in with women. Oh, that was wild. *(laughs)* They were lucky they got out of there alive.

[While at the camp we were] well fed: food trucks [were] coming in twenty-four hours a day. Some of them . . . one time there was a truck came in that had some fresh fruits and vegetables on it, and I don't think he got a hundred feet inside the gate, and the POWs just peeled off everything that was in that truck. Get it as fast as you can steal it.

Les Schrenk was on the forced march from Luft IV. In the first days of May, his column encountered advancing British troops.

It was just a British [reconnaissance unit] that liberated us. They told us that we had to march to their outpost, which was quite a distance away. . . . [At this] British outpost, there we got our first shower, and I could shave, and we got our first meal. . . . [The shower] was like heaven.

Harold Brick (left) and fellow POW Wilfred Ritzman, last days of April 1945. In late April, after the guards of their forced-march column melted away, Harold and two other former POWs simply were on their own. This was a period of limbo: the war wasn't over, but German civilian authority had broken down and the military occupation had yet to begin.

We always had somebody telling us what to do, and now we were all by ourselves. . . . I think for one thing we felt good that we weren't under German control. But we didn't feel so good because we weren't in *anybody's* control. During the daytime, we'd browse around the countryside. After several days, we commandeered a car. It was a German car, a four-speed Opel. One time . . . this was in Chemnitz, went into a beer hall, and the place was packed. Germans. We ordered beer. We drank our beer. We didn't have any money to pay for it. We just walked out.

I can still remember what a relief it was to get rid of the beard. Then to get out of the clothes that were just absolutely reeking, stinky, and get deloused with DDT. That was just like heaven.

I have to laugh at this to this day. We got ready to take our shower. There were two German girls—I'm sure that the British army had made them work for them—one of them had little cakes of Cashmere Bouquet soap, which smelled real nice, like springtime. The other one had Lifebuoy. Lifebuoy at that time had almost an odor to it; it did not smell good at all. But it was also known for body odor. Everybody took a bar of Lifebuoy, and I can remember this one with the Cashmere Bouquet, "I don't know what's wrong. This smells so good; that smells so bad, and nobody wants mine."

Bob Knobel was in another of the columns that had departed Luft IV back in February.

The day that we were liberated, 6 May, . . . we didn't have any idea. We figured the next day would just be another day, and the next day all of the sudden . . . the tank force came up over a hill some distance away. That's when the Germans just said, "You want my gun? Here." And they took off. I don't know where they went.

When we were liberated, then we headed for this one [British] guy who had been there for some time. The English had been captives for two, three years. . . . We headed up to the main house of this great big farm where we were. He came back with turkey eggs and ham and stuff. We probably ate at least one or two turkey eggs and a slice of ham and some bread that was better than our bread. But we got violently sick. Our stomachs just couldn't take that.

Unfortunately, these joyous scenes of liberation also had darker sides. Bob speaks openly about his actions later that day.

Then two other fellows that were in the group—*(three second pause)* that's right, they were from our room, but I never buddied with them or knew them well—we commandeered a car that was in a garage. *(chuckles)* It had fuel. We just took it. . . . Didn't think a *thing* of it, really. I mean, they'd taken everything from us. So we just took it. Commandeered it. . . . It ran out of gas finally, [after] twenty miles or thirty miles maybe, so we just left it.

Evacuating tens of thousands of men from the overcrowded Moosburg camp took several weeks; order was almost impossible to maintain. Dick Lewis talks frankly about abuses carried out on the local German civilian population.

Once we'd been opened up to the city [of Moosburg], a lot of the guys would go into town. They'd get German clothes and get German cars and rob and take anything they wanted in town. I guess even women. You could hear women screaming in the town.

Yes, that was [a nightmare]. No one seemed to keep order for quite a while, although we had officers, regular officer compounds there. I think, according to my notebook, they took the officers out first.

I stayed [in camp]. I didn't want to go out of camp. *No way.* I didn't want to get out and get involved with any of that chaos. I suppose to some

Warren Claypool's forced-march column crosses a makeshift bridge immediately after their liberation on April 26, 1945. The U.S. troops photographed the men as they walked by.

degree it was [fearing for my safety]. There were so many different camps or compounds of different soldiers. I didn't want to get involved with a lot of others, and I *certainly* didn't want to get into the town, that's for sure. I stayed where I thought was the safest place to be.

Warren Claypool was part of still another Luft IV group, wandering near the central German city of Bitterfeld on April 26, 1945. Some focused on revenge.

We got to a bridge near Bitterfeld, Germany. But before we got to the bridge . . . that's when we were liberated. We were in a small farm. Our group wasn't very big at that time. I suppose two hundred. We were asleep. It was still dark. We heard this commotion in the yard, and we looked out, and there was an American Jeep in the yard and a United States major from the [army's] 104th Timberwolf Division standing up in the Jeep, firing his pistol in the air. He got attention from the Germans and gave them orders to have us headed for the river by daylight or they'd shoot them all.

We finally came up on a wide gravel road, and it was going straight toward this village, toward this town. Anyway, when we got out on that gravel road, this same major sat in his Jeep, and he gave every man to know as he went by if you didn't like some of those Germans—they'd been mean to you—they'd shoot them right there. And they would have.

Herb Kohnke was with a small group of prisoners evacuated from a work detail and marched south, toward Munich. When their German guards vanished one night, the men drifted to the nearest town. There Herb saw one of the German guards, whom he refers to as Fred, that had been with their group.

This Fred, I ran into him in the town. I thought I was going to say goodbye to him. I wasn't mad at him. I was just going to shake his hand goodbye and good luck. He came up the street, and he had civilian clothes on.

They all had packs. He told me afterward, they all carried packs. There was no food or anything like that in there—it was civilian clothes. So if they got in a bind, they'd throw on civilian clothes, to become a civilian in a hurry. He recognized me, too. We just had a big laugh. I had to laugh at him because he was in civilian clothes.

Then, after we were talking for a little bit, I heard a tank. It came down another road in the town. It was kind of a crossroads there, and it came down that road, in[to] the heart of town. A sergeant was on the top. One [American] tank. That's all.

He was wild. He was swearing like the devil and calling . . . "Who's in charge of this?" That was the first thing he wanted to know. And he wanted to know . . . "Anybody giving you a bad time?" Well, a lot of guys, me included, I pointed to . . . this captain; he was at the front of the line [of marching prisoners]. He was the boss. He was just like little Hitler. That's about what he amounted to. He had a little moustache just like him and everything. . . . He was giving us the bad time.

He was down the street, still in his uniform. So they just went after him. They took him by a barn, one of the farmer's barns, [to] the side of it. Just shot him down. . . . And there were a couple of civilians that were with him; they took them, too.

I thought it was the wrong thing to do. Why? Because they only were doing what they were ordered to do. . . . They had to do it. . . . But I couldn't see that. That was uncalled for. I thought he was just going to

Captured German guards, April 26, 1945. These guards had accompanied the Warren Claypool march column until U.S. forces liberated the men. The photo was taken minutes after the Americans' arrival; note the tension in the faces of the two men at right.

take him and have him as a captive and interrogate him or whatever. I didn't know they were going to do that.

This was no isolated incident. Frank Linc shares a memory from VII-A Moosburg as American soldiers first arrived.

A Jeep came by us, and [the soldiers] stopped to ask how things are. I remember they gave me an orange to eat. Then they asked how the conditions were, and . . . how did the guards treat us. One of the fellows said they were all pretty good, except that one over there. *(points with index finger)* And he was a bad one.

So believe it or not, these GIs grabbed that guard. They took him into the woods and shot him. I didn't like it. But then . . . these fellows lost buddies. It didn't take much for them to react the way these guys did. I think probably we all would do the same thing if we were under those circumstances. [As a pilot] I never saw people killed. I never saw blood. This sort of thing. So it's an altogether different world.

Soviet liberators exacted ferocious revenge on the vanquished Germans—soldier and civilian alike. On April 23, advancing Red Army troops freed IV-B Mühlberg. Floyd Dahl bears witness.

I was asked to go on another detail to pick up some bodies. The German guard we called Popeye, he was a mean one, and he must have been meaner to the Russians because when we picked up his body . . . *(trails off)*. He had been dragged behind a horse and kicked to death or kicked. . . . He was hardly recognizable. They must have beat him up terrible, and then they put him behind a horse and just dragged him around.

When they liberated Luft I, the Red Army also roared through nearby Barth. Waiting to be evacuated to American lines, some men took the opportunity to wander into town. Fighter pilot Bill Schleppegrell recalls the before:

When we arrived [in January 1945] in Barth, this little town that the camp was close to, it was really a quaint, really pretty little town. Spotless. I mean it was winter, of course, and the snow—everything was clean. We marched down the street and out to the camp.

Bill struggles for words to describe what he witnessed in Barth after liberation.

When the Russians came then and we had a chance to get into the town . . . *(trails off)*. We weren't supposed to leave the camp at all. But at one point I got back into the town, and it was just utter devastation. Everything had been . . . the Russians had gone through and . . . you'd see pianos on the street that had been pushed out of balconies. Windows, everything was broken. It was just a mess. It was like the place had been bombed. It was [pretty much a ghost town].

LeRoy Shaw:

The first thing we encountered . . . about halfway to town, here was a baby buggy sitting there with an infant in there with a black spot right in the middle of its forehead and the mother and the grandmother just a little ways away. They were all dead. But I knew that none of our guys had done it. And whether it was done by the Russians or not . . . *(trails off)*. They were pretty wild.

[In Barth] there were German [civilians] around. As a matter of fact, I saw one of these Russians walk up to . . . there were about four or five German girls standing talking. He walked over there, and he grabbed one of them and hauled her off to the side and threw his machine gun up over his back and mauled her right there.

For some prisoners, it was their terrible physical condition that dominated discussions of liberation. Russ Gunvalson had endured hungry weeks at IX-B Bad Orb and IX-A Ziegenhain. He recalls the day of his liberation, March 30, 1945.

Geez, I was nothing but skin and bones. My clothes just hung on me, and I hadn't had a bath since November, in England. I put long johns on the day after Thanksgiving in England because we were going over into the continent and winter had set in over there. . . . I took the long johns off on the front steps of the Rouen, France, hospital on 10 April 1945.

By the time of his liberation on April 13, John Kline had been through the grim camps at IV-B Mühlberg and VIII-A Görlitz and force-marched hundreds of miles. Advancing U.S. forces found him lying in a German hospital in the city of Helmstedt.

There was a string of [army] ambulances came up. They hauled us back to an evacuation hospital, . . . and that was my first treatment by Americans. When I arrived at the hospital, they put me in a tent and told me to take off all my clothes and throw them into the fire. I had no socks. No gloves. My boots were on my feet like a pair of galoshes at that time because I had lost fifty pounds. . . . They would bring me a glass [half] full of pills, about three times a day, to stop the diarrhea.

Paul Peterson describes the relief he felt when he knew his ordeal was over. British troops had rescued him, ill with dysentery, from the Lazarett (camp hospital) of XI-B Fallingbostel.

When we got back to England and got off the plane, they wouldn't even let us in the building at the hospital with the clothes on. "Put them all right there, and we'll burn them, boots and all." . . . We stripped off all our clothes, showered, with soap and in hot water. Stand there and just let it go.

They let us into the ward, which is a Quonset hut, and there must have been fifty beds. All white. White blankets. White sheets. *(pauses three seconds)* Then it hit us: we were home.

In certain cases, evacuation and repatriation fell prey to international wrangling. There were instances of the Soviets delaying the release of U.S. and British soldiers from camps in the area of Germany now under their control while the three Allied powers worked to settle complex questions of repatriation. For weeks after the German surrender, men were forced to sit in camps and wait for news.

Reuben Weber was at II-A Neubrandenburg, one of the camps in the Soviet zone. Liberation meant no more Germans, "but also no more food." After several days with no indication of evacuation, Reuben and three other Americans decided to leave camp and head in the direction of U.S. or British forces.

We saw this weapons carrier coming by and different vehicles, six by sixes and what have you. These are Russians. We thought maybe we could hitch a ride. One of them stopped, and they had room in their weapons carrier there, and we crawled [in the] back, and he took off. I had my pack of cigarettes, so I handed them the pack of cigarettes so he could have one. He took it and put it in his pocket, the whole pack—what was left of it. I thought, oh well. We're getting a ride, so that's okay.

There was two of them: a driver and an assistant driver. They finally figured out we were American. Oh! Then he said, "This Studebaker!" *(chuckles)* It *was* a Studebaker. So then he reaches in his pocket and gives me my cigarettes back. *(chuckles)* Then we were okay. We were friends.

For a twenty-year-old man from rural North Dakota, the days spent on the road with the Red Army proved to be a cultural experience.

The Russians, they were a little different. They carried musical instruments. . . . I saw six by sixes filled with Russian soldiers, and some of them even had women in them. They'd [be] play[ing] their accordions and singing songs. Making the best of it.

From that time on, we had not a worry in the world because [if] we'd come into a town and we were hungry, why they'd find a nice-looking house and go in there and get food, and we'd eat. The place to sleep would be one of the nicest houses in town, too. They rousted the people out of there, and we'd take over.

And one of the strangest things I saw, too, is . . . there were a lot of dead soldiers laying around yet. And they'd pick up a dead Russian and bring him over to a real nice home, and they'd have the people [German civilians] dig a trench. And they'd have to bury that Russian right there in their front yard.

Seven days after striking out from II-A, Reuben and the three other men reached British lines.

Evacuation at III-A Luckenwalde took place on May 20—nearly two weeks after V-E Day. By that time, though, some men already had set out on their own, headed for U.S. lines. Army machine gunner Bill Hall estimates he and a group of friends waited about a week after the liberation before deciding to leave.

One morning we just . . . you walked through the gate of the camp, and there was a woods not much from here, maybe a couple blocks over. So you walked through the woods. You came to the main road.

Well, the four of us sat down on the main road, and vehicles were going by. Down the road come a three-wheeled vehicle . . . small, but it had a back with a tarp over it. It was weaving down the road with two Russians, and they were really bombed out of sight. Drunk. So we waved them down. We thought this was our opportunity. So they had big smiles, and they motioned in the back of the truck. So we got in the back, and there were two dead pigs in there. So the four of us just squatted down under that tarpaulin with those pigs. Pulled the tarp over us, and they proceeded up to the roadblock. That's how the Russians were keeping people in and out [of the area].

When they got there, we—of course, we didn't dare move in there. We heard all kinds of laughter and backslapping and jovial . . . bottles clinking. They knew these two clowns that were driving that thing, and security was at . . . was lost. They let them go right on through, with us in the back. So we drove down probably, oh, maybe fifteen miles. Finally, we came to a screeching halt, and the Russian got out, still a big grin on his face, and told us, "Out! Out!" So we got out and began our march from there to the Elbe River and the Americans. That's how we did it.

For several days after the cart trip, Bill's group moved west toward American lines and safety. They repeatedly encountered Soviet soldiers.

Well, we ran into a few firefights. There were pockets of Germans that were still in the countryside, and the Russians had bypassed them and were now ferreting them out. Every once in a while you would hear some firing going on, and you'd see some Russian scurry across the field here and Germans out here, and they'd be shooting the Germans down.

[We could have been captured] by the Russians or whoever, yes. Captured by the Germans, we probably would have been shot. But I think that they were probably at that point, thank goodness, too busy trying to control their own life, trying to *save* their own life. Because the Russians were all over the place.

We just moved . . . we just marched west. We knew the Russians were east, so we just . . . the sun . . . we kept going west all the time until we came to the Elbe River. The bridge between . . . the German side and the American side . . . was blown, so the only way you had to cross the bridge, you had to cross those girders.

The first thing we saw [on the other side] was a patrol of Americans. One guy was a corporal; he said, "Who *are* you guys?" We told him we were POWs. My gosh! He had a camera. He took pictures. *(chuckles)*

That patrol took us back to their camp. There was a large cook tent out there. So they brought us in there, and two doctors came in. And the doctor said, "Where are the POWs here?" And I said, "Right here, sir." So they came over, and he said, "Don't you guys move." So they brought us in bowls of oatmeal, toast, and coffee. Gourmet. The finest restaurant in the world didn't compare. *(laughs)*

The Pacific

Prisoners of the Japanese were liberated from far-flung camps across Asia. Walter Miller and Glenn Wohlferd, for example, both were prisoners in Mukden, Manchuria. Advancing Red Army troops overran Mukden in mid-August 1945; Japanese guards were removed from the main camp and administration handed over to the U.S. Army. Walter recalls the chaos in Mukden during the first day after liberation.

The next morning when we got up, we started roaming around; then we saw the Russians on the streets [of Mukden]. . . . I can remember downtown . . . because the Chinese, they confiscated all the Japanese arms they could get their hands on, and they were on top of the buildings downtown, and they were shooting at anything that moved. Me and this guy from Pennsylvania, we were there trying to get back to the main camp, and we got caught in the crossfire there. We found a space between two buildings. There was nothing but dirt between the two. So we spent the night there.

You didn't know who was shooting at who. The Russians were down the road with artillery shooting at the top of the buildings, and the Chinese were shooting at everything that moved down below. Now I don't know if they didn't like the Russians or what the hell was going on. We got caught in that situation.

USS Houston *survivor Al Kopp was moved in mid-1944 to a POW camp in Saigon, Vietnam. The U.S. Navy pharmacist's mate previously had spent more than eighteen months on the Burma-Thailand Railway detail.*

One day a plane came over Saigon. It was a B-24 Liberator, dropping leaflets over the camp. They dropped them, but unfortunately there was enough breeze, and not a single leaflet fell in the camp. But the Vietnamese, they put a leaflet on a little rock and pitched it [over the fence] into the camp. Then the Japs told us they were going to shoot us if we read it. *(chuckles)* We picked up leaflets. We were tickled to death. It said, "Stand by. The war is over." It didn't say *will* be over. It said *it's over.* We'll be back.

The next day they came again, and they dropped more leaflets, but they dropped people. They dropped paratroopers. [We found out later] that they had read the Japanese were going to kill all the prisoners. They knew that, so they dropped a whole bunch of paratroopers. This guy came up to the camp. Great big tall man. He must have been six and a half foot. With a beard. He had a carbine slung over his shoulder, and he had ammunition all around and hand grenades. He had the whole works. And he had full colonel's insignia.

He came up to the gate, and he rattled it, and he said, "Let me in." The Japs were kind of frozen. They didn't know whether they should shoot at him or not. They must have known the war was over, too; people told them. But they didn't open the gate, either. They didn't shoot, and they didn't open the gate. Finally he used some real roughy words: "You sons of bitches! The war is over." He talked to them like a woodsman. He pulled a hand grenade out and said, "I'll open it if somebody doesn't."

The sergeant ran over, and he quickly opened it. He walked in. He had a lot of guts.

We thought they were going to kill him because that's all they had done to us for years. He ran up to this [Japanese] guy, and he must have knocked him twenty feet. He rolled him right away. Big guy.

Turned out he was a sergeant—he wasn't a full colonel at all. He said, "Don't pay any attention to these. I'm a buck sergeant." He was tough. The first American we saw. Big ugly guy. Oh, man, I told him, I said, "I'm about to kiss you." He said, "As ugly as I am?" or something like that. "Nobody wants to kiss me." *(chuckles)* . . .

They took some [Japanese] away. I wasn't going to look to see what happened to them. Some guy said they took them out in the jungle and shot them. I don't know if they did. I didn't think any Americans would do that. Then again, you don't know about people that just come out of action, what they'd do.

Marine Irving Silverlieb was at Hakodate Camp 3, on the northern island of Hokkaido.

It was at least ten days after the war ended that we heard about it. Some B-29s flew over and dropped messages written in English and Dutch. Different languages on the note, that the war is ended. If it's a prison camp, spread blankets or do something [for aerial recognition]. . . . Once they found out the war was over, we had no more work. Our rations—which is the most important—we started getting a little bit more rations. [According to the Japanese,] we were now friends and stuff. *(laughs)*

American aircraft dropped supplies to camps as they were located and identified. Irv describes this process at Camp 3.

Once a day the army would come over and drop us food. The next day the navy came and dropped us food. What it was: they came down in parachutes. Two fifty-five gallon drums welded together and skip it, come down low and release them. They skidded into the camp . . . [and] split open. Any kind of food you could imagine. Everything. We were eating probably better than we had ever eaten in our lives, which we thought anyhow. All the cigarettes you wanted. All the medication that we needed.

At the Kamioka lead mine on Honshu, Ray Makepeace and Howard Swanson recall war's end and the aftermath.

Howard Swanson:

There were kind of rumors, because we could hear airplanes. This is the first time that we heard airplanes in Japan because, see, we were in the interior. Rumors start, but you hold back on rumors, because we heard rumors before that never came true, and you just didn't want to state what you might even believe.

Through an interpreter, says Ray, the camp commandant made a formal announcement: the war was over.

Then there was peace. But none of the men—there was no cheering or emotion or anything. We were too far down the drain. . . .

Most of us . . . everybody in the camp was in terrible . . . bad shape. But what happened then, you know, the Japanese military, the sergeants and the corporals and whatever were guarding us, took off. The commandant stayed with us. We called him Onion Head. I don't know what his name was; we called him Onion Head. He said that he would stay with us because he didn't know how the civilian population would accept this.

The English or the Dutch more or less took over [the camp]. They outranked our—we only had a second lieutenant. The Americans, that's the only officer we had. So then we went to the warehouse, and we took out the food there. There was a lot of food in there. Could have been issued to us but never was. There was corned beef and squid and soy sauce. Hardtack. Rations that these [Japanese] troops eat. Wool blankets. Clothing. We got it all. So we ate. Just sat up and ate all the time. I don't remember sleeping. I was eating all the time. . . . Everybody was in what you might call . . . euphoria. Joy.

They identified the camp, Howard reports.

We put [painted] a big "PW" on the roof of the warehouse, and it was an American that came up to our camp. Military. This is the first American that we saw. And at the time he explained to us too that the transportation wasn't available. We'd have to wait first for . . . I think for the rail tracks, yes, the railroad tracks were damaged from bombing. And they had to repair those, and then when they got repaired, then we could get out of there. But he just came into the camp. One guy. One person.

Some weeks passed; finally, Ray remembers, came departure day, September 7, 1945.

I said I wanted to walk out of this camp, but I still had to be carried out by a truck. I couldn't walk down that mountain. . . . We had one old, beat-up truck, and there was several of the guys in the camp, about twenty or thirty of us, who were in pretty bad shape. I was one of them.

When the war ended, Glenn Oliver was on a canal-digging detail of some two hundred prisoners at Maibara, near Lake Biwa. Men here were concerned that Allied forces wouldn't locate their small camp, so Glenn and two other Americans decided to return to their first camp, Wakayama, near the city of Osaka.

We wanted to go back to Osaka because we knew that was a big-name camp and we knew that they would be able to get us in contact with the military to locate our small little camp that was at the base of the mountain there.

Everybody was traveling around. We had guys come to visit our camp. That's where we got the idea: just get on the train and go wherever you want. We learned that the Japanese emperor had told the civilians that they were not to retaliate and harm anybody. That's the way they were.

We walked downtown and went to the railroad station. They wanted us to buy tickets, and we said no. They have turnstiles there that you go through to get to the rest of the platform, so we ducked under them and walked out to the platform, and there was a train sitting there. There were Japs all over the engine, riding on the sideboards there, and hanging on the steps. It was going the right direction, so we went and got on it.

They acted like we were lepers or something. They'd back up and make room for us. I think I was in the lead and walked down the aisle, and I was looking for a place to sit. No way you're going to sit because they were standing; the aisle was so full. [There were also] soldiers of different ranks, some with guns. . . . Couldn't hardly get through. They'd crowd away from you and let you by.

The seats face each other. We motioned to [some Japanese] to get out. We [sat down]. One of them sat next to me, and another guy sat on the other seat. . . . We sat there for a while, and pretty soon a civilian worked his way up through the aisle where we were. He bowed two, three times and could speak good English. He wanted to know if he could help us, where we wanted to go. We told him we wanted to go to Osaka. He said, "You're on the right train for that." We told him we wanted to go to Wakayama House. He said, "I'll help you find the right street to go there." So we let him sit with us.

With information from this Japanese man, the three found their way from Osaka Station to Wakayama House.

There was a Jap hanging by his feet in the entranceway; somebody had cut his throat. I looked at him, and I figured out it was the medic that used to chew me out [when I was at Wakayama House].

I asked one of the POWs there, "What happened to him?" He said, "We gave him the job of emptying the *benjo* [toilet] buckets, and he tried to take off, and they caught him and brought him back and cut his throat." He was still hanging there. So we went upstairs, up to the room up there with the radio, and contacted [American forces] and told them where the camp was.

Then we went down, and we got food, K rations, and we all got clothing. Trousers . . . most of them were too long. We got shoes, socks and underwear, shirt and trousers. Hurried down the street to the railroad station. Got on the train and started back up to Maibara.

The three men arrived back at Maibara that day. On September 10, U.S. forces reached the small camp and evacuated the prisoners.

Alf Larson was liberated from Camp Nomachi, near Takaoka.

We didn't have any official word, and the next day the Swedish consulate from Tokyo came up and said, "The war is over. You're living in an atomic age." What the heck is an atomic age?

Ken Porwoll experienced the end of the war in the city of Niigata, where the Bataan survivor had endured twenty-two months as a slave laborer in a coal yard. In early August, there was talk of "big things."

It was kind of surprising in that after the second "big thing" happened—and later we learned it was the atomic bombs—three of our men said, "This war is over guys. We're going to Tokyo and find the Yanks."

Whatever these two "big things" were, they produced changes.

After the first "big thing," [the] atomic bomb, the commissioned officers left. And then [after] the second one, the noncoms left, which left the privates. These guys don't know what to do if somebody doesn't tell them. So a hundred guys got together, and they marched to the guardhouse and took their rifles away, and they put them in the latrines, down in the bottom of the latrines, and then took down the, opened the gates and opened all the warehouses, the storage rooms around, and found one meal of rice.

There was one meal of rice in the warehouse. So the men get in groups of four or five and go out in the countryside and take ducks and chickens and produce from the farmers. If they resisted, they'd get beat up. But they for the most part did not.

Then you bring it back into camp, and there were people that had fires started, and they're tearing the barracks down to build a fire to boil this stuff in a five-gallon can. If you put an item in a pot someplace, then you could come back and dip out a bowl of soup. I think we fed ourselves for at least a week before the air corps found us and dropped supplies and clothing and medicines.

By war's end, hundreds of prisoners were crowded into Camp Omori in Tokyo. Bill Connell was one; he remembers sensing that something was about to happen.[12]

[A few days before the surrender,] a new prisoner came into our group. He was just shot down. When it came mealtime, we served him his share of the food, and he wouldn't eat it. We said, "Hey buddy, you better eat, or you're going to starve to death. This is all you're going to get." He said, "I'm not eating that slop! This war is going to be over in just a matter of days." . . . He knew that the atomic bomb had been dropped on Hiroshima, and he knew the one had been dropped on Nagasaki. And it *was* just days later that the Japanese capitulated, agreed to sign the surrender papers.

Bill was on an eighteen-man work detail outside camp the day Japan agreed to surrender.

When we were out there working, it was a rural area. The houses were well spread apart, because there was a lot of rice paddies and so forth. All of the houses have the sliding panels, and they had the whole house wide open. We noticed that they had their radios wide open [volume up]. There was somebody giving a speech, and we couldn't understand what it was. [We found out later] it was the emperor, announcing to the Japanese population that the war was over.

The guards came and got us and said [to] pick up all the tools. We took all of our things, and we were going back to camp. They made sure that we were lined up in four files, and the people on the outside files had tools in their hands: shovels, picks, whatever. We were marching back to camp. We had to go through two small villages on the way back.

When we first entered this first village, some of the people were smiling and happy and others were very, very bitter. The guards were a little bit afraid that we might get attacked. But fortunately we didn't, and we got back to the main highway [back to camp]. We were walking down that highway, and some of the old timers, they had worked down in the rail yards, unloading boxcars. They were on a truck because they couldn't walk that far. They were whizzing by us, jumping up and down, screaming their heads off that the war was over, and we thought they must be crazy. We didn't believe them. We got back to camp. We did discover that the war was over.

At Camp Omori, men sensed impending change. B-29 gunner Bill Price had been in solitary confinement at Omori since April; without explanation, that August day his existence changed.

They took us out [of solitary], and I remember they sat us down outside the building, and I just sat there in the sun wondering what's going on, because things were different. In the meantime, they'd taken out all the sadistic guards and just left the token guards around there. As I say, I didn't know what was going on, but I got my first bath, shave, and a haircut. And [I was] put in with . . . the "special prisoners" for a few days because we still weren't allowed to converse with [regular prisoners] in the camp. But after about the third day or so, we were allowed to mingle throughout the camp and talk to everybody.

But, Bill Connell recalls, on that momentous day at Omori, there still was reason to fear.

Then we began to be very apprehensive because the guards had said that if the Japanese lost the war that we would be executed. So the rest of that afternoon we were *very* apprehensive of what was going on. In that evening none of us . . . that night none of us slept very much because we were up talking about what we would try to do if the Japanese attempted to execute us. We would go down fighting, so to speak. We didn't know exactly what we would do, but we were going to do something.

Bob Michelsen describes the following day.

The next morning, we woke up, and it was very silent; there were no Japanese, except for one Japanese person, the interpreter. All the guards, the commandant—they had all left. Gone. Overnight, they were gone. [We were] dumbfounded. Amazed. Particularly those that had been there a long time, the Corregidor and Bataan POWs: for them it was unbelievable.

Submariner Floyd Caverly:

Everybody was gone, including one camp doctor that we had there. He disappeared, too. We found him a little bit later—the Aussies had killed him and stuck him headfirst down the benjo and then nailed the door shut. They didn't find him for about two weeks, after the Americans took the camp over.

The former Omori prisoners were transported to a hospital ship, the Benevolence, *anchored in Tokyo Bay. On board, the men were the center of attention. Floyd Caverly has strong memories of the food.*

They picked us up in these Higgins boats [36-foot infantry landing craft] and took us off of the island of Omori and took us out to the *Benevolence.* Gave us kind of a fast check to find out who was about ready to die and who was in bad shape and didn't have legs and couldn't walk. *(chuckles)* I was in pretty good shape yet. They fed us. God, they just fed us *so* much. We ate until we got sick, and we heaved it up and turned right around and went back down to that crazy chow line again. We done some awful crazy things.

For Bill Price, clean beds stand out in his memory.

We got a shower and clean clothes and so forth and stood in line for a quick physical. I remember, too, you know, it may seem trivial, but standing in line there in these wards with their clean sheets on the beds and

The end: ex-POWs at Camp Omori greet advancing U.S. Navy landing craft, August 29, 1945. The evacuation of Omori took place several days before the removal of POWs was scheduled to begin. With clearance from MacArthur's headquarters, the navy sent a rescue force to the camp, which was clearly visible from the ships anchored in Tokyo Bay. Bob Michelsen remembers.

We could see all the [American ships] in Tokyo Bay. One of those afternoons, large motor-boats came toward the island. We watched them coming. There was a dock going out into the ocean, and [the boats] came right up to the shore and close to the dock. Marines jumped out with rifles and machine guns. . . . Shortly after that, boats, small motor craft, were relaying prisoners out to the larger ships.

nice fluffy pillows with white pillowcases. I—and I found other POWs doing the same thing: punching our fingers into the pillow and stuff like that and feeling it.

Bob Michelsen remembers trying to contact home.

At some point or another toward evening, I was relayed [from there] to a small ship and allowed to try to phone home to tell my mother and my family that I was okay. I couldn't get through, but somebody on that ship said they would call the newspaper in my hometown and let them know. Cedric Adams was a newscaster on WCCO radio [Minneapolis] at that time, and that's how my mother first learned that I was alive. From Cedric Adams, the newscaster on WCCO.

Navy pilot Bill Connell tries to describe the excitement.

They gave us navy enlisted clothing, consisting of dungarees, and, no matter what your rank was, you wore a white hat. Everybody had a white hat, a shirt, pair of pants, and a pair of navy shoes. We all looked alike.

The first night, none of us went to sleep. We could walk anywhere we wanted on the ship, and they gave us free cigarettes, all the cigarettes we wanted. We just smoked cigarettes, one right after the other. I must have smoked half a carton of cigarettes the first day.

Of course, the ship was just full of reporters wanting stories. They sent us up, and we were interviewed just for a matter of a couple of words. They just wanted to identify us: who we were, where we came from.... And our physical consisted of, "Are you okay? Are you hurt anywhere?" *(chuckles)* Because they were just processing one right after the other.

Bob Michelsen was more introspective in considering his time on the Benevolence.

There were two things that I wanted to do. The first thing: I wanted to go back into Tokyo and see what it was like. I wanted to find out where we had been and what the conditions were from the outside where we had been interred. And to see what the town was like. But there was no availability; could not do it. The other thing [going through my mind], I think it was just a matter of being alive. It was just the joy of being alive and being secure. That was my main feeling.

[What did I feel in those first days?] *(pauses five seconds)* . . . It was all in my mind, and I didn't care about anything else. I did not care. I was proud of the fact that I was still alive. I think pride was—yes, it was—it was pride in *everything*. Not only in being alive, but pride in the country that had defeated Japan.

[Other guys,] some were more cheery and hollering; they were so happy, you know. A lot of them wanted to, wanted to get drunk. *(laughs)* They had, the navy had said, "Yeah, we got some drinks on that ship out there; go get it!" And the ones that got drunk, they got really sick. Now the food, my first meal was bacon and eggs, and I got *really* sick. My stomach wasn't ready for that.

Floyd Caverly has the final word in this extraordinary chapter of these men's lives.

When the armistice was signed [on September 2] on the *Missouri*, they wanted to know if I wanted to go over to see MacArthur accept the surrender. I said, "Are the Japanese surrendered?" And they said, "Yes." And I said, "That's all I give a damn. That's all I care about. I'm staying right here. It's over."

The Road Back

After evacuation from Japan, the majority of RAMPs passed through the large tent camp set up outside Manila. Alf Larson was evacuated from Camp Nomachi to Manila. Like many men, he recalls the food—anything, anytime.

At the rest and recuperation, they told us any time day or night that we felt hungry or something, go to any kitchen and ask them to do it. If they had it, they would fix it for you. Like if you wanted fried eggs, if they had the eggs they would do it. You could do that to any kitchen in the camp. I didn't splurge. Now there were some people that just really splurged. They paid for it. But, no, I paced myself. I just figured that you're not supposed to eat all this at one time.

The only thing, the air force recruiters came through. . . . They were there a few days after we got to camp. They asked me to sign up. They said, "We'll fly you home right away and get you out there." At that time I didn't want anything to do with it. I wanted to get out. That was it.

At a British military hospital in Rangoon, Jim Whittaker had an experience similar to that of the Americans in Manila.

> Oh, we were very, very happy. We were met at the plane by Red Cross ladies with mugs of hot tea, with milk and sugar in it, and with white bread sandwiches of cheese, and we thought we were really . . . free. Then they put us in the hospital, and we were halfway afraid to sit on beds with white sheets we hadn't seen for years. . . . They put us through the hospital for a couple of days. When they saw that we were fit—and that's a relative term, as more people came in, in worse shape—they moved us out of the hospital into canvas.

Bob Heer (right) and buddy Lewis Taylor enjoy bottles of cool beer at the tent city set up for repatriated POWs, Manila, September 1945. Both had been liberated earlier that month from Akabira, a remote mining camp on Hokkaido.

The first few days, they warned us, just don't eat too much at first, until your body gets used to it. . . . I managed to do that. But then after a while there was nothing left to do. . . . We just found ourselves eating and just talking and lazing around. So you put on weight real quick.

Another ex-POW, Ken Porwoll, agrees: "If you didn't see a buddy within a week's time, you didn't recognize him when you saw him—he changed that much in weight and appearance."

Red Cross workers took our home addresses and sent cables to notify families we had been repatriated. I didn't get any mail in the time I was a POW and did not know how things were at home. I did not know if my family had heard from me. . . . To be able to contact loved ones and to know we were finally free brought on a feeling of euphoria.

Then we were on a boat to England. We went first to Colombo, in Ceylon, or what is now known as Sri Lanka, then through the Red Sea into the Mediterranean to Port Said [Egypt], and from there on to England. It took about a month. I was about a month getting home.

For a small number of ex-POWs, there was air transport to the United States. Navy pilot Bill Connell caught a grueling flight back stateside, with four refueling stops just to reach California. Louis Bailen also remembers "three or four stops: Guam, Wake, Hawaii. I saw Wake Island. We landed. Stayed there a day or so."

The majority of American servicemen, though, were transported back to the United States on ships. Marvin Roslansky, who had spent much of the war at Zentsuji on Shikoku, was evacuated to Guam. After two weeks there, he boarded a ship for San Diego. Some ships departed from Okinawa; even more sailed from the Philippines. For men like Douglas MacArthur and Harold Kurvers, journeys to West Coast ports like San Francisco or San Diego were long and tedious. One shipboard memory comes from navy veteran Manuel Aguirre. After the Japanese surrender, his ship, USS Ozark, *was used to transport ex-POWs from Japan to several locations.*

[W]hen we came back from Japan, we had over a thousand American ex-prisoners on there, American repatriated prisoners of war. . . . They had this pay coming for all the time that they were over there as prisoners. Three and four years, and they paid them aboard ship. You should have seen the crap games. Boy! Fifty-dollar bills, hundred-dollar bills, and one pile that had two or three thousand dollars in it. A lot of the guys lost all their money. Yes, a lot of those guys lost all their money before they got to the States over here. . . . They were so happy, they were spending all their money in the crap games and card games. Blew a lot of money.

In Europe, RAMPs were processed through Camp Lucky Strike in France. Harold Brown remembers the camp as an assembly line repatriation facility.

We flew into Lucky Strike. They had one landing strip there. Then they started the real processing. They gave you X amount of money, and you signed for getting so much money. Then they even gave you additional clothes. They got our name, rank, what outfit were you in—all that basic stuff. Basic information. . . . A couple other questions: How were you treated? Did you sustain any injuries?

They did have medical people look at you. They were looking at you more from a *physical* point of view. Okay, you lost a few pounds, but physically. . . . I can remember the guy—they weren't flyers, but they were army guys—"You're fine. You're okay." I said, "I feel fine. I'm just a little hungry. And now I'm no longer hungry." They said, "Yes, you're okay. Next guy."

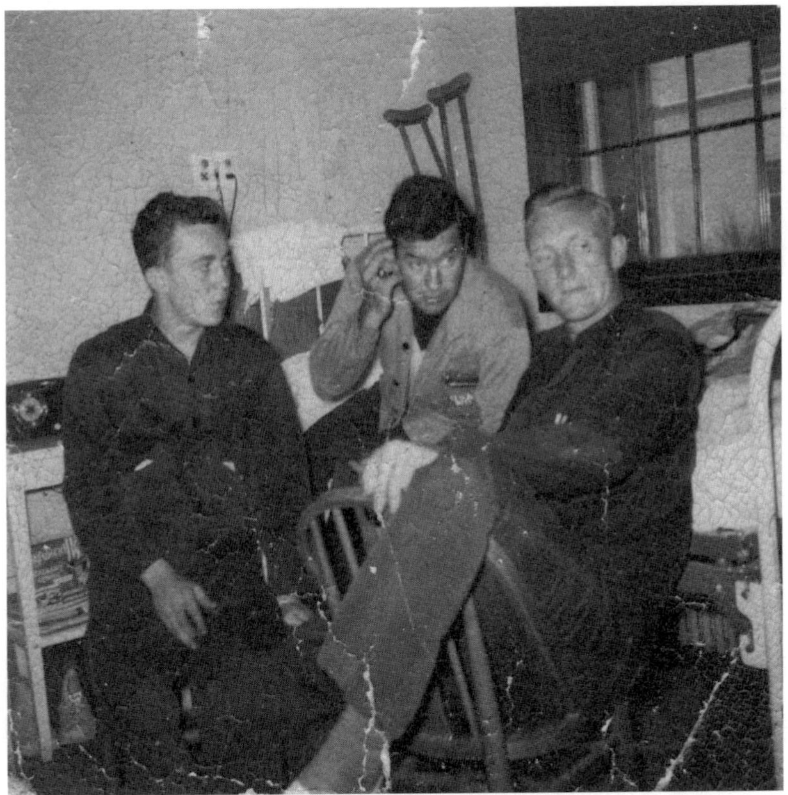

Gerald Wakefield (right) recovering in a stateside military hospital, late 1945. Like most returning Pacific POWs, Gerald suffered the aftermaths of malnutrition, tropical diseases, and physical and psychological abuse. Some effects lasted a lifetime.

Arnold Sprong voices a common complaint of the ex-POWs at Lucky Strike: he couldn't keep down food.

First we were in these eight-man tents or whatever they were. We got no medical attention. This bothered us, because we should have. We heard—somebody came and said the Red Cross is giving out eggnog. So they gave us a canteen cup. . . . I went up and got a cup of eggnog. Oh, it was just delicious. So I went back, and I got another one.

And talk about sick. My stomach! I couldn't tolerate normal food for weeks. Probably . . . might even be a month or so before I could eat heavy food. Had to eat small amounts and try to keep it more on the liquid side. Nothing heavy. Go for digestible stuff.

It was much the same for paratrooper Earle Bombardier, the D-Day veteran.

While I was at Lucky Strike, I went up to see a doctor, and he asked, "How are things going?" I said, "Not too bad, I guess, but I can't keep any food down." And he said, "What are they feeding you?" I said, "I've been eating pork chops and mashed potatoes and gravy and green beans." He said, "Good God, man. Don't you know how big your stomach is? About the size of a teacup. No wonder you can't handle all that food."

9

Long Hard Road

MEMORIES OF reunions with family proved to be a poignant subject. Many a former POW became very emotional when reliving that moment when he once again felt the touch of an anxious parent, wife, or other loved one.

Numerous reunions came after years of separation. Many men had been gone for a long time: the bulk of Pacific POWs had been captured in early 1942, meaning nearly four years had passed since they shipped overseas. In addition to concern about those behind barbed wire, families at home also faced periods of uncertainty when their serviceman was listed as "missing in action," before his status as prisoner was confirmed. For some Pacific POWs, this confirmation took years, if it happened at all. To many former prisoners—but also for those left behind to wait and worry—it had seemed as if this reunion might never arrive.

Upon landing stateside, RAMPs received sixty days leave. For many, a period of time at a military recreation and rehabilitation center followed; married men often were joined by their wives. By the end of 1945, most ex-POWs had been discharged from service; all but a handful were out by mid-1946. In outward appearance often healthy, with their uniforms in mothballs, these men found that civilian life and postwar "normalcy" beckoned: families, jobs, mortgages.[1]

If only it had been that simple. Historian of medicine Charles G. Roland, author of a detailed study of the effects of malnutrition and poor health on POWs, writes, "[t]oo often [POWs] arrived home with unwanted and sometimes unrecognized baggage." Another expert estimates that three and a half years as a prisoner of the Japanese aged a man by ten to fifteen years. The effects of beriberi, malaria, and other tropical illnesses would ravage men for decades.[2]

But other effects for POWs were much more insidious; these men "carried the seeds of restless dissatisfactions and dysfunctions." Some simply didn't make it: returning POWs were more than twice as likely to die in their first years of freedom as other veterans. For others, the seeds bore fruit that included self-destructive behavior, tortured nightmares, broken marriages, alcohol problems, and workplace difficulties.[3]

The U.S. government, specifically the Veterans Administration (VA), is complicit in this tragedy: for many years, ex-POWs failed to receive adequate treatment. In the immediate postwar period, many former prisoners recall being disbelieved by VA doctors regarding their symptoms or having their disability payments reduced or even eliminated. For its part, the Department of Defense for decades rejected the idea of a medal for former POWs because "there was opposition to honoring men who had surrendered. It did not fit well with the historic image of the American fighting man." Only in 1986, after a long campaign, was the Prisoner of War Medal finally authorized by Congress.[4]

The 1980s also saw an about-face by the VA. In the aftermath of the Vietnam War and the Iran hostage crisis, when returning captives received public sympathy and recognition, World War II POWs finally were viewed as deserving of attention. It became easier for the tens of thousands of ex-POWs to qualify for health and disability benefits; in addition, local VA medical centers started POW support groups to facilitate conversations among the men themselves. The American Ex-POWs organization (AX-POW) also experienced strong growth during this time. Founded in 1949 and still viable today, AX-POW makes members aware of various benefits, lobbies on their behalf, and provides a family-like community of men with similar experiences. Decades after war's end, and by that time into their seventies, thousands of ex-POWs felt they could share their stories without shame and stand up proudly with other veterans.

Reuniting

Reliving moments when ex-POWs first saw their loved ones frequently brought to the surface intense emotions. Liberated from Camp Omori, Bill Price was back stateside by mid-October 1945.

I got back to the Presidio in Frisco, and I got a three-minute telephone call . . . home. Well, my good mother, she wanted to know if I had all my arms and legs, and I said, "Yes, mom." I said, "I'm in good shape. Don't worry about it." In three minutes, you can't say really too much.

It wasn't until Omori was liberated in late August that Bill's parents even knew he was alive. Since his B-29 was downed over Nagoya on April 7, 1945, he had been listed simply as "missing in action."

But it was peace of mind for [my mom] because when I was . . . when they gave her the telegram that I was missing in action, that had an effect on my dad. He had a mild stroke because [of] I guess what went through his mind. I was daddy's boy. I'll admit it. I did have one sister that died in 1934 at the age of thirteen. She was the oldest. Died of TB [tuberculosis], and of course now here I was just turned twenty, and they thought I was dead. Of course, dad was beginning to wonder if he could raise a family to adulthood.

I spent a couple weeks in the Presidio there. Then they flew me to Vaughn General Hospital in Hines, Illinois, just outside Chicago. After I was there a while, I managed to get a pass home. Didn't tell my folks. I took a train home and got off the train, and I got on a streetcar . . . and I took a taxi home from there. The folks didn't know I was coming home.

James Fager at home, reunited with his mother, summer 1945. Gunner on a heavy bomber, Jim had believed that as a young guy, he "was going to make it." Make it he did—but only after his bomber was shot out of the sky and he spent months in German POW camps.

I walked in the back door, and my folks were always sitting in the living room in the evening like that. My mother saw me. My dad didn't. . . . I came in the back door, and she jumped up, and she yelled, "Bill!" Well, my dad's name was Bill. Although it was Edward, but they called him Bill. And the way she said it, he thought she was having a stroke or something, you know, until he saw me. Then of course there were all kinds of tears and hugs and stuff. But that was quite a reunion. Quite a reunion.

After a long ship journey that had begun in Odessa, on the Black Sea, Vern Kruse arrived in Boston in mid-April 1945. Then he took a train home to Minneapolis.

I called mom at home, from Fort Snelling [in Minneapolis], and I said, "This is Vern." *(voice begins to tremble)* She didn't believe it. I talked to her. She says, "You wait where you're at, and we'll come and pick you up." My dad was at work. He worked at Sears, Roebuck at the time, most of the time. But she called him up at Sears, and he got out of Sears right away and came home to pick her up, and they went out to Fort Snelling to get me.

(very emotionally) I don't know how my dad could even drive the car, but they came out there. Here I'm standing there at the curb, and I heard a car horn beep. Here I had come back to the States; I hadn't called from out there. I wanted to surprise them. *(pauses ten seconds)* It was happy. I'm not much of a person for hugging and kissing. I know I shook hands with my dad, and I gave Mom a hug. They were awfully happy to see me. *(pauses five seconds)* That was my arrival home.

After a hospital stop in Iowa, in October Alf Larson finally had a chance to return to Duluth, Minnesota, to see his parents. The Bataan March survivor had shipped out to the Philippines in 1939—nearly six years before.

They didn't question me at all. They just . . . my mom, when she saw me, said, "Oh!" Grabbed me and hugged me. She said, "I'm so glad to see you." She never gave up hope. *(pauses five seconds)* When we were over in the Philippines and we were prisoners, the government, after a period of time, tried to get my mother to accept the ten thousand dollar insurance that I had. She wouldn't take it because if she did then that was admitting to herself that I was dead. And she would not admit to that.

She went to a movie one time . . . and they had these newsreels, and she swears up and down she saw me on it because they showed something about the prisoners walking. Where they got the footage, I don't know, but apparently they did some. But she swears up and down she saw me. I never saw [it], so I don't know. Like I say, she kept that memory alive, and she would *not* turn it loose.

In early May 1945, John Kline was repatriated from Europe to the United States on a military transport plane. Within two weeks, he was heading home to his family's residence in Terre Haute, Indiana.

I decided to get off the bus just south of my home, about a mile and a half. You know, Main Street comes into town. I made the bus driver stop, which he didn't mind doing, because I said I want to get off here. I'm going to walk home. I practically *ran* home because I was so anxious to get home.

I had a bulldog. Mother told me later that the bulldog was going wild just before I got home. With no indication of why she was. She was at the back door, scrabbling on the back door. There's got to be a connection. That was me, running from Main Street, twelve blocks, fourteen blocks. As I got home, just before I came home, my mother said that my bulldog was practically clawing the rear door down. Never did that before.

So when I got home, I was greeted by my mother and my wife and my bulldog. That was the greatest thing in my life. . . . You just hug each other and thank God you're there. It's a great experience. What days those were. I choke up just thinking about them.

Irving Silverlieb was captured in December 1941 on Wake Island and spent the rest of the war in Japanese camps. His parents heard little, then nothing.

[My folks] had heard that—[the] first notification that they got was the first day of the war. They got a note that I was wounded in action right after the first day of the war. . . . I was MIA for a long time. Then I was transferred from an MIA to a KIA. . . . They had the telegram.

I did write from late '43. We wrote little [form] letters that the Japanese are treating us good and stuff like that. Then they didn't believe the letters.

I was dead. They had a funeral for me. I got a picture somewhere, a picture of my funeral. At that time there, the Torah where I graduated from was on Eighth and Fremont Avenue North [Minneapolis] . . . and they had my funeral there. Of course, they didn't have a body to bury. I was with another guy who played taps at my funeral, and he still laughs at it. He played taps at my funeral.

After evacuation from Japan, Irv was transported by ship back to the United States.

When I called my folks up from San Francisco, they said, "What!?" They didn't believe it was me. *(emotionally)* They didn't . . . you know. Fortunately, one of my uncles who was in the service at that time was home, discharged and home. I talked to my Uncle Joe, and he had to convince my folks that I was still alive.

I talked to my uncle, and I let him know from Great Lakes, or wherever it was I called up, "I'll be home by such and such a time." I came home, and they were waiting for me. *(emotionally, pauses ten seconds)* My mother went nuts. Just literally. My father, I thought he was going to squeeze me to death.

For some returning ex-POWs, memories were less pleasant. Earl Miller completed fourteen bombing missions over Europe, then spent nineteen months as a POW. His parents were happy to see him, but they didn't provide an opportunity to talk about what he had been through.

Well, I guess we were both kind of shy. My parents . . . we weren't very demonstrative, so . . . *(trails off)*. I know my father got a tear in his eye. My mother hugged me. *(emotionally; pauses ten seconds)* So then they were staying with friends here in St. Paul [Minnesota]. I think we went back to Cold Spring that same day, in the car.

My father said, "It's all over. We'll forget it now. It's all over with." Even before I could say a word. That bothered me for years; it still does. I don't know [why]. I just don't know. [Dad] never wanted to [know]. Never asked me. *(pauses five seconds)* Never indicated any desire at all.

They were living by this thought that came after the First World War: don't talk to these people, just don't bring it up anymore—that attitude. And they carried that over to World War II and my experience. I felt they thought that if we don't talk about it that you would forget about it. *(pauses five seconds)* Little did they know.

Some reunions weren't just with family; Harry Magnuson also faced the grieving family members of his bomber crew. When Harry bailed out of the burning B-29 over Tokyo, he was the only man of the eleven-member crew that returned: the bomber exploded in mid-air. For a long time afterward, however, the Tokyo Trolley *and crew officially were listed as "missing in action."*

The only thing I discussed about my experiences was with the families of the flight commander, the families of the copilot, the families of the radar operator, the families of the engineer. They all came to my place where my wife and I were staying. Because they didn't know. I was the only one that knew what happened to those guys. So they came to see me. Well, there wasn't much I could tell them because I didn't know at the time that the plane blew up.

The copilot's folks, he was an attorney, so he had a lot of things that he could do. So he researched; they sent people over there, to Japan, to find out if they're still there or what it was. Because I couldn't, I really couldn't help them at all. . . . But they wanted to talk to me first, to see if I could give them—if I could tell them anything.

But I had no—I couldn't tell them what happened to the crew. If I would have seen that airplane, and if I would have seen. . . . If I would have had any brains or thoughts to watch where the plane is going [after

USS Houston *survivor Al Kopp, 1946. When Al returned to the family farm near Raleigh, North Dakota, in late 1945, eight years had passed since he left home to join the navy.*

I bailed out], which I never even *thought* of the plane. Although I did see planes going by, flying over me.

I was kind of . . . I felt bad, that I couldn't help them. I felt bad.

There was yet another sad chapter to this postwar reunion. Charlie Snell was tail gunner on the Tokyo Trolley; *he, too, managed to bail out but, badly burned, died in the same cramped Kempeitai prison cell where Harry was kept.*

They had a memorial service for Charlie Snell in Faribault [Minnesota], and I went to that. That's where he was from, he and his wife.

One of the things that hurt me was Charlie Snell's wife. They were divorced. But when you lose your life in the war, you get ten thousand in insurance. So his wife called me and said . . . "Did Charlie sign anything over to me, because he signed everything over to his folks" So his folks got the ten thousand. But his wife had two kids, and they were divorced. And she wanted me to say that on his deathbed, Charlie said, "Tell my wife that the ten thousand belongs to her and not the folks." She called me about it, and I said, "I'm sorry, but he never said boo." I *could* have said it. I could have said it, but I said, "I'm sorry; Charlie never mentioned it."

Adjusting

Adjusting to the civilian world and its expectations proved to be a complex process, unique for each man. Some ex-POWs, for example, struggled with a feeling of guilt upon their release. There existed a sense of "giving up" while other comrades in the unit continued to fight and in some cases to die. Infantryman Harold Brick admits he felt this way. He became a prisoner in January 1945 when his commanding officer surrendered their unit.

I'd talk about *those* kind of things [my combat experience] but very little about the prisoner of war deal and especially the part about that we surrendered. That was a taboo. Nobody pushed it. . . . I felt that I shouldn't have been a prisoner. I think that's what it was: that I let my country down.

Paratrooper Earle Bombardier was part of the June 6, 1944, invasion of

France. Some days after dropping behind enemy lines, he was captured following a firefight with SS troops.

I guess it isn't that easy to explain, but you know when you think about your buddies that were killed and those around you that were taken prisoner, you feel guilty because you feel you weren't doing your job. A lot of other guys were out there fighting, and here you were a prisoner and couldn't do a thing about it. You felt guilty in that respect.

It's something I guess I'll deal with until the day I die. The guilt is still there. I know our doctor at [my] VA talks about that. We don't linger on that type of thing. We talk about other things. I guess the guilt feeling is something that we probably all have and will retain. It's there, but you don't talk about it that much.

Aaron Kuptsow was radar navigator on a B-17 bomber shot down over Germany. He, too, talks about the presence of guilt but also how he got past that feeling.

One of the [Germans'] expressions that became famous, "For you, the war is over," made the average soldier feel guilty. And it certainly was true in my case. The fact that I only flew eight missions was a concern. I felt that I had let the country down. While others were out there still fighting, I was sitting in a camp—relatively safe. That feeling of guilt was with me for the next fifty years or so.

One of my closest friends in med school had flown in the Pacific Theater, had completed fifty missions, then had come back to the States and was sent around the country boosting sales of U.S. bonds. Then when I went to the VA to sign up for medical benefits, lo and behold they notify me that I am entitled to special benefits as an ex-POW. Why? Apparently, I'm considered some kind of a hero. But I only flew eight missions. It goes with the category. Then I find out I'm entitled to some disability benefits.

It bothered me to some extent. It wasn't the kind of thought that kept popping up in my mind, but it did occur from time to time. As I look back, I think that is one of the reasons that I never talked about my experiences during the first fifty years. Now I feel better about it. I have learned that only about one in three [bomber crews] ever finished a complete tour. At our recent [Eighth Air Force] reunion, one of the POWs was shot down on his first mission. What the hell—I didn't do too badly. So the feeling is passing. Good riddance.

Other former prisoners displayed evidence of self-destructive behavior. Alcohol abuse was a serious problem for a number of men, including Irv Silverlieb. By the time of his repatriation, the Wake Island veteran had spent forty-five months in Japanese camps.

We were in a different world, and we were scared. Most of the guys will say they did not know how to act among civilized people. We *didn't* know how to act. And the easiest place to hide, and a lot of guys will tell you, was in a bottle. It's nothing I'm proud of right now. I still take a drink or two, but not like I *was* drinking. At that time, I was drinking between a pint and a fifth every day. This was every day, for years.

For months after a March 1946 discharge, Pacific POW Bill Price lived at a reckless pace.

When I came out I tried to make up—at first, before I was married—I tried to make up for things that I thought had been taken away from me by being . . . a prisoner of war. I really burned the candle at both ends and

Gerald Wakefield (right) at home, probably 1946. The Litchfield, Minnesota, native worked hard to readjust—after Corregidor, two years on Palawan Island, a hell-ship journey, and months of slave labor in Japan.

in the middle, too, I think there for a short time. I worked. I had a motorcycle. I'd go flying. I was really living and doing a lot of drinking, with a lot of other people.

I had a little bit of money accumulated because my pay accumulated while I was a prisoner of war and they gave me one lump sum. In fact, they gave me two hundred dollars there in the Philippines before I came home. What the hell did they give me that for? Because the only way I could spend it is on the boat. There's no place on the boat to spend it. So when I got back, then I got discharged. I got the full amount. I went through it. I found out who my true friends were when I ran out of money.

Fellow Pacific POW Al Kopp talks frankly about his readjustment process after three and a half years in Japanese camps.

In the first year I guess I did a lot of partying. Drank whiskey to beat hell. We were married in 1946, in September. But anyway, before that, we'd party. First of all we were stationed briefly at Wold-Chamberlain Field, here in Minneapolis. We didn't work; we just had a good time.

Al feels he always has been a flexible person, a trait that helped him survive prison camp—and the transition phase out of his POW life.

I'm easy to adjust to most any situation. It kind of bugs me when people can't, because it's so easy to do. You can adjust to so many situations and not be miserable, by just adjusting. For the most part, [the inflexible guys,] they didn't get back. They couldn't adjust to a prison camp. You can't live in a place like that if you don't. It's hard enough if you do.

Yet after liberation and repatriation, there were men who struggled with the transition back to civilian life.

Some of the guys didn't readjust. Guys that I had been with in camp, [they] couldn't adjust. There's [self-inflicted] gunshot wounds, and then you don't even count the car wrecks. I just have the feeling that some of those were brought on [by the fact that] they couldn't handle it. . . . Couldn't adjust to living, I guess.

My first reaction: you've got to feel sorry for them, or else they were damn fools. Or both. But you have to feel sorry for them because nobody would take their own life if they're all there. . . . But you saw that plenty of times, quite a lot of them.

Some men didn't readjust; for others this process proved to be a long—and tortured—road on which there were other victims in addition to the former POW. By the time he arrived home in May 1945, Glen Naze had a lot of experiences behind him: twenty-two completed bombing missions over Europe and more than ten months as a POW. He felt the stress—and believes those around him did, too.

There's really three different parts to your life: the flying, the POW, and the coming home. They were all . . . at the time it was difficult. When you're flying you say, well, I might not make it back. And the period of the camp, well, I'm safer now. I went home, and I was so run down that I couldn't do anything. I was pretty hard to get along with when I came back. I think my nerves were shot. . . . Somebody would say something cross to me; I would fly off the handle. My nerves were on edge. . . . I suppose it was two, three years [before I started to feel like my old self again].

Bill Connell noticed his POW experience in Japan had an impact on him, but it took the military decades until it was able to diagnose the problem.

It used to be that I was very argumentative, very opinionated, and I just wasn't a very nice guy. . . . I still have a flash-type temper, but now when I find myself really ready to explode, I try to turn around, walk away from whatever it is.

The Veterans Administration, they refer to that as the delayed stress syndrome. I *still* have trouble with it. There's an awful lot of people that are affected by that, and they're discovering now that the soldiers and marines over in Iraq are suffering from that quite a bit. But the military medical services as well as the VA are becoming much more adept at treating that.

[When I first was an ex-POW,] they didn't have the faintest idea. Neither did the navy. I couldn't go to the flight surgeon and complain about that, because then they would have come to the conclusion at that time that I was psychologically not adept for flying. That would have been their decision—not that something else was causing it. That's what they would have said.

To the best of my knowledge, up until about, until the late seventies, there wasn't anybody to go to or anything. The navy didn't give *diddly* about that. There was no concern. Nobody really cared about it.

This ex-prisoner remembers the impact of his POW experience in Germany on his marriage. He and his wife had been married in 1944, prior to him shipping out.

I got discharged right after Thanksgiving [1945]. I was working by the first of December at [my pre-service job], so I didn't have vacation in between. It had to be very difficult for my wife because I was moody. I was angry quite a bit of the time. I didn't drink. I didn't smoke. But I wasn't very good company. I wasn't. . . . I wanted to do what I wanted to do, and that was it. Like I was a dictator again.

I'm quite sure she did [notice I had changed]. Yes, I'm quite sure she did. . . . I can remember one night when we got in an argument over some little thing; I don't remember what it was. But I got so angry I ran out of the house, and I ran for several miles. This was eleven, twelve o'clock at night. I wasn't very stable, and she wasn't very stable either.

This former POW and his wife were separated in 1948 and later divorced.

Sam Nenadich had a difficult POW experience. In August 1944 when his bomber was shot down, he suffered a leg wound that became infected; there was talk of amputation. He later endured the eighty-six-day forced march from Luft IV. When Sam returned home, what he had gone through was still very much with him.

Just . . . I was on the edge, you know. Somebody would say something, and boom! I'd had enough of that in prison camp, where they told me where to shit and where to eat and when to eat. [At work or home,] I didn't talk too much about prison camp. That was a sore spot with me, so I didn't. . . . [I'd] get a relapse and start getting nervous and shaky all over again.

Sam's relationship with his wife, Flossie—they were married in summer 1944, just before he shipped overseas—was strained.

The first year after I got out of the service was kind of rough for us. We weren't cat and dog, but it was rough in general. Sometimes I'd flare up, but really now that I think of it, at my age I had no reason to flare up, but [it was] just one of those things: typical reaction from being a prisoner. It affected her pretty much. She really, really outdid herself trying to cater to me. I'd be sitting here reading the newspaper, and she'd come and put her arms around me and stuff like that.

Sam speaks openly about his next action, which he is sure helped him on his own long, hard road back. He made the decision to seek help through the Veterans Administration.

I did get help from the VA. I saw a shrink. Probably a couple years after the war ended. It was down at the Superior [Wisconsin] VA. Psychologist. [Deciding to seek help] wasn't hard really. Because I figured, well, I'm going to be going down to the Vets. Who in the hell in this neighborhood [Chisholm, Minnesota] is going to know that I went down to see a shrink?

My wife said to me, "You need help." Because she came down there [to Superior] with me, and [the] doctor . . . said, "What did you want?" She said, "I want my husband back. I don't want Sam. I want my husband."

We talked about it. We just talked about it. He said, "Things will pass over. Don't be afraid to talk about it." Things worked like that. Now I see [a VA psychologist] probably once every six months. Just checking up. I think it's just a friendly chat: "How are you doing? Last time you were here you said this. How are things going with that?" . . . I'm *positive* it helped me.

There are other powerful stories of former prisoners and their individual paths to recovery. Ken Porwoll, for example: against the odds, he was still alive in September 1945 after Bataan, Camp O'Donnell, a hellship journey, and nearly two years of slave labor in Japan. But along the way Ken had contracted tuberculosis of the spine; after evacuation from Japan, he remained in army medical facilities for nearly a year. Here he talks about his physical and spiritual healing.

August of 1946 I was discharged from the Hopkins TB Sanitarium. One of the first things I did is, I went down and signed up for unemployment insurance, and then I went for walks. Every day I walked. I would walk three or four hours a day, by myself. Listening to the birds and looking at the flowers and absorbing the peace around me.

Well, I was dealing with my healing. I had a lot of healing to do. I was still wearing a steel brace over the shoulders and up the back so that I couldn't bend or stoop. So that was kind of a constant reminder, too. I was really focused on getting out of that harness.

Then the other thing I did was go out to that cottage [at Brainerd, MN] and live out there for summer and early fall. And there, too, I would go for walks. I would go to the next little lake, and I would get up on the knoll and look down over the lake and watch the sunfish come up and take the bugs off the lily pads and all that. Good feeling experience.

You know, sometimes I would sleep out all night on the beach. I would have a little fire in the beginning when the mosquitoes are out, and after ten thirty, eleven o'clock the mosquitoes left, and [in] the moonlight night . . . I would just lay down and go to sleep.

After the war, Tuskegee Airman Luther H. Smith, Jr., spent many long months in hospitals recovering from the serious injuries he sustained when bailing out of his aircraft. He used this time to carefully consider what had happened, how to interpret events, and how to move ahead.

What happened is that . . . because of my physical condition, I was deeply depressed. . . . I obviously was feeling sorry for myself, and why did this have to happen to me, and how could this happen to me after all I'd gone through and the things I had accomplished as a combat pilot and have it end like this. Really feeling sorry for myself, until one day it dawned on me that on that Friday the thirteenth of October 1944, I was almost killed.

At this point, Luther's faith provided strength.

I was miraculously—my life was saved and spared by only God. It wasn't because of what I did, of what my airplane was able, my parachute was able to do. It was God's doing that I was alive, where hundreds of thousands of men had been killed in that war. Killed daily throughout that war. And my life was spared. And I realized that I had something to be thankful for and to live for. I knew not what I could do in appreciation or gratitude for my life being spared, but I better start working at it and making sure that I showed some acknowledgment that my life was spared.

Several wives of former POWs shared perspectives on the postwar adjustment, a process that in many cases lasted for decades. Betty Bigalke's husband, Vernon, was a POW in Germany during 1945.

When he got back, he was so thin, and he was sick for a whole year afterwards. He had dysentery, and it was a tough time for him.

Even after he recovered physically, Vernon still kept his story to himself and shared little about what he had been through as a prisoner of the Germans.

Donald Norris was an army medic; he was captured in the Philippines in early 1942 and was a POW until war's end. His wife, Marion, recalls the postwar years, when she and Donald lived in Willmar, Minnesota, and he worked for the state as a dairy and food inspector.

When he was in Willmar, he was under the care of a psychiatrist most of the time and [took] a lot of Valium. . . . [H]is nerves were pretty shot. He could hardly hold a pencil or write his name. So his reports, he had to type up.

He would get distant, you know; he'd be thinking real distantly, but he would never really *say* anything to me about it. Well, he told about how they slept out on the ground and different things and how he had gone through a lot, but you know he just went about his work and making a living. But he didn't really give me too many answers. He was pretty quiet about it.

Norma and Bill Schleppegrell were married in 1948. Bill, a fighter pilot, had been a POW in Germany during the last four months of the war. Norma knew few details of Bill's POW time until the 1980s; as she gradually learned more, she realized just how much that experience had affected Bill over the years.

It was only in coming to know him over the years that I realized what a terrible impact that had been. It's only in learning about that and then going back and recognizing the decisions that he made throughout our life because of that experience that I could begin to put the two things together and recognize that there were lots of places where he was very careful not to push something or do something because he dealt internally with what happened to him.

L. recalls a tough adjustment after her air corps husband returned from Germany.

At first he was . . . it was just like he hadn't been gone. But then, oh, I don't know how long it would be, but I never could do anything right.

Anything that I did was wrong. [Like] cooking. I don't know. Just *everything*. . . . I *was* happy, yes, but there was always this. . . . I wasn't right up to his expectations.

K.'s husband was a POW in the Pacific from 1942 to 1945; he suffered damage to his eyes that plagued him the rest of his life.

He was very sensitive. You couldn't mention eyes to him. I mean, he would just go . . . very high-strung. He didn't want anybody to know he had any problem. But, of course, I knew he did.

About '47, I guess, he went down, and [the doctors] . . . well, they knew they could never bring back his sight. He said there was nothing they could do about it, but he didn't think it would get any worse, and he'd just have to live with the fact that he just has to see from the side vision. He trained himself to do that. . . . I mean, to pick up a newspaper, he'd have to put it so close to [his] eyes that you *knew* he had problems. But he wouldn't talk about it. He didn't . . . *(trails off)*. He was always so worried about getting a job. He didn't want anybody to know that his vision wasn't good and that he had been in prison camp.

Dreaming

Many former prisoners were plagued for years, even into the present, by recurring dreams that feature specific images or individuals from their time as POWs. For Dick Carroll, who was a prisoner at Luft I, his dream involves dogs. As the Germans patrolled the camp compound at night, guard dogs roamed under the barracks, which were constructed several feet off the ground to discourage tunneling. Lying in his bunk, Dick could hear the dogs growling beneath him.

With all my experience, the only nightmares I have are of a pack of dogs chasing me. And I can't do anything about it because they catch up and they drag me down. And then you try to cover your face and your throat so they don't get you there, which would be fatal. And so then the only defense you have is your feet. So you kick, and you kick your wife. Not very pleasant.

And of course, you know, you're convinced that you can overcome, you say that, you *will* yourself to wake before the dogs drag you down. But it doesn't work. So then you stay up late at night. You can do [work] and spend less time sleeping, so you sleep more soundly. And it did help a little bit. It seemed to expand the time element between the bad dreams, but you never . . . *(voice trails off)*. [I still have them.] *(softly now, with emotion)* Yes. Maybe every other month. *(pauses five seconds)* That's about the way it is.

Ray Toelle was at Camp Ofuna. While his POW-related dreams were more numerous in the period right after 1945, they haven't disappeared. Ray describes an image that recurred: the prison cell at Ofuna where for months he was kept in solitary confinement.

I used to dream about being in this room [prison cell]. Because it was such a small room. And you didn't know what was going on. That was the worst thing. Because it was dark in there all the time. . . . There was no lights in there, day or night. The windows were boarded up, and there was no lights in the room. There was just the light that came through the door. They had a little, about a foot square window in the door where the guards could look in. And that was it. . . .

One thing I still do: I have to have a night-light on in the house.

Other men didn't dream about specific images, but the results could nevertheless cause anxiety. Pacific POW Howard Swanson:

I had one very bad, bad dream. And it lasted. For a number of years I've had that dream. . . . I always dreamed that the Japanese started another war against the United States and that the government rounded up all us guys, because they knew that there were going to be prisoners taken. For some reason they knew that at a certain place there was going to be American prisoners taken by the Japanese again. But they had to have soldiers at this place. So they came to us because we had the experience being prisoners of war. *(pauses three seconds)*

Isn't that a horseshit dream to have? That's just a terrible, terrible . . . *(trails off)*. I would struggle; I think I actually physically struggled in my sleep with that kind of a dream. I'd just be pooped out when I woke up.

Bill Connell was another Ofuna prisoner. His experiences there influenced how he dreams and also how he sleeps.

Well, surprisingly, the first twenty-five years after the war I had a *lot* of [dreams]. I really did. . . . I still dream every now and then. About life at

Ofuna and things that didn't happen that *could* have happened. Execution. Beatings that I saw. Things that didn't happen to me but I dream about them *anyway*.

Even today when I sleep, I don't sleep soundly. I toss and turn. I'm awake. . . . I wake up, oh, every hour and a half at night. I wake up. I fall back asleep again, but I wake up. And part of that is developed from the fact that I was a POW, that we didn't sleep soundly. [At Ofuna,] we were always afraid one of these guards were going to come in and do something to us while we were asleep. So that we were semi-awake I guess. That stuck with me forever.

Talking

Army ranger Don Frederick was captured in Italy in November 1943 and spent eighteen months as a POW. He and his wife, Carolyn, were married in 1946.

To this day I don't think she knows a lot of what happened. I never discussed it much with her. I would say, "I'll tell you about it tomorrow." When tomorrow came, I just dropped it and wouldn't talk about it. It came up; I just ignored it.

It may be tempting to consider Don's case—keeping events from family and loved ones for decades—to be an exception. Today, media coverage of similar stories—for example, that of Jessica Lynch, the soldier captured and held briefly during the 2003 U.S.–led invasion of Iraq—would be extensive, with psychological services at the ready for military personnel and families alike. Talking would be encouraged. But this was another era, and when these men returned home, they received little if any encouragement to share their experiences with others. Evidence from scores of conversations with former prisoners revealed that talking was difficult.

On the one hand, some recall they had little difficulty speaking about what they had been through: B-17 tail gunner Dick Brownlee, for example, spent six months in German camps.

[Family or friends,] they all kind of wanted to hear. It got to be kind of a joke because everybody has a story, you know. All of us had a story. Everybody was happy to deliver his story. Yes, people asked me about it. Prac-

Air corps officer Marcus Hertz (right) recalls it was nearly impossible to talk about his POW experiences, even with friends and family: "My neighbors, my children, they can't associate anything I'm saying with a guy freezing to death or starving to death. It isn't in their world."

tically everybody I knew. I guess I was willing to tell them anything I've told you. I really don't . . . it was not a bad experience.

It was enough of an experience to me so that if the opportunity provided itself I'd be happy to talk about it. It was fun to listen to other people talk about where they'd been and what they'd done. *(chuckles)* You get a bunch a guys together, and lots of times the war experience is the only thing that they had that's worth talking about.

Charles Woehrle echoes these sentiments. He was navigator on a four-engine bomber and was captured in France in 1943.

It just came out rather easily in conversation, but [my family] didn't just grill me, as I remember. Some people apparently did have trouble talking, but I did not. I didn't have that problem. We were a very vocal family, anyway. We were talkers. That was not hard for me, no.

People have said about these psychological experiences that they have, either they close down or hold it all inside. I was not built that way, nor did I suffer from that. I mean, I was there, and it was a sad moment in my life, but it didn't . . . just like I'm talking to you. It's not going to ruin my day.

Fighter pilot Harold Brown reports that he was prepared to talk about his wartime experiences but that his parents didn't ask him—neither about his time flying combat missions in Italy nor about the months as a POW in Germany.

Why didn't they raise those kinds of questions? I just don't know. They never asked what happened to me. They never—you were home, and they were so happy that you were home. They didn't even raise the question. I don't know if they didn't raise it because perhaps he doesn't want to talk about it and if he wants to tell us about it then he'll tell us when he feels like telling us about it. We aren't going to intrude. I suppose if I was going to give an answer, that would probably be the best answer. Our parents really didn't intrude into our personal lives. No part of it. Even when I became a pilot, Dad never sat down and said, "Hey, Harold, how is flying?" No. For them to have asked me would have been out of character.

As a matter of fact, it was years and years before we even talked about it here, in just lowly little bits and pieces. And it isn't that I felt . . . it isn't that it caused me any pain or discomfort at all. I just didn't do it. I just saw no reason to do it.

[Over the years] I shared a number of things with my brother [who also served in Italy]. I shared a few things maybe with a few people. Not all of the details, but bits and pieces. Later on, even with the kids. Occasionally I say a few things. Sometimes, if the parents were around, I might expand on a story. "I didn't know that, Harold. Did you such and such? You haven't said that before." Oh, well, there's a whole lot of things I haven't said before.

Bomber pilot Dick Carroll held his memories inside because of the pain they may have caused those he loved. After bailing out over German-occupied Hungary in 1944, Dick had been shot in the chest by a civilian when he hit the ground. He nearly died, and the bullet remained lodged next to his heart.

[My folks,] they never asked, and I never told them. Besides, my father and mother were quite old. I was the eighth child. They were much older. *(pauses three seconds)* How would they feel if I told them what I told you

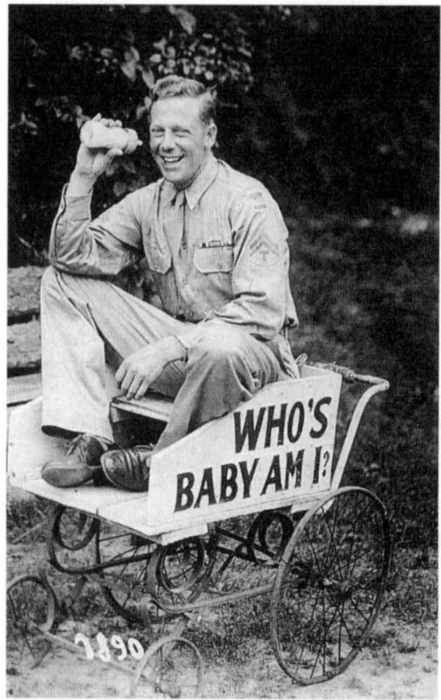

Sam Alle, gag photo taken at Hot Springs, Arkansas, June 1945. After his repatriation, Sam spent time at a rest and recuperation facility for ex-POWs in Hot Springs. On the surface happy and carefree, Sam remembers the reality of the postwar period was rather different: "Prison camp was just like a bad dream. . . . I mean, I never talked to anyone."

today? Because that would cause them so much heartache that it would be harmful to them. I didn't want to do it. . . . My father and mother died without ever hearing my story.

[My wife,] she picked up little bits of this when we were called to active duty, recalled down to Florida. She'd hear us talking and recalling things. So she'd pick up little bits, and she never, I never told her the whole story. So much of it was rather gory. It would make her feel sad. Did she really need to know? We didn't . . . back in those days, we didn't talk so freely.

At times, the barrier to communication was the experience itself. Army infantryman Floyd Dahl offers one account.

[My folks] wanted to know everything, but I couldn't tell them anything because when I started to tell them something it was like . . . ahhh!!! *That* didn't happen; that *couldn't* happen. I got the impression . . . not that they didn't believe me, but that they couldn't understand. They couldn't comprehend. They couldn't understand . . . what no food was like, what no *nothing* was like. No clean clothes. Stay in your underwear almost the time you got there until you went to the camp and then got deloused and got my underwear back. I don't remember the next time we got deloused or washed or clothes cleaned or anything like that. It was months. So you're always in the same. . . . They couldn't understand that.

I think they *tried* to understand, but I got the impression that they just didn't understand. Conversations [were infrequent].

Ken Porwoll develops this idea a bit further. When people back home failed to comprehend, he censored what he related about his own experiences, from Bataan March to hellship to slave labor in Japan.

You know, our story was so unusual that if I talked to some ordinary citizen, they would walk away scratching their head and look askance at you. And then you begin to wonder if you were dreaming this stuff up or making it up. Because it was out of the ordinary. And it was only when you got together with another POW that you got verified and you said, hey, I'm not crazy; I'm not making stuff up; I'm not lying. That's what *happened* to me.

Amongst the POWs, it was shared experience. That was another thing. You felt at ease with that group, and you could say whatever you wanted to say, and you didn't have to hold back or plan on what you were going to say. But out in the general public I just really didn't want people to know that I had lived through that kind of a terrible experience, because they might think I'm goofy. Because they might think that I've been mentally deranged, and maybe that's what they thought my stories were coming from, was a mental derangement.

In addition, there could be pain in recollecting.

So it was . . . like I went to a couple of families who the guys got left over there, and one of them, one of the dads said to me, "What did you know that my son didn't know?" I don't need that kind of hassle. So then I quit doing that.

Then there was another one's dad. You kind of hated to go around there, because every time you did he was crying and crying. And so it was miserable. . . . We'd always meet him in the VFW up there at Brainerd [Minnesota] because he would hang around there quite a bit. So it got so that I wouldn't go there anymore. Just avoid those kind of people.

Several men state that their recollections were called directly into question. Because of this, even today Irving Silverlieb chooses carefully who to talk to. In frank language, this Marine Corps veteran of Wake Island explains why.

Most of the people . . . first thing, how they treat you. You try to tell them the truth. "Oh, bullshit! Nobody would do. . . . That's impossible. Nobody does that to nobody." . . . Not only that, but, "Nobody could take that kind of shit." That's the thing. "Nobody can do that to you. You're making it all up," and stuff like that. That's the part that gets to trouble even talking about it. You're not going to be believed.

Irv offers an example. In February 1942, in a Japanese POW camp in China, evidence proves that Irv had his appendix removed—and that the Japanese provided no medical supplies and no anesthetic.

My operation [in China]. People heard about it, but they never ran into anybody. I'm living proof. These guys [other POWs] know it. They had a convention, reunion here in Minneapolis a few years back, and some guys knew about it. The guys who I was with know I'm not bullshitting them. But when you tell that to other people, that a guy cut you with a razor blade, and you passed out . . . *(trails off)*. Would *you* believe that?

Earle Bombardier relates a difficult experience from 1956, the consequences of which remained with him for more than two decades.

I distinctly remember [a lunch with our] neighbors, who belonged to our church. . . . He asked me a few questions about it, and before that I'd never talked about my experience at all. I told him about [being strafed while locked in a boxcar]. . . . I just told him, I said, "I'm living proof that you can exist after going through something like that."

He called me a liar. I didn't say anything at all. It wasn't easy, but I just let it go at that. I didn't say any more about it. And afterwards it was even worse. It wasn't until, oh, gosh, it must have been about 1981 or '82 that we had a fellow, an engineer at the company where I worked that was quite a historian. He was a World War II veteran, too, a wounded veteran. Very intelligent guy. Very compassionate guy. He started one day making up a history of the veterans that worked with the power company.

He came to me, and he wanted me to tell him my story, and I said, "No, I won't do it." He kept after me and after me, and finally he came around one day, and he said, "I've got everybody except you. Now," he said, "I think you better reconsider." So I finally told him. I said, "Against my better judgment, I'll give you just a few minutes." We sat down and started talking, and, my God, it just like opened the floodgates. It just poured out.

Many who have talked about, or written about, their painful experiences are confident that doing so has helped them on their own long, hard road. Yet the ability to take action required the right forum or situation or partner, and for some that didn't come along for many years after war's end. The American Ex-Prisoners of War organization (AX-POW) provided help for many. Russ Gunvalson, captured at the Battle of the Bulge, was among those who felt a stigma attached to having been a prisoner.

Somewhere along the line, it was told to us through some Legion meeting that being captured was not a very honorable thing to do. So we didn't let anybody know that we were a POW. Even my wife says that I didn't say anything. . . . I never, I didn't say anything to anybody. My diary [of my POW time] lay dormant for thirty-seven years.

AX-POW helped him move past this feeling.

In 1982, I got introduced to the POW organization. Greatest thing that ever happened to my being. It helped me to where I am today. Just talking about . . . .the psychiatrist at the VA told me that we have to talk about this. You have to talk about it. So they got the whole story, and he said, "Now we want this for our record, but you have to go out and tell your story," he said, "because it's not only good for historians to hear but also it's good therapy for you to get it off your chest."

I organized the Hiawatha Chapter here in Rochester [Minnesota] back in 1985, and there was POWs that I called up to join us. They would have no part of it—they'd just hang up on you. They don't want to talk about it. And some of those still are that way today—they *still* won't talk about it. . . . If it's up in your mind someplace and you don't get it off, it's still there.

For Dick Lewis, AX-POW has provided fellowship—but it took time for him to decide to join the organization.

I just don't know what it was that . . . I thought maybe in these latter years of my life, all these guys have gone through the same thing I've gone through. We've got a lot in common: maybe I just should be in fellowship with all of them. You know, for the longest time, I didn't even want to get into it. . . . I had a vision of POWs—all they do is get together and talk about their experiences. I've gone through that. I don't want to relive it all over and over and over again.

Once I finally decided—thought, gosh, maybe I better get into this—thankfully I did. I got into the [local] chapter and got to know [the commander] and, like I say, he got me going through here on the state level and changed my whole life. Now I'm the [chapter] commander. . . . It's been very good. I've appreciated it so much.

Other venues now exist for gathering with fellow ex-POWs and talking about shared experiences. In the 1980s, Veterans Administration offices reached out to World War II ex-POWs across the country and began to organize support groups. Pacific POW Stan Galbraith has been a participant in a support group organized by his local VA.

It's been beneficial to the extent that I have a, a little companionship with some guys that know where you've been and what you've been and they know you're not bullshitting. . . . And if they think I'm full of bull, I have no qualms about telling them, "This is the goddamned truth and nothing but the truth." And, of course, I won't talk to anybody about that unless they know I'm telling . . . I've got proof to back it up.

Stan can relax around other ex-POWs of the Japanese: "Sure," he says, "you can say what you want with them." With some men who had been prisoners of the Germans, though, he finds it's different. Stan recounts an incident from 2004.

(laughing) There's one that got, he kind of got out of my skin with the ones that meet out at the VA there. . . . Honest to God, I listened to him for two years. Jesus! It was *constant. (sarcastic tone)* God, he had it [tough]. Three months [he was a POW]. I didn't say too much. We're going out [from our group session at the VA] . . . and he came up behind me. He patted me on the butt and says, "That's how we pushed them along [on the forced march]." And he never had it out of his mouth. I spun it. . . . I had my hand right here up [on his neck] and put him up against the wall. And I said, "*This* is the way we did it in the Pacific."

John Kline was captured during the Battle of the Bulge. He joined a POW support group organized by staff at his local VA. He talks about the value of this group for him.

I think it's just the camaraderie, the getting together with somebody that had similar experiences. When I was first asked to join the group, [the doctor in charge] said, "Why don't you join our group?" I said, "You've got guys who were prisoners of the Japanese for three and half years. I was only a prisoner for four months." He said, "That doesn't make any difference." It doesn't. Their remarks to me: . . . "You were a prisoner, and you got pretty roughly treated the four months you were a prisoner."

You know, you talk to these guys, and you're just buddies. You're part of a group. You're part of a group. . . . It's the greatest thing in the world. I wouldn't miss one if I had to.

Support groups aren't the solution for everyone, though. In the past, Corregidor veteran Douglas MacArthur attended a regular monthly lunch of former Pacific POWs, but no more.

I used to go, but there are just certain people in the group that won't let it lie. And I'm not interested in thrashing it all over again. I don't *need* it. It's history, and I want to *leave* it there. I don't want to get into the conversations, and I don't want to *listen* to it, either, so I quit going. I don't *want* to.

Reflections

Forgiveness

With difficult, at times horrible experiences finally behind them, the former prisoners faced many challenges as they attempted to put their lives back together. One of the more complex challenges was to deal with their feelings toward those who had been their captors—individual guards or prison camp officials, as well as German and Japanese people in general. Men grappled with the question: what about forgiveness?

More than a few ex-prisoners, sixty years later, still harbor bad feelings toward their former captors. As one former POW of the Germans put it, "I guess I still hate them. . . . It's still there [inside me]." For others, the question is more complex—and the answers, too.

Arnold Sprong says he has negative feelings only about some Germans. He makes a careful distinction between those on the other side.

I have a bad feeling about *Nazis,* and so on and so forth. But the German people, they got caught up in something. A lot of it wasn't really their fault, I think. They just . . . they were in the wrong place at the wrong time, and they were in trouble, and some guy [Hitler] was going to give them what they thought they needed, and it ended up being a bad thing.

Reuben Weber relied on his faith to deal with residual anger he felt for an especially abusive guard at his camp, II-A Neubrandenburg. One day, not long after his return, he was working the fields on the family farm in Hillsboro, North Dakota.

I was out cultivating corn with a single-row cultivator, team of horses. I was out there in the field all by myself, and I got to thinking about this guy, and it made me so angry that I started slapping the horses. Then I realized, hey, those poor horses are working hard. That's no way to treat them.

Then I thought, what am I going to do? Am I going to go over to Germany and see if I can prosecute this clown, or what? I thought that wouldn't sound like a very smart idea either. Then I realized I'd have to do something to get him off my mind. So I forgave him. I got to the end of the row, and I said the Lord's Prayer: "Forgive us our trespasses *as* we forgive those who trespass against us." And that did it. After that, didn't bother me then.

For some men, this theme of forgiveness was more nuanced, with evidence of conflicting emotions. As Dick Carroll explores his feelings, it's clear the matter still is a complex one.

Bitterness . . . at first I hated them. But I soon found out that that was really not helping me at all. I then began to hate the system that would provide that sort of treatment. But as far as the people are concerned, do you condemn them all? How guilty is this one versus this one versus this one? We know the SS were completely . . . real bad, right? But then how about the *Wehrmacht* [German Army]? Some of them treated us very decently. They protected us. Kept us from being killed. Literally.

Each day the hatred dies down. You realize that it's wasteful to hate and that it's more constructive to do something about it. But you can hate the system that provides for that sort of treatment.

For example, I don't hate the Germans or the Japanese, because I know the Japanese treated us worse as POWs than the Germans did. But I know that if I were a Russian, the Germans would have treated me quite different than the way they treated me. So, you know, you have all these relationships and . . . that's why I say, before you get into hatred, my attitude is no, I don't hate them. But would I buy a German or a Japanese car? Why should I? Because, did the Germans or the Japanese ever *apologize* for their treatment of POWs? I haven't heard it.

For Pacific POW Al Kopp, his view of the Japanese is also more than a black and white issue. On the one hand, there is bitterness.

I disliked them very intensely [when we were liberated]. I had the feeling you should never trust them ever again because they were just not trustworthy. They lied and cheated and mistreated.

I don't feel very much different towards the Japanese today, and I don't care if they are two generations younger. I don't think they'd probably be as bad nowadays, but I think this ruthless, killer instinct in them is just inherent. I wouldn't trust them with anything civilian now. You wouldn't ever see me buy a Japanese car. You'd never see me buy a Japanese TV if you could get an American one. *(laughs)* I have no desire to [travel to Japan], unless I went over there with intent to do some bodily harm. I think I overstated that a little bit. I don't want to go over there and beat them up, but I don't want to go, either.

Yet in one sense, he is still able to see his former captors as human beings.

I really got a lot of empathy for people, generally. I don't know if that exactly included the Japanese. I could feel at times, just like when we were out in the jungle. . . . Even their guards, as mean as they were, they had an awful life. They had to be in a constant state of disorganized mess themselves. They had no liberty, no leave. They had no place to go except back on the railroad the same day with the prisoners and beat on them. I could feel something for them. After the war, after our people came in and the guards were cowering in the corner, I actually felt a little sorry for them.

Going Back

A number of ex-POWs of the Germans have returned to that country, specifically to search out locations where they were captured, held prisoner, or force-marched. Cal Norman and Arnold Sprong are just two of the men who did so, Cal in the 1980s and Arnold in the 1990s; both described their trips as positive and successful. Speaking of his experience, Arnold said, "I enjoyed the trip and even managed to talk a little bit of German and make myself understood. We had a good time."

Far fewer prisoners of the Japanese have ventured back to where they were held captive—remote Pacific locations or Japan itself. While the majority expressed no desire whatsoever to return, there were a few who did go back. Two men talk about what they were searching for and what they found.

Irv Silverlieb spent forty-five months as a prisoner of the Japanese. Decades later, the former marine returned to Japan.

We were there once in the 1980s and once in the 1990s. I really wanted to see [the country] because of the progress they had made. I wanted to see what the people were like.

Japan is a young country. The population, they are basically young. You go there today, the kids know *nothing* about the war. But the kids there, they want to learn. They want to know everything they can about the United States. And they're nice. They're nice kids.

Yet when he encountered Japanese men his own age, men who could have been in the military during the war, Irv had a quite different response.

I saw the guys *my* age, I'd be ticked off at him because I knew I was better than he was. That was my personal feeling. We beat you guys.

But on these trips to Japan, Irv says, "Nobody knew that [I had been a POW]. That was my own business."

Another Pacific POW, Howard Swanson, described a different experience. In the 1960s, the Corregidor veteran returned to Japan on a quest to visit the location where he had been a slave laborer: the Kamioka lead mine in central Honshu.

I was working in San Diego, California, at the time. I was a parole officer in San Diego. I decided I wanted to go to Japan and go to that prison camp [at Kamioka]. I wanted to go back and pay my compliments, my respects, [to] guys that died in the camp there, at Kamioka.

Then I had to find my way to Kamioka. I had to take a train so far and then a bus, because it's up in the mountains. There was a lady, a Japanese lady on the bus. And I was the only Caucasian. But there were other Japanese men and women on the bus. But this one lady kept looking at me, and I wondered what in the hell she was looking at me for. When I got to Kamioka, she—now I didn't know that she left and went to the police station, but that's where she went. She came right back to the bus where I was, and . . . the police wanted to know why I was at Kamioka.

She thought—this is what I was told—she thought I was coming back to scold the Japanese for mistreating prisoners. She used the Japanese word for *scold. (chuckles)* I told her that Americans were killed, died in the camp.

With the help of the Japanese, Howard located the Kamioka mine compound. Some buildings were still standing, but the lead mine where he worked was closed.

This story of return has another chapter: Howard elected to remain in Japan. During the late 1960s and early 1970s, he was a civilian employee at an American naval base in Japan.

I was in special services. I worked in recreation. I got the job and worked there for about ten years. I had quite a bit of contact with the local civilian population. Musical groups from the United States would perform in Japan, [in] some of the large nightclubs in Tokyo. I had a Japanese secretary. I would have her contact the Japanese, who invited the entertainers to come to Japan. So then, wherever that band or vocalist or whatever it was entertained at a nightclub in Tokyo, my secretary and I would go and check out the Japanese, check out the place.

Howard is sure his time in Japan helped him move past the POW years.

I think I'm different than some of the other ex-POWs in the way they think of the Japanese. . . . I changed my attitudes, and [my Japanese secretary], she helped me in a lot of ways. Maybe helped heal.

Bill Schleppegrell returned to Germany, but his goal was more than just to revisit personal sites. Ironically, Bill's POW experience was the beginning of a lifelong interest in the language and people of Germany. After his discharge from the service, the former fighter pilot completed an education degree at the University of Minnesota and became a high school teacher of the German language in Hibbing, Minnesota.

I was in pre-med . . . before I went in the service. But I was not happy with that. When I got out, then I went back to school under the GI Bill, and I didn't know what I actually wanted to do. . . . But I did want to take some German. I went into teaching German and getting to know the Germans, the culture.

While on a 1962 fellowship trip to Germany, Bill decided he wanted to do more.

I went to Germany and was there for six weeks. So that was my first time back to Germany since I'd left it in 1945. . . . When I was over there and went around to different spots in Germany, I realized that I really enjoyed different things over there, and I thought, I've got to get groups together and bring them over here and show them these things. So in 1966, I put together a program and took twenty-five students, by myself. We spent eight weeks in Germany. We'd stay in youth hostels. We traveled by train. We stayed in places . . . and I had the kids go out and really get involved with the communities.

In addition to student trips, Bill worked many years with the Concordia College summer language camps in Bemidji, Minnesota. Near the end of his career, the German government and the American Association of German Teachers honored Bill with an award for his years of work with young people, for striving to build a bridge between people of different cultures.

Final Thoughts

Is it possible to put the difficult POW experiences into a larger perspective? To close, several former prisoners attempt to do so.

Les Schrenk focuses on the practical, everyday effects of having been a POW.

Actually, I think it perhaps was for the better. I wouldn't for any amount of money go through it again, but I'm very proud that it did happen.

I think it made me a lot more tolerant. I think it gave me a much wider perspective of what other people go through. It most certainly made me realize how important food and water is, and how fortunate we are to live in the United States. We are really blessed. Everybody takes it for granted that you've got food and water and a place to sleep. You don't realize how fortunate you are to be able to go to bed at night and not have hunger pangs. I think it was by far the worst of all the POW experiences . . . being hungry a hundred percent of the time. And being so starved of water. To this day, when we go to a restaurant or even [at] home here, by the time I'm done eating, without even thinking about it, there isn't a scrap of food on my plate. It almost looks like it's been licked clean. If I've got a glass of water, you notice right now, it's completely gone, without even thinking about it. There's nothing left.

Navy pharmacist's mate Al Kopp reflects on his three and a half years as a prisoner. In keeping with his optimistic character, he focuses on the positive.

I think I learned a lot. I think I probably learned so much more than I would have if I hadn't been there because it was an experience that I wouldn't connect with any other way. I think you learn a lot of tolerance in a place like that, for other people. To tolerate them. I think you become better for managing for yourself and the guys around you. I don't think I'm the wisest guy in the world, but I got smarter along the way. I think that was good for you. And you look back, and you think, hey, when you die—and we all do that—you can say, well, I *did* something. I tried. I tried as hard as I could. You'd like to think you saved a few lives, which was very important—I'm almost positive I did that. You left the world a little better than you found it. Maybe that was part of the reason.

Dick Lewis believes his POW experience helped him put the positive aspects of his life in better perspective.

Right. *(with emphasis)* Absolutely, it did. . . . I'm sure it helped mature me to some degree, although I always felt I was a rather immature kid, I think because of not having any parental guidance or direction throughout my life, [being raised by my grandparents]. I guess it made me want to be married and have my own family and to have a foundation of a family, which I didn't have when I was growing up. I think that made a big difference for me. I wanted to get home and get through this whole ordeal of being a POW and start a whole new life with my wife. And go on from there.

And maybe that's why I didn't want to look back over all of this until the last number of years here. [But now,] you know, you're in the end of your life.

Others showed a harder edge when reflecting back: Lex Schoonover came back to civilian life after hard months at IX-B Bad Orb.

I always refer to my prison experience as a maturing experience. I went in a little boy, and I came out a man. I always said when I was working, I said, "Nothing's tough. If they're not fooling with my life, it's not tough." That's where they really fooled with my life. And it made me more hard-nosed. I just didn't want anybody to take advantage of me. Didn't want *anybody* [to] take advantage of me.

Stan Galbraith, a prisoner on Java and on the Burma-Thailand Railway, closes with a word about survival and why he believes men made it—or didn't.

I think 98 percent was your own mind. I'm not a very religious man, I'll tell you frankly. But I respect anybody, and I respect [them] if they live up to what is practiced. But I don't expect the Lord to pull me out of any mess. I either knew I was—and my friends around me—we were going to get out or . . . *(trails off)*. Getting down and praying every day wasn't going to make a *damn* bit of difference.

When the going was tough there, if you didn't make up your mind, if you gave up, you were a *goner.* To me, I have always thought there isn't too much in luck. You make your *own* damn luck.

Bob Michelsen, who survived imprisonment by the Kempeitai secret police, also reflected on survival and religion. Back home, he wondered about the role of a god.

I remember being at home one night in early 1946, and there's a bed that I could have slept in, but it was too soft; I slept on the floor. I was used to sleeping on a wooden floor. And I was on this floor, thinking about everything that had happened and wondering, and the thought came to me, why *am* I alive, when friends of mine are obviously dead? I thought, how can I *(pauses three seconds)*, how can I join my friends? And there was only one way, and I remembered that gun I had left behind [in the airplane]. So I briefly entertained suicide, to join my friends, and it actually was to join my friends . . . the thought did enter my head.

The thought, why am I alive? That is a very difficult question, because some people say, "God has saved you." Well, why didn't he save the others? So you get these questions, and "No, you're alive because you are going to do something great." Well, you are dead because you do nothing great? So all of these questions. . . . I think that it's just a matter of good fortune, and that's all I can attribute it to. I cannot say religion, or my own will, or my own pride, or anything else. Good fortune. I don't want to say chance—good fortune. *(pauses three seconds)* So for months and months, maybe years, that was my reaction at home to all that episode. That was my main reaction.

Paul Peterson, too, has thoughts about faith. Paul switched life paths in his forties, becoming an ordained Lutheran minister.

I think I have a deeper appreciation for life and a more profound trust in God, something that carried me through that experience. People ask me about that in terms of my calling as a clergyperson: does this have an effect, and is this why you went into ministry? No, I can't say that it is. But it certainly is formative in terms of helping you understand that, no matter how desperate life becomes, a person of faith can survive with the awareness that you're not alone.

Pacific POW Ken Porwoll paused for a moment before talking about how he still wrestles with his emotions.

Man alive! That's a hard one. I think I still do a lot of vacillating between the anger and revenge and forgiveness. I still do some of that. I . . . more on the forgiveness side or on the move on, Ken, move on—you've been there long enough. And what good is it going to do you to be vengeful or hateful? I've learned early in the game that to be hateful is very self-destructive. Very self-destructive. I've seen men go to their grave because they were frothing with hate, just absolutely.

If you conquer the ego, it's no problem. The ego is the big thing in the whole picture. The bigger your ego gets, the harder those things become. And the more you can put it down as to you're just . . . you're just Joe out there on the street, Ken. I think volunteering down there at St. Paul Listening House [a drop-in center for the homeless in St. Paul, Minnesota] has had that kind of effect on me, too, that I'm no better than those guys down there and the difference between us is maybe one paycheck.

After discharge from the service, Aaron Kuptsow went to medical school and became a physician. He is certain that after the war he was a different man.

You become very introspective. It did change my personality quite a bit, I think. I was, I think prior to the war, I was very carefree. Joked around a lot and everything was . . . nothing was too serious. In school I guess I was an average student. Not too aggressive or anything like that. But I think that the solitary and then the prison experience afterwards . . . *(trails off).*

When I came back, I was much more reserved. Right now I'm talking to you . . . but usually I'm very quiet. And student-wise, I became, you know, a strictly A student. I guess I learned a lot from it. I became much more conservative and more determined to have a goal and to go for it and count for something.

And I think also I always considered myself a very compassionate physician. I never ran one of these mills where you come in and go out and make a fast buck. I think I [have] more clemency for the feelings of other people, how different things affect them and the way I should treat them. I guess in a way I did benefit from a horrible experience.

Prisoners of War Interviewed for This Book

Cities and counties are in Minnesota unless otherwise noted.

Alle, Samuel Born (1919) and raised North St. Paul. Army medic. Captured near French-German border. POW Sep 44–Jan 45, in Germany. Postwar: Postal Service, St. Paul.

Anderson, Warren Born (1924) and raised Grand Rapids. Army paratrooper. Captured in Belgium. POW Dec 44–Apr 45, in Germany. Postwar: lawyer, Grand Rapids.

Bailen, Louis Born (1921) near Benoit, WI; raised Superior, WI. Navy mechanic. Captured on Corregidor. POW May 42–Sep 45, in the Philippines, on Palawan Island, and in Japan. Postwar: public school maintenance, St. Paul.

Bedsted, Lee Born (1923) and raised on Lyon County farm. Air corps: flight engineer and gunner on heavy bomber. Shot down over Germany. POW Jul 44–Apr 45, in Germany. Postwar: industrial arts teacher and high school counselor, Austin.

Bigalke, Vernon Born (1917) and raised Little Falls. Army infantry. Captured near French-German border. POW Feb–Apr 45, in Germany. Postwar: farmer, near Little Falls.

Bombardier, Earle Born (1922) and raised Crookston. Army paratrooper. Captured at Normandy D-Day invasion. POW Jun 44–Apr 45, in France and Germany. Postwar: power company employee, Fergus Falls.

Brandanger, Merlyn Born (1923) and raised Roberts, WI. Air corps: gunner on heavy bomber. Shot down over Italy. POW Mar 44–May 45, in Germany. Postwar: accountant, South Dakota and Minnesota.

Brick, Harold Born (1924) and raised Lake Henry. Army mortar squad. Captured in eastern France. POW Jan–Apr 45, in Germany. Postwar: Postal Service, Twin Cities.

Brown, Harold Born (1924) and raised Minneapolis. Air corps officer, fighter pilot. Shot down over Linz, Austria. POW Mar–Apr 45, in Germany. Postwar: career air force; later college administrator, Ohio.

Brownlee, Dick Born (1925) Pittsburgh, PA; raised St. Paul. Air corps: gunner on heavy bomber. Shot down over Germany. POW Oct 44–Apr 45, in Germany. Postwar: industrial management, Twin Cities.

Brummond, Bruce Born (1917) Buffalo Lake; raised Hutchinson. Army infantry. Captured in Luxembourg. POW Dec 44–Apr 45, in Germany. Postwar: retail sales and sales rep, Midwest.

Carlson, Raynold Born (1919) and raised Hibbing. Army infantry. Captured at Salerno, Italy. POW Sep 43–Apr 45, in Italy and Germany. Postwar: railroad employee, Minnesota.

Carroll, Richard Born (1920) and raised on farm near Rosemount. Air corps officer, copilot on heavy bomber. Shot down over Hungary. POW Jul 44–May 45, in Hungary and Germany. Postwar: various federal agencies, Twin Cities area.

Cartier, Richard Born (1923) St. Paul; raised on farm near Hugo. Army infantry. Captured at Belgian-German border. POW Dec 44–Apr 45, in Germany. Postwar: carpenter, Twin Cities.

Caverly, Floyd Born (1917) and raised near Hill City. Navy, crewman on submarine USS *Tang*. Ship sunk off Formosa. POW Oct 44–Sep 45, on Formosa and in Japan. Postwar: career navy; later defense industry employee.

Claypool, Warren Born (1919) and raised on farm in Ottertail County. Air corps, gunner on heavy bomber. Plane crash-landed in German-occupied Denmark. POW May 44–Apr 45, in Germany. Postwar: farmer, near Bemidji.

Clem, Onnie Born (1919) and raised Dallas, TX. Marine Corps. Captured at Bataan. POW Apr 42–Sep 44, in the Philippines. Postwar: retail lumber business, Dallas.

Connell, William Born (1924) Bakersfield, CA; raised Seattle, WA. Navy officer, dive-bomber pilot. Shot down over Chichi Jima island. POW Jul 44–Sep 45, on Chichi Jima and in Japan. Postwar: career navy; later insurance sales, Minnesota.

Dahl, Floyd Born (1923) and raised Minneapolis. Army, field artillery. Captured in Belgium. POW Dec 44–Apr 45, in Germany. Postwar: salesman for bookkeeping systems, Twin Cities.

Fager, James Born (1923) and raised Minneapolis. Air corps, gunner on heavy bomber. Plane crash-landed near Dutch-German border. POW Jan–Apr 45, in Germany. Postwar: carpenter, Twin Cities.

Frederick, Don Born (1923) and raised Albert Lea. Army officer, ranger battalion. Captured in Italy. POW Nov 43–Apr 45, in Italy and Germany. Postwar: hardware business (service rep and store owner), Minnesota and Iowa.

Galbraith, Stan Born (1918) and raised Virginia (MN). Army, artillery battalion. Captured on Java. POW Mar 42–Sep 45, on Java and Singapore and in Burma-Thailand jungle. Postwar: retail sales, Iron Range and Twin Cities.

Gall, Ernest Born (1918) and raised on farm near Turtle Lake, WI. Army, heavy weapons company. Captured at Belgian-German border. POW Dec 44–Apr 45, in Germany. Postwar: auto collision repair, St. Paul.

Gunvalson, Russ Born (1923) and raised Spring Valley, WI. Army, field artillery. Captured in Belgium. POW Dec 44–Mar 45, in Germany. Postwar: Postal Service, Spring Valley area.

Haider, Ed Born (1921) and raised St. Paul. Army paratrooper. Captured on Sicily. POW Jul 43–May 45, in Italy and Germany. Postwar: railroad employee, Midwest area.

Hall, Bill Born (1924) and raised St. Paul. Army machine gunner. Captured in France. POW Oct 44–Apr 45, in Germany. Postwar: banker, Twin Cities area.

Heer, Robert Born (1921) Dubuque, IA; raised Waterloo, IA. Air corps, support staff. Captured on Mindanao, Philippines. POW May 42–Sep 45, in the Philippines, on Formosa, and in Japan. Postwar: career air force.

Hertz, Marcus Born (1922) and raised St. Paul. Air corps officer, navigator on heavy bomber. Shot down over Germany. POW Jul 44–Apr 45, in Germany. Postwar: retail sales, St. Paul.

Joswick, Earl Born (1923) Minneapolis; raised Deephaven. Air corps, gunner on heavy bomber. Shot down over Germany. POW Jul 44–Apr 45, in Germany. Postwar: auto mechanic, Wayzata.

King, Charles Born (1920) and raised Cherokee, IA. Army, ranger battalion. Captured in Algeria, North Africa. POW Dec 42–Sep 43, in Italy. Postwar: Postal Service, Minnesota.

Kline, John Born (1925) and raised Glen Ayre, IN. Army infantry. Captured at Belgian-German border. POW Dec 44–Apr 45, in Germany. Postwar: sales and insurance, Midwest area.

Knobel, Bob Born (1923) and raised Altoona, WI. Air corps, flight engineer and gunner on heavy bomber. Shot down over German-occupied France. POW Jun 44–Apr 45, in Germany. Postwar: broadcasting industry, later industrial management, Twin Cities.

Kohnke, Herb Born (1914) and raised St. Paul. Army infantry. Captured in Belgium. POW Dec 44–May 45, in Germany. Postwar: quality control for industry, Minneapolis.

Kopp, Alois Born (1918) and raised on farm near Raleigh, ND. Navy pharmacist's mate, USS *Houston*. Ship sunk in action off Java. POW Mar 42–Sep 45, on Java, in Burma jungle camps, and in Vietnam. Postwar: sales, Upper Midwest.

Koshiol, Milton Born (1924) and raised St. Cloud. Army, armored infantry battalion. Captured in Germany. POW Mar–Apr 45, in Germany. Postwar: shoe repair shop owner, Paynesville.

Kruse, Vernon Born (1923) and raised St. Louis Park. Army, reconnaissance. Captured in France. POW Aug 44–Jan 45, in Germany. Postwar: radio and electronics repair, St. Louis Park.

Kuptsow, Aaron Born (1922) and raised Philadelphia, PA. Air corps officer, radar navigator bombardier on heavy bomber. Shot down over Germany. POW Nov 44–May 45, in Germany. Postwar: physician, Philadelphia.

Kurvers, Harold Born (1918) and raised St. Paul. Army tank crewman. Captured at Bataan. POW Apr 42–Sep 45, in the Philippines and Japan. Postwar: Postal Service, St. Paul.

Larson, Alf Born (1918) Orebro, Sweden; raised Duluth. Air corps, materials squadron. Captured at Bataan. POW Apr 42–Sep 45, in the Philippines and Japan. Postwar: engineering firms, Crystal.

Lewis, Dick Born (1922) and raised Faribault. Air corps, gunner on heavy bomber. Shot down over Germany. POW Nov 44–Apr 45, in Germany. Postwar: architect, Upper Midwest area.

Linc, Frank Born (1919) and raised North St. Paul. Air corps officer, copilot on heavy bomber. Shot down over Germany. POW Apr 44–Apr 45, in Germany. Postwar: mechanical engineer, Midwest area.

Luoma, Edwin Born (1919) and raised Eveleth. Army, mail clerk. Captured in Belgium. POW Dec 44–Apr 45, in Germany. Postwar: railroad employee, Eveleth and Duluth.

MacArthur, Douglas Born (1920) Ashland, WI; raised Northfield. Army, quartermaster detachment. Captured on Corregidor. POW May 42–Sep 45, in the Philippines and Japan. Postwar: sales, Minnesota area.

Magnuson, Harry Born (1923) and raised Minneapolis. Air corps, gunner on heavy bomber. Shot down over Tokyo. POW May–Sep 45, in Japan. Postwar: retail sales, Minneapolis.

Makepeace, Ray Born (1915) and raised Minneapolis. Army, coast artillery. Captured on Corregidor. POW May 42–Sep 45, in the Philippines and Japan. Postwar: insurance sales, Minneapolis.

Martinson, Kelly Born (1924) Annandale; raised Minneapolis. Air corps, gunner on heavy bomber. Shot down over Germany. POW Mar 44–Apr 45, in Germany. Postwar: factory rep for machine tool company, Minneapolis.

Meader, Les Born (1920) Detroit, MI; raised Columbia Heights. Air corps, gunner on heavy bomber. Shot down over Belgium. POW Nov 43–May 45, in Germany. Postwar: sales and transportation, Minneapolis.

Michelsen, Robert Born (1925) and raised Minneapolis. Air corps, gunner on heavy bomber. Shot down over Tokyo. POW May–Sep 45, in Japan. Postwar: sales rep, book publishing firm, Minneapolis.

Miller, Earl F. Born (1922) and raised Cold Spring. Air corps, gunner on heavy bomber. Shot down over Germany. POW Oct 43–Apr 45. Postwar: Postal Service, St. Paul.

Miller, Walter Born (1919) and raised Hibbing. Army, coast artillery. Captured on Corregidor. POW May 42–Sep 45, in the Philippines and Mukden, Manchuria. Postwar: mechanic and bus driver, Hibbing.

Morrett, John Born (1916) and raised Springfield, OH. Army officer, field artillery. Captured at Bataan. POW Apr 42–Sep 44, in the Philippines. Postwar: Lutheran minister in China, Hawaii, and the United States.

Naze, Glen Born (1919) and raised on farm near Jamestown, ND. Air corps, flight engineer and gunner on heavy bomber. Shot down over Germany. POW Jun 44–Apr 45, in Germany. Postwar: auto mechanic, Twin Cities.

Nenadich, Sam Born (1923) and raised Chisholm. Air corps, gunner on heavy bomber. Shot down over German-occupied Czechoslovakia. POW Aug 44–Apr 45, in Germany. Postwar: mineworker, Chisholm.

Norman, Caldon Born (1925) and raised Minneapolis. Army, infantry. Captured in eastern France. POW Dec 44–Apr 45, in Germany. Postwar: public school teacher and administrator, Portland, OR.

Oliver, Glenn Born (1919) and raised Brainerd. Army, tank crewman. Captured at Bataan. POW Apr 42–Sep 45, in the Philippines, on Formosa, and in Japan. Postwar: railroad employee, Washington.

Pearson, Lyle Born (1921) Montevideo; raised St. Peter. Air corps officer, pilot on heavy bomber. Shot down over Italy. POW Dec 44–May 45, in Germany. Postwar: probation officer, several Minnesota counties.

Peterson, Dale Born (1921) St. Paul; raised Osceola, WI. Air corps officer, pilot on heavy bomber. Shot down near Dutch-German border. POW Mar 44–May 45, in Germany. Postwar: career air force (retired 1960), then Federal Aviation Administration.

Peterson, Paul Born (1924) and raised Minneapolis. Army, scout/observer. Captured in Belgium. POW Dec 44–Apr 45, in Germany. Postwar: university faculty, Minneapolis; later Lutheran minister, St. Paul.

Pfaffinger, Richard Born (1920) and raised Blue Earth. Air corps, flight engineer and gunner on heavy bomber. Shot down over the Adriatic. POW Apr 44–May 45, in Italy and Germany. Postwar: farming, turkey retail business, both Blue Earth.

Pflueger, Ted Born (1913) Circleville, OH; raised Omaha, NE. Army officer, Corps of Engineers. Captured at Bataan. POW Apr 42–Sep 44, in the Philippines. Postwar: engineering field, California.

Porwoll, Ken Born (1920) St. Cloud; raised Brainerd. Army tank commander. Captured at Bataan. POW Apr 42–Sep 45, in the Philippines and Japan. Postwar: manufacturer's rep for machinery firm, St. Paul.

Price, Bill Born (1924) and raised Dearborn, MI. Air corps, gunner on heavy bomber. Shot down over Nagoya, Japan. POW Apr–Sep 45, in Japan. Postwar: management, auto industry, Michigan.

Ringgenberg, Jack Born (1924) and raised Rochester. Army paratrooper. Captured at Anzio, Italy. POW Jan 44–Apr 45, in Italy and Germany. Postwar: grocery retail, Forest Lake and Mankato areas.

Ritchie, Richard Born (1924) and raised Waterloo, IA. Army medic. Captured in Belgium. POW Dec 44–Apr 45, in Germany. Postwar: instructor, engineering and computer firms, Twin Cities.

Roslansky, Marvin Born (1922) and raised Lakefield. Marine Corps. Captured on Guam Island. POW Dec 41–Sep 45, on Guam and in Japan. Postwar: auto body repair, Racine, WI.

Sabbatini, Abraham Born (1913) Glen Lyon, PA; raised Italy. Air corps, ordnance company. Captured on Mindanao, Philippines. POW May 42–Sep 45, in the Philippines and Japan. Postwar: plumber, San Francisco, CA.

Schleppegrell, Bill Born (1923) Hibbing; raised Littlefork. Air corps officer, fighter pilot. Shot down over Germany. POW Jan–May 45, in Germany. Postwar: high school German teacher, Hibbing.

Schmidt, Alvin Born (1917) and raised on farm near Fergus Falls. Army, machine gun crew. Captured in France (Normandy). POW Jul 44–Jan 45, in Germany. Postwar: lumber business, North Dakota and Minnesota.

Schoonover, Hewitt "Lex" Born (1923) in Stroudsburg, PA; raised in several locations. Army, jeep driver. Captured in Belgium. POW Dec 44–Apr 45, in Germany. Postwar: retail store manager, Ohio and Minnesota.

Schrenk, Lester Born (1923) and raised Long Prairie. Air corps, gunner on heavy bomber. Shot down over German-occupied Denmark. POW Feb 44–Apr 45, in Germany. Postwar: warehouse manager, Twin Cities.

Shaw, LeRoy Born (1922) and raised Minneapolis. Air corps, gunner on medium bomber. Shot down over German-occupied France. POW May 44–May 45, in France and Germany. Postwar: airline mechanic, Minneapolis.

Shogren, Rodney Born (1921) in Taylors Falls; raised Shafer. Air corps, gunner on heavy bomber. Shot down over Germany. POW Mar 44–Apr 45, in Germany. Postwar: Postal Service, Shafer.

Silverlieb, Irving Born (1922) on North Dakota farm; raised Minneapolis. Marine Corps. Captured at Wake Island. POW Dec 41–Sep 45 in China, Korea, and Japan. Postwar: scrap metal business, Twin Cities.

Smith, Jr., Luther H. Born (1920) and raised Des Moines, IA. Air corps officer, fighter pilot. Shot down over Hungary. POW Oct 44–May 45, in Austria. Postwar: electrical engineer, New York and Pennsylvania.

Sprong, Arnold Born (1925) and raised Michigan City, IN. Army infantry. Captured in France. POW Jul 44–Apr 45, in France and Germany. Postwar: engineering field, Michigan City area.

Swanson, Howard Born (1921) and raised Minneapolis. Marine Corps. Captured on Corregidor. POW May 42–Sep 45, in the Philippines and Japan. Postwar: parole officer, Minnesota and other states; U.S. Navy employee in Japan, 1960s.

Toelle, Ray Born (1923) Arpin, WI; raised Wisconsin Rapids, WI. Air corps, gunner on heavy bomber. Shot down over Tokyo. POW May–Sep 45, in Japan. Postwar: grocery retail, Wisconsin Rapids.

Van Every, Harold Born (1918) and raised Minnetonka Beach. Air corps officer, pilot on heavy bomber. Shot down over Germany. POW May 44–Apr 45, in Germany. Postwar: insurance industry, Twin Cities area.

Velasquez, Simon Born (1920) Dolores, TX; raised Lovell, WY and St. Paul. Air corps, gunner on heavy bomber. Shot down over Germany. POW Apr 44–May 45, in Austria. Postwar: auto mechanic, Twin Cities.

Wakefield, Gerald Born (1920) and raised on farm near Forest City. Army, coast artillery. Captured on Corregidor. POW May 42–Sep 45, in the Philippines, on Palawan, and in Japan. Postwar: self-employed, Litchfield area.

Weber, Reuben Born (1925) and raised on farm in Hillsboro, ND. Army infantry. Captured near French-German border. POW Nov 44–Apr 45, in Germany. Postwar: telephone company employee, North Dakota and Minnesota.

Whittaker, James Born (1921) and raised Manchester, England. British Army, signal corps. Captured on Sumatra. POW Mar 42–Sep 45, on Sumatra and in Burma-Thailand jungle camps. Postwar: railroad employee, Minnesota.

Winter, Ray Born (1918) and raised Watkins. Army infantry, scout. Captured in Belgium. POW Dec 44–Apr 45, in Germany. Postwar: delivery driver, Maple Lake.

Woehrle, Charles Born (1916) Nashua, IA; raised Pine City. Air corps officer, bombardier on heavy bomber. Shot down over France. POW May 43–Apr 45, in Germany. Postwar: photography and engineering, Twin Cities area.

Wohlferd, Glenn Born (1921) and raised Pepin, WI. Army, coast artillery. Captured on Corregidor. POW May 42–Sep 45, in the Philippines and Mukden, Manchuria. Postwar: career air force.

Notes

Notes to Preface

1. Donald A. Ritchie, *Doing Oral History* (New York: Twayne, 1995), 11, 14.
2. Samuel Hynes, *The Soldiers' Tale: Bearing Witness to Modern War* (New York: Penguin, 1997), 25.

Notes to "It's Never Going to Happen to Me"

1. David Rolf, *Prisoners of the Reich: Germany's Captives, 1939–1945* (London: Leo Cooper, 1988), 4; U.S. War Department, Pamphlet No. 21–7, "If You Should Be Captured These Are Your Rights," May 16, 1944.
2. Rolf, *Prisoners of the Reich,* 3.

Notes to Chapter 1

1. "Europe" here includes continental Europe and Italy but also North Africa and the Mediterranean. No navy or marine corps personnel were listed on this document: see Military Intelligence Service, War Department, "American POWs in Germany," November 1945; quoted in John Nichol and Tony Rennell, *The Last Escape: The Untold Story of Allied Prisoners of War in Europe, 1944–45* (New York: Viking, 2002), 466. On pages 462–66, these authors also explain the difficulty of determining accurate numbers for British and American POWs in Germany and review various sources. Breakdown for airmen and ground forces in David Foy, *For You the War Is Over: American Prisoners of War in Nazi Germany* (New York: Stein and Day, 1984), 12.
2. Quote from Foy, *For You the War Is Over,* 37.
3. S. P. MacKenzie, *The Colditz Myth: The Real Story of POW Life in Germany* (Oxford: Oxford University Press, 2004), 37–41; researcher Greg Hadley documents this with his thorough examination of the downing of a B-29 on July 19–20, 1945, outside the city of Niigata. See *Field of Spears: The Last Mission of the Jordan Crew* (London: Paulownia Press, 2007), quote, p91. Also Gavan Daws, *Prisoners of the Japanese: POWs of World War II in the Pacific* (New York: William Morrow, 1994), 320–22.
4. Tom Lansford, "Bataan Death March," in Stanley Sander, ed., *World War II in the Pacific: An Encyclopedia* (New York: Garland, 2001), 101–3; John W. Whitman, "Fall of the Philippines," in Sander, ed., *World War II in the Pacific,* 478–83.
5. Donald Knox, *Death March: The Survivors of Bataan* (New York: Harcourt Brace, 1981), 118–71; Daws, *Prisoners of the Japanese,* 73–83; Lansford estimates 650 Americans died: see "Bataan Death March," 103.

6. Extensive evidence in Brian MacArthur, *Surviving the Sword: Prisoners of the Japanese in the Far East, 1942–45* (New York: Random House, 2005); Daws, *Prisoners of the Japanese.* Both works also contain bibliographies of firsthand accounts. S. P. MacKenzie, "The Treatment of Prisoners in World War II," *Journal of Modern History* 66 (Sep 1994): 513–14, quotes, p512–13. See also John Dower, *War Without Mercy: Race and Power in the Pacific War* (New York: Pantheon, 1986), 67–68; Saburo Ienaga, *The Pacific War, 1931–45: A Critical Perspective on Japan's Role in World War II* (New York: Random House, 1978), 49–50; Jonathan F. Vance, "Prisoners of War," in Sander, ed., *World War II in the Pacific,* 486–87.
7. There were 11,000 prisoners held at the 92nd Garage: 4,000 Americans and 7,000 Filipinos. Van Waterford, *Prisoners of the Japanese in World War II* (London and Jefferson, NC: McFarland & Company, 1994), 254; E. Bartlett Kerr, *Surrender and Survival: The Experience of American POWs in the Pacific, 1941–1945* (New York: William Morrow, 1985), 69–75; John A. Glusman, *Conduct Under Fire: Four American Doctors and Their Fight for Life as Prisoners of the Japanese, 1941–1945* (New York: Viking, 2005), 203–6.

Notes to Chapter 2

1. MacKenzie, *The Colditz Myth,* 49–54; the official name was *Durchgangslager Luftwaffe,* or German Air Force Transit Camp. Opened in 1939, the Dulag Luft complex housed a main interrogation center, a hospital facility, and a transit camp at the nearby town of Wetzlar, where prisoners were sent after interrogation and prepared for the move to a permanent camp. "Dulag Luft," at http://www.b24.net/ (accessed Mar 27, 2007). Also MacKenzie, *The Colditz Myth,* 54–56, and Foy, *For You the War Is Over,* 53. Some camp locations shifted late in the war due to Allied air strikes: Arthur A. Durand sorts this out in *Stalag Luft III: The Secret Story* (Baton Rouge and London: Louisiana State University Press, 1988), 57–58.
2. Interrogation techniques: Rolf, *Prisoners of the Reich,* 11–26; Foy, *For You the War Is Over,* 45–60. "Geneva Convention statutes," at http://www.icrc.org (accessed Mar 17, 2007); MacKenzie, *The Colditz Myth,* 51–52, 56.
3. Ofuna was established in April 1942 and operated by the navy: "Ofuna POW Interrogation Center," at http://www.mansell.com/pow_resources/camplists/tokyo/ofuna/ofuna.html (accessed Mar 27, 2007). Also Toru Fukubayashi, "POW Camps in Japan Proper," trans. Yuka Ibuki, at POW Research Group of Japan, http://homepage3.nifty.com/pow-j/e/POW%20Camps%20in%20Japan.doc (accessed Mar 21, 2007), 14. Kempeitai: Hadley, *Field of Spears,* 106–7. Kempeitai methods of torture: Waterford, *Prisoners of the Japanese,* 120–22.
4. "Stalag" is an abbreviation for *Stammlager,* or main camp; "Oflag" is an abbreviation for *Offizierlager.* The German Navy, the *Kriegsmarine,* had its own, much smaller camp system, abbreviated as *Marlag und Milag*; few American POWs entered this camp, and then only in the war's final chaotic weeks. On the camp system, see MacKenzie, *The Colditz Myth,* 93–106, and Foy, *For You the War Is Over,* 61–64.
5. The seven Stalag Luft camps were: Dulag Luft; I Barth; III Sagan; IV Gross Tychow; VI Heydekrug; VII Bankau; XVII-B Krems. Extensive information on all Luft camps at "WW Two Stalag Luft Research," at http://www.b24.net (accessed

Mar 27, 2007). On the Luftwaffe camp system, see also MacKenzie, *The Colditz Myth,* 93–106.

6. Transit camps: Rolf, *Prisoners of the Reich,* 11–21; MacKenzie, *The Colditz Myth,* 66–67. Foy addresses the overcrowding and steadily deteriorating conditions: see *For You the War Is Over,* 65–70.
7. On in-camp activities, see Foy, *For You the War Is Over,* 91–96; on boredom and mental health, see MacKenzie, *The Colditz Myth,* 154–92.
8. The Geneva Convention regulated work performed by POWs. See "Convention Relative to the Treatment of Prisoners of War," Geneva, July 27, 1929, articles 27–34, at http://www.icrc.org (accessed Mar 17, 2007), quote, Article 31. On the various types of labor on *Arbeitskommandos,* refer to MacKenzie, *The Colditz Myth,* 193–200, and Rolf, *Prisoners of the Reich,* 62–74.
9. Vance, "Prisoners of War," 487; Tojo Hideki's directive was read at two meetings (in June and July 1942) of high-ranking officers of the POW Information and Control Bureaus: see Sibylla Jane Flower, "Captors and Captives on the Burma-Thailand Railway," in Bob Moore and Kent Fedorowich, eds., *Prisoners of War and Their Captors in World War II* (Oxford and Washington, DC: Berg, 1996), 234–35. The document was presented as evidence at the International Military Tribunal for the Far East (IMTFE), held 1946–49. Quoted in Kerr, *Surrender and Survival,* 88.
10. Kerr, *Surrender and Survival,* 107–24. For information on camp locations across Asia, see "Center for Research, Allied POWs of the Japanese," at http://www.mansell.com (accessed Mar 27, 2007).
11. MacArthur, *Surviving the Sword,* 43–48, 146–47; also Robert S. La Forte and Ronald E. Marcello, eds., *Building the Death Railway: The Ordeal of American POWs in Burma, 1942–1945* (Wilmington, DE: Scholarly Resources, 1993), 113–20; statistics: Flower, "Captors and Captives on the Burma-Thailand Railway," 240–47. Americans were among the 62,000 POWs, USS *Houston* survivors, and men of the army's 131st Field Artillery captured on Java. On the human experience building the railway: MacArthur, *Surviving the Sword,* 52–147; Daws, *Prisoners of the Japanese,* 183–252; oral history excerpts form the basis for La Forte and Marcello's *Building the Death Railway.* See bibliographies in MacArthur and Daws for firsthand accounts.
12. Yasuo Kobayashi "spoke excellent English, had grown up in California, and attended Ohio University," Fiske Hanley, *Accused American War Criminal* (Austin, TX: Eakin Press, 1997), 114–15. Kennichi Yanagizawa had studied in Los Angeles before the war; his command of English was better than Kobayashi's: Hadley, *Field of Spears,* 108.

Notes to Chapter 3

1. Detailed discussion in MacKenzie, *The Colditz Myth,* 231–64.
2. Daws, *Prisoners of the Japanese,* 98–104; MacArthur, *Surviving the Sword,* 59–62.
3. Ienaga, *The Pacific War,* 46–54. Also Glusman, *Conduct Under Fire,* 269–70; Daws, *Prisoners of the Japanese,* 81–82.
4. While the majority of escapees were recaptured, a handful did manage to reach Allied control or neutral Sweden or Switzerland: See MacKenzie, *The Colditz Myth,* 319, 342–43; Geneva Convention 1929, Article 50, at http://www.icrc.org

(accessed Mar 17, 2007). German policy: In March 1944, seventy-six officers escaped Stalag Luft III through a tunnel system. Of these men, fifty were executed after being apprehended; only three men made it to England. Durand details the escape and its consequences in *Stalag Luft III*, 282–302.

5. Vance, "Prisoners of War," 489; Daws, *Prisoners of the Japanese*, 100.
6. Documented accounts of prisoners tortured and killed after attempting escape: three men at Cabanatuan, September 1942, in Glusman, *Conduct Under Fire*, 260–61; nine prisoners in Singapore, March 1942, in MacArthur, *Surviving the Sword*, 20; six men from Tamarkan, Burma railway detail, January 1943, in MacArthur, *Surviving the Sword*, 62; Daws, *Prisoners of the Japanese*, 99. Men interviewed for this book also provide confirmation.
7. Corroborating evidence for these events described in MacKenzie, *The Colditz Myth*, 241–42.
8. Major Caplan was assigned as flight surgeon to 719th Squadron, 449th Bomb Group, 15th Air Force, based in Grottaglie, Italy. On October 13, 1944, Caplan was flying a combat mission as a medical observer when the B-24 bomber was shot down. In sworn testimony of December 1947 for the War Crimes Office, Civil Affairs Division, Dr. Caplan confirms physical abuse of prisoners by Big Stoop. Document reproduced in Laura Caplan, *Domain of Heroes: The Medical Journal, Writings, and Story of Dr. Leslie Caplan* (privately printed, 2004), 177–84; bio, 89–118. Accounts of brutal treatment also in Nichol and Rennell, *The Last Escape*, 116–18.
9. Nichol and Rennell, *The Last Escape*, 376.
10. The Germans attempted to move POWs from Italian camps north into Germany. Some prisoners, like Charles King, escaped in the chaos, but the majority ended up in camps in Germany. Nichol and Rennell, *The Last Escape*, 43–45.

Notes to Chapter 4

1. On relationships in German camps: MacKenzie, *The Colditz Myth*, esp. 125–53.
2. On food and diet, Rolf, *Prisoners of the Reich*, 53–57, 95–96; Foy, *For You the War Is Over*, 71–80. On Red Cross parcels: Foy, *For You the War Is Over*, 74–78; Durand, *Stalag Luft III*, 164–68.
3. Good discussion of tribes in Daws, *Prisoners of the Japanese*, 134–40.
4. Food supplied by the Japanese, also POWs eating anything: detailed discussion in MacArthur, *Surviving the Sword*, 175–88. U.S. Army daily food ration for an enlisted man: 2,013 grams (combat rations higher). The Japanese set the level for a prisoner performing hard labor at 790 grams; later in the war it fell lower. Caloric value of rations supplied by the Japanese: Kerr, *Surrender and Survival*, 120; MacArthur, *Surviving the Sword*, 175.
5. Glusman describes certain direct effects of malnutrition; these included pellagra, optical neuritis, and beriberi: see *Conduct Under Fire*, 228–29, 265, 277–78. Also Daws, *Prisoners of the Japanese*, 267–68. Craving of food: Daws, *Prisoners of the Japanese*, 110–14. Quote: MacArthur, *Surviving the Sword*, 219.
6. "Preliminary Hearing, 29 January 1945," Document at Veterans History Project, American Folklife Center of the Library of Congress, Johann Karl Friedrich Kasten papers, at http://lcweb2.loc.gov/diglib/vhp-stories/loc.natlib.afc2001 001.12002/#vhp:other (accessed Jun 7, 2007).

7. There are no records indicating that any prisoners were shot as a result of this incident.

Notes to Chapter 5

1. Quote from Foy, *For You the War Is Over,* 129. See also Mitchell G. Bard, *Forgotten Victims: The Abandonment of Americans in Hitler's Camps* (Boulder, CO: Westview, 1994), 36–38. Roger Cohen provides a complete account of the prisoners taken in February 1945 from Bad Orb to the concentration camp at Berga and the subsequent abuse and death of more than seventy. See his *Soldiers and Slaves: American POWs Trapped by the Nazis' Final Gamble* (New York: Knopf, 2005).
2. Foy, *For You the War Is Over,* 128. David Killingray, "Africans and African Americans in Enemy Hands," in Moore and Fedorowich, eds., *Prisoners of War,* 199.
3. Hadley, *Field of Spears,* quote, p105–6.
4. Hadley consults several sources in reconstructing life in the Kempeitai cells and the interrogators and their methods in *Field of Spears,* 106–21. Corroborating firsthand account found in Hanley, *Accused American War Criminal.* Daws provides perspective in *Prisoners of the Japanese,* 317–22, 433. He also concludes that some hokaku beihei were executed by their captors.
5. The U.S. military remained segregated during the war. Richter, "Black Units in the U.S. Military," in David Zabecki, ed., *World War II: An Encyclopedia,* 2 vols. (New York and London: Garland, 1999), 1:651–56.
6. Other African American officers taken prisoner report similar accounts, of being asked by their German interrogators "why they fought for a country that despised them." See Killingray, "Africans and African-Americans in Enemy Hands," 181–204, quote, p196.
7. Cohen, *Soldiers and Slaves.*

Notes to Chapter 6

1. Historian Gerhard L. Weinberg details the final six months of the war in Europe in *A World at Arms: A Global History of World War II* (Cambridge: Cambridge University Press, 2005), 780–826.
2. MacKenzie, *The Colditz Myth,* 358–60; Nichol and Rennell, *The Last Escape,* 91–113.
3. MacKenzie, *The Colditz Myth,* 358–83, quote, p359.
4. Forced marches are the theme of Nichol and Rennell, *The Last Escape;* the estimate of deaths is theirs, based on statistical research (447). See also Rolf, *Prisoners of the Reich,* 151–69; Foy, *For You The War Is Over,* 139–50; MacKenzie, *The Colditz Myth,* 358–68.
5. Dawn Trimble Bunyak, *Our Last Mission: A World War II Prisoner in Germany* (Norman: University of Oklahoma Press, 2003), 133–48, covers the history of Luft IV.
6. Departure conditions and length of march documented in Nichol and Rennell, *The Last Escape,* 114–38.
7. Conditions and numbers at the camp and departure in February 1945: "Stalag VIII-A," at http://www.pegasusarchive.org/pow/ (accessed Mar 27, 2007).

8. Reliable information in English or German on this camp is scarce; some helpful information in "1992–1996 Findings of the WW II Working Group. Section A.2. Camp. Stalag III-C, Küstrin, Poland," at http://www.aiipowmia.com/wwii/wwiiwkgrp.html (accessed Mar 27, 2007). Numbers of prisoners in "Kriegsgefangenen-Bestandsmeldungen des Befehlshabers des Ersatzheeres/Stand 1. Dezember 1944," at http://www.gedenktafel.info/ (accessed Mar 27, 2007).
9. Agreement among the United States, Britain, and the Soviet Union on the repatriation of prisoners proved to be very difficult; an atmosphere of mutual suspicion hung over the negotiations. Two authors try to sort out the dealings: Nichol and Rennell, *The Last Escape,* 232–50; and the more detailed study of Patricia L. Wadley, "Even One Is Too Many: An Examination of the Soviet Refusal to Repatriate Liberated American World War II Prisoners of War" (PhD diss., Texas Christian University, 1993).

Notes to Chapter 7

1. Gregory Michno, *Death on the Hellships: Prisoners at Sea in the Pacific War* (Annapolis, MD: Naval Institute Press, 2001), 281–83, has data and discussion of sources. See also Appendix 309–17, listing all transports, 1941–45.
2. Michno, *Death on the Hellships,* ch. 4, "1944: Fleeing from the Allies," 151–262.
3. Daws, *Prisoners of the Japanese,* 295–96. Michno, *Death on the Hellships,* 295–96.
4. Michno, *Death on the Hellships,* 306. Ex-POWs interviewed for this project affirm this conclusion.
5. Charles Roland, *Long Night's Journey into Day: Prisoners of War in Hong Kong and Japan, 1941–1945* (Waterloo, ON: Wilfrid Laurier University Press, 2001), 225–302, details this system of camps and industry coordination; Linda Goetz Holmes, *Unjust Enrichment: How Japan's Companies Built Postwar Fortunes Using American POWs* (Mechanicsburg, PA: Stackpole Books, 2001), documents several dozen of the Japanese companies that profited from their use of slave labor; list of companies, p149–50.
6. Deteriorating conditions in Japan during 1944–45: Haruko Taya Cook and Theodore F. Cook, *Japan at War: An Oral History* (New York: New Press, 1992), 169–257; Ienaga, *The Pacific War,* 181–202; Edwin P. Hoyt, *Japan's War: The Great Pacific Conflict* (New York: Cooper Square Press, 2001), 340–50, 375–87. The complete collapse at the surrender in August 1945 is best captured by John Dower, *Embracing Defeat: Japan in the Wake of World War II* (New York: W. W. Norton, 1999), 33–64. How POWs endured the war's final year: Glusman explores the human dimension well in *Conduct Under Fire,* 368–430; see also Roland, *Long Night's Journey into Day,* 225–302.
7. Survivor Andrew D. Carson, quoted in Michno, *Death on the Hellships,* 185.
8. Michno, *Death on the Hellships,* 189.
9. Multiple survivor testimonies exist documenting this; quote from Michno, *Death on the Hellships,* 260. Extensive evidence on *Oryoku Maru,* with survivor testimony and photos, at "Oryoku Maru Online," at http://www.oryokumaruonline.org (accessed Mar 27, 2007).
10. Michno, *Death on the Hellships,* 250–58 and notes 74–77.

Notes to Chapter 8

1. On the last weeks of the war in Europe, see Weinberg, *A World at Arms,* 810–41.
2. Refer to MacKenzie, *The Colditz Myth,* 370–73, on varying reactions.
3. On the complicated matter of repatriation and Big Three negotiations, see Wadley, "Even One Is Too Many." Nichol and Rennell, *The Last Escape,* esp. 204–31 (on III-A) and 248–50 (on Luft I).
4. Recent works on the final months of the Pacific War have illuminated the complex scenarios and negotiations by the United States, Japan, and the Soviet Union. See especially Tsuyoshi Hasegawa, *Racing the Enemy: Stalin, Truman, and the Surrender of Japan* (Cambridge, MA: Belknap Press, 2005), and Richard B. Frank, *Downfall: The End of the Imperial Japanese Empire* (New York: Random House, 1999).
5. Captured Japanese documents cited in Daws, *Prisoners of the Japanese,* 322–27.
6. Daws, *Prisoners of the Japanese,* 338–40; Kerr, *Surrender and Survival,* 282, 286.
7. Daws, *Prisoners of the Japanese,* 340–42; Kerr, *Surrender and Survival,* 284–85.
8. Kerr, *Surrender and Survival,* 286–91, Glusman, *Conduct Under Fire,* 442–49. Daws, *Prisoners of the Japanese,* 332–61, has accounts of evacuations from Japan and other locations. Evacuation from German camps: MacKenzie, *The Colditz Myth,* 387–89; Camp Lucky Strike: Nichol and Rennell, *The Last Escape,* 398–402.
9. Glusman, *Conduct Under Fire,* 460–61, cites and discusses several pieces of medical evidence related to medical and psychological effects.
10. There is information on the liberation of VII-A Moosburg, and much more on the camp, its history, and the town, at http://www.moosburg.org/info/stalag/index.html (accessed May 31, 2007). See also the vivid account in Durand, *Stalag Luft III,* 352–57.
11. Liberation of III-A Luckenwalde: Nichol and Rennell, *The Last Escape,* 217–31.
12. Accounts of Omori liberation: Daws, *Prisoners of the Japanese,* 342; Glusman, *Conduct Under Fire,* 442; Kerr, *Surrender and Survival,* 286.

Notes to Chapter 9

1. Nichol and Rennell, *The Last Escape,* 412, and interviews for this project.
2. Roland, *Long Night's Journey into Day,* 321–28; Glusman, *Conduct Under Fire,* summarizes medical findings on 467.
3. Roland, *Long Night's Journey into Day,* 322. Glusman, *Conduct Under Fire,* 467. Statistics on POW mortality in Bernard M. Cohen and Maurice Z. Cooper, *A Follow-Up Study of World War II Prisoners of War* (Washington DC: GPO, 1954).
4. VA doctors and medical care, reduced benefits: numerous interviews for this project, of both Pacific and Europe POWs; also Daws, *Prisoners of the Japanese,* 385–91. Nichol and Rennell, *The Last Escape,* 440.

Sources

Primary Sources and Reference Materials

Center for Research, Allied POWs of the Japanese. At http://www.mansell.com (accessed Mar 27, 2007).

Cohen, Bernard M. and Maurice Z. Cooper. *A Follow-Up Study of World War II Prisoners of War.* Washington, DC: GPO, 1954.

Convention relative to the Treatment of Prisoners of War. Geneva, July 27, 1929. At http://www.icrc.org (accessed Mar 17, 2007).

Dear, I. C. B., ed. *The Oxford Companion to World War II.* Oxford: Oxford University Press, 2001.

The Encyclopedia of Aircraft of World War II. London: Amber Books, 2004.

Fukubayashi, Toru. "POW Camps in Japan Proper." Translated by Yuka Ibuki. At POW Research Group of Japan, http://homepage3.nifty.com/pow-j/e/POW%20Camps%20in%20Japan.doc (accessed Mar 21, 2007).

Oral history interviews. See complete list of interviewees.

POW Research Network Japan. "List of POW Camps and Chart of Casualties." At http://homepage3.nifty.com/pow-j/e/list/chart.htm (accessed Mar 21, 2007).

Sander, Stanley, ed. *World War II in the Pacific: An Encyclopedia.* New York: Garland, 2001.

Waterford, Van. *Prisoners of the Japanese in World War II: Statistical History, Personal Narratives and Memorials Concerning POWs in Camps and on Hellships, Civilian Internees, Asian Slave Laborers and Others Captured in the Pacific Theater.* London and Jefferson, NC: McFarland & Company, 1994.

Zabecki, David, ed. *World War II: An Encyclopedia.* 2 Vols. New York and London: Garland, 1999.

Secondary Literature

Bard, Mitchell G. *Forgotten Victims: The Abandonment of Americans in Hitler's Camps.* Boulder, CO: Westview, 1994.

Beatty, John D. "Prisoner of War Operations." In Zabecki, ed., *World War II: An Encyclopedia,* 2:1247–50.

Bunyak, Dawn Trimble. *Our Last Mission: A World War II Prisoner in Germany.* Norman: University of Oklahoma Press, 2003.

Burdick, Charles, and Ursula Moessner. *The German Prisoners-of-War in Japan, 1914–1920*. Lanham, MD: University Press of America, 1984.

Caplan, Laura. *Domain of Heroes: The Medical Journal, Writings, and Story of Dr. Leslie Caplan*. Privately printed, 2004.

Carlson, Lewis. *We Were Each Other's Prisoners: An Oral History of World War II American and German Prisoners of War*. New York: Basic Books, 1997.

Cohen, Roger. *Soldiers and Slaves: American POWs Trapped by the Nazis' Final Gamble*. New York: Knopf, 2005.

Cook, Haruko Taya, and Theodore F. Cook. *Japan at War: An Oral History*. New York: New Press, 1992.

Daws, Gavan. *Prisoners of the Japanese: POWs of World War II in the Pacific*. New York: William Morrow, 1994.

Dower, John. *Embracing Defeat: Japan in the Wake of World War II*. New York: W. W. Norton, 1999.

———. *War Without Mercy: Race and Power in the Pacific War*. New York: Pantheon, 1986.

Doyle, Robert C. *Voices from Captivity: Interpreting the American POW Narrative*. Lawrence: Kansas University Press, 1994.

Durand, Arthur A. *Stalag Luft III: The Secret Story*. Baton Rouge and London: Louisiana State University Press, 1988.

Faber, Peter. "Strategic Bombing." In Zabecki, ed., *World War II: An Encyclopedia*, 2: 1266–69.

Falk, Stanley. *Bataan: The March of Death*. New York: Curtis Books, 1962.

Feuer, A. B., ed. *Bilibid Diary: The Secret Notebooks of Commander Thomas Hayes, POW, the Philippines, 1942–1945*. Hamden, CT: Archon Books, 1987.

Flower, Sibylla Jane. "Captors and Captives on the Burma-Thailand Railway." In Moore and Fedorowich, eds., *Prisoners of War*, 227–52.

Foy, David. *For You the War Is Over: American Prisoners of War in Nazi Germany*. New York: Stein and Day, 1984.

Frankland, Noble. "Strategic Air Offensives. 1. Against Germany." In *The Oxford Companion to World War II*, 832–33.

Fussell, Paul. *Wartime: Understanding and Behavior in the Second World War*. Oxford: Oxford University Press, 1989.

Glusman, John A. *Conduct Under Fire: Four American Doctors and Their Fight for Life as Prisoners of the Japanese, 1941–1945*. New York: Viking, 2005.

Hadley, Gregory. *Field of Spears: The Last Mission of the Jordan Crew*. London: Paulownia Press, 2007.

Hanley, Fiske. *Accused American War Criminal*. Austin, TX: Eakin Press, 1997.

Holmes, Linda Goetz. *Unjust Enrichment: How Japan's Companies Built Postwar Fortunes Using American POWs*. Mechanicsburg, PA: Stackpole Books, 2001.

Hoyt, Edwin P. *Japan's War: The Great Pacific Conflict*. New York: Cooper Square Press, 2001.

Hynes, Samuel. *The Soldiers' Tale: Bearing Witness to Modern War.* New York: Penguin, 1997.
Ienaga, Saburo. *The Pacific War, 1931–45: A Critical Perspective on Japan's Role in World War II.* New York: Random House, 1978.
Kelnhofer, Guy J. *Understanding the Former Prisoner of War: Life after Liberation.* St. Paul, MN: Banfil Street Press, 1992.
Kerr, E. Bartlett. *Surrender and Survival: The Experience of American POWs in the Pacific, 1941–1945.* New York: William Morrow, 1985.
Killingray, David. "Africans and African Americans in Enemy Hands." In Moore and Fedorowich, eds., *Prisoners of War,* 181–204.
Knox, Donald. *Death March: The Survivors of Bataan.* New York: Harcourt Brace, 1981.
La Forte, Robert S., and Ronald E. Marcello, eds. *Building the Death Railway: The Ordeal of American POWs in Burma, 1942–1945.* Wilmington, DE: Scholarly Resources, 1993.
Lansford, Tom. "Bataan Death March." In Sander, ed., *World War II in the Pacific,* 101–3.
MacArthur, Brian. *Surviving the Sword: Prisoners of the Japanese in the Far East, 1942–45.* New York: Random House, 2005.
MacKenzie, S. P. *The Colditz Myth: The Real Story of POW Life in Germany.* Oxford: Oxford University Press, 2004.
———. "The Treatment of Prisoners in World War II." In *Journal of Modern History* 66 (Sep 1994): 487–520.
Michno, Gregory. *Death on the Hellships: Prisoners at Sea in the Pacific War.* Annapolis, MD: Naval Institute Press, 2001.
Moore, Bob, and Kent Fedorowich, eds. *Prisoners of War and Their Captors in World War II.* Oxford and Washington, DC: Berg, 1996.
Nichol, John, and Tony Rennell. *The Last Escape: The Untold Story of Allied Prisoners of War in Europe, 1944–45.* New York: Viking, 2002.
Ritchie, Donald A. *Doing Oral History.* New York: Twayne, 1995.
Roland, Charles. *Long Night's Journey into Day: Prisoners of War in Hong Kong and Japan, 1941–1945.* Waterloo, ON: Wilfrid Laurier University Press, 2001.
Rolf, David. *Prisoners of the Reich: Germany's Captives, 1939–1945.* London: Leo Cooper, 1988.
Ruehrmund, James C. "Germany Air Campaign (September 1939–April 1945)." In Zabecki, ed., *World War II: An Encyclopedia,* 2:1505–10.
Taiwan POW Camps Memorial Society. "Taiwan POW Camps." At http://www.powtaiwan.org/ (accessed Mar 21, 2007).
Towle, Philip, Margaret Kosuge, and Yoichi Kibata, eds. *Japanese Prisoners of War.* London and New York: Hambledon and London, 2000.
Vance, Jonathan F. "Prisoners of War." In Sander, ed., *World War II in the Pacific,* 486–91.

Wadley, Patricia L. "Even One Is Too Many: An Examination of the Soviet Refusal to Repatriate Liberated American World War II Prisoners of War." PhD diss., Texas Christian University, 1993.

Weinberg, Gerhard L. *A World at Arms: A Global History of World War II*. Cambridge: Cambridge University Press, 2005.

Whitman, John W. "Fall of the Philippines." In Sander, ed., *World War II in the Pacific*, 478–83.

Index

Numbers in *italic* refer to pictures.

abuse of civilians, 170, 173, 209, 211, 213–14
abuse of prisoners, 13, 15, 48, 50–51, 67, 76, 77, 131, 162; Bataan Death March and, 6–11; in German camps, 82–84; in Japanese camps, 26–27, 86–91, 194, 200. *See also* executions
Adams, Cedric, 227
Africa, 70, 96, 99
African American POWs, 130, 132–34, 282
Aguirre, Manuel, 230
aircraft carriers, 26
airdrops, 203, 223
airmen, 4, 5, 9, 18, 22–29, 235, 244, 247, 253; burn injuries and, 57, 87–88, 240; downed in Europe, 79, 82, 84, 93, 94, 105, 110, 117, 135–36, 137, 241, 245, 251–53; downed in Pacific, 85, 86, 87, 127, 239; interrogation and, 39, 40, 43, 44–46, 54, 58; preparation for capture and, 3, 94; "special prisoner" status and, 130–31, 138–41,144–48; threat of lynch justice and, 6, 26–38, 142–43, 224
Akabira, Japan, 191, 229
alcohol abuse, 173, 242, 243
Alle, Samuel (Sam), 54, 59, 166, 169, 170, 254, 269
Allied forces, 97, 149
American Association of German Teachers, 265
American Ex-POWs organization (AX-POW), 234, 257–58
Anderson, Warren, 269
anti-Semitism, 33, 34, 130, 134–37
Anzio invasion, 21, 110
Arbeitskommandos. *See* work details
Ardennes Offensive, 95. *See also* Bulge, Battle of the
Arisan Maru (cargo ship), 188, 198
army enlisted men, 106, 119, 122, 135
atomic bombs, 203, 222, 223
Augsburg, Germany, 79
Austria, 31, 158. *See also* Stalag XVII-B Krems

Bad Orb, Germany. *See* Stalag IX-B
Bailen, Louis, 114–15, 230, 269
Balanga, Philippines, 9, 10
Barger, Herman, 114
Barth, Germany, 213–14. *See also* Stalag Luft I Barth
Bataan (Pacific), 47
Bataan Death March, ix, 6–7, *8*, 9–12; survivors of, 68, 74, 101, 123, 236, 246, 255
Bedsted, Lee, 4, 53–54, 151, 154–55, 157, 269
Belgium, 30, 51
Benevolence (hospital ship), 225, 227–28
Berga (German concentration camp), 130, 135, 282
Bicycle Camp (Java), 113
Bigalke, Betty, 247–48
Bigalke, Vernon, 17, 247–48, 269
Big Stoop (German guard), 83–84, 281
Bitterfeld, Germany, 210
Bombardier, Earle, 18, 232, 240–41, 256–57
bombing, 6, 185, 220; aftermath in Europe, 170, 171; of Germany, 31, 63–64; of Japan, 130, 140, 145, 191, 192–93; of ship convoys, 183–84
boredom in camps, 41, 59–63, 78; importance of diversions and, 60–61
Brandanger, Merlyn, 155–56, 269
Braunau, Austria, 158
Brazil Maru (ship), 185
Brick, Harold, 51, 134–35, *208*, 240, 270; on sharing of food, 119–20; on theft of food, 121–22
Bridge on the River Kwai, The (film), 72, 102
British Army, 88, 97, 99, 127
Brodsky, Phil, 189–90

Brown, Harold, 31–33, 207, 230–31, 253, 270
Brownlee, Dick, 24–25, 62–63, 251–52, 270
Brummond, Bruce, 55, 106, 108
B-17 Flying Fortress (bomber): crew members of, 4, 23–25, 29–30, 33, 93, 94, 241–42, 251
B-24 Liberator (bomber), 218; crew member of, 22, 152
B-29 Superfortress (bomber), 140, 145, 192, 219
B-29 Superfortress (bomber): crew members of, 6, *27*, *28*, 36, 127, 141, 145, 224, 235, 239–40; Japanese mistreatment of, 130–31, 138–39; threat of execution as war criminals and, 142–44, 146–47, 225
Bulge, Battle of the, 80, 111; survivors of, 52, 91, 121, 205, 257, 258–59
Burma, 41, 66, 176
Burma-Thailand Railway, 42, 70–71, 89–90, 99–100, 112, 124, 218

Cabanatuan (Camp Number 1, Philippines), 74–76, 86, 100, 114, 123
Camp Lucky Strike (France), 204, 230–32, 284
Camp Nomachi (Japan), 196–97, 222, 228
Camp O'Donnell (Philippines), 10, 68, 74, 101, 183
Camp Ofuna, (Japanese naval interrogation facility), 40, 49, 86, 91; difficulty of escape from, 100–101; solitary confinement cells at, 131, 140–41; survivors of, 126, 143, 144, 250, 251, 279
Camp Omori (Japan), 143–46, 147–48, 223–25; prisoners liberated from, *226*, 234–35
Capas, Philippines, 10
Caplan, Leslie, 83–84, 281
capture, 3–6; of airmen, 22–29; Bataan march and, 8–12; of ground troops, 16–22; lynch justice and, 28, 30–38, 142; at sea, 14–15; seen as shameful by Japanese, 7
Carlson, Raynold, 66, 270
carrier-based aircraft, 176
Carroll, Richard (Dick), 34–36, 44–45, 105–6, 249–50, 253–54, 261, 270
Cartier, Richard (Dick), 81–82, 270
Caverly, Floyd, 48–49, 90–91, 141, 225, 228, 270
censorship of prisoner mail, 107
Chemnitz, Germany, 208
Chichi Jima, Japan, 26, 86, 100
civilians, 28, 29, 44, 94, 170, 177, 220–23; end of war and, 209, 211, 213, 214, 215–16; food for prisoners and, 81–82, 158, 163–64, 168, 171, 173; as interrogators, 50, 51, 138, 147, 280; kindness of, 65–66, 156, 167, 192; potential for lynch justice and, x, 6, 22–25, 30–38, 49; unpredictability of, 30, 161–62, 224; work details and, 41, 64, 197–98, 200
Clark Field, Luzon (Philippines), 10, 100, 101, 115–16, 178, 197
Claypool, Warren, 153, 156, *210*, 211, 270
Clem, Onnie, 185, 186–87, 270
communication: creative means of, 141; from outside world, 79–80, 192; with prisoners' families, 107, 227, 230, 234–35, 237
Connell, William (Bill), 223–25, 227, 230, 244–45, 250–51, 271; at Camp Ofuna, 86–87, 126, 140–42; at Camp Omori, 143–46; capture and, 26–27
Corregidor Island (Philippines), 6, 12–14, 47, 68, 86, 179; veterans of, 259, 263

Dahl, Floyd, 61, 120, 213, 254–55, 271
deaths of prisoners, vii, 14, 42, 76, 185; Bataan march and, 6–7, 8, 9, 11; burial detail and, 74–75; forced marches in Germany and, 150; hellships and, 176, 180, 185; Kamioka work camp and, 195–96; loss of compassion and, 76; psychological factors and, 73
D-Day veterans, 18, 85, 240–41
Department of Defense, U.S., 234
disability benefits, 234, 241
discrimination, 130, 224; against African Americans, 133–34; against air crew prisoners, 83, 138–48; against Jews, 33, 34, 130, 135–37; against Mexican Americans, 131; against supposed collaborators, 116, 197–98
Doane, Bert, 164
Dulag Luft (German interrogation facility for airmen), 39, 40, 43–46; record card from, *58*

Eighth Air Force (U.S.), 63, 241
803rd Engineers, 47
80th Infantry Division, 59
escape, 95–96, 280–81; attempts at, ix, 78, 93, 94–95, 136; difficulty of, in Asia, 100–103; end of war and, 168–75; execution and, 76, 86; successful, 97–99; thoughts of, 91–92
Europe, x; capture of American servicemen in,

16–26, 29–36; discrimination in, 131–37; hunger in, 116–23, 155–58, 160–64; interrogation of POWs in, 42–47; prison camps in, 51–63, 105–12, 151, 164–65; reciprocity regarding prisoners in, 130; trek to freedom across, 169–75; war's end in, 202, 204–17; work details in, 64–66
evacuation of prison camps, 149, 151, 165, 187, 204, 215, 216; hospitals and, 214–15. *See also* liberation
executions, 78, 116; attempted escape and, 76, 86; fear of, 146, 147, 224–25; of prisoners from sinking ship, 186, 187; threat of, 142, 144, 177–78, 203

Fager, James, 4, 235, 271
faith, 10, 106, 184, 247, 260–61, 266, 267
Fallingbostel, Germany. *See* Stalag XI-B
families of prisoners, 239; communication and, 107, 227, 230, 234–35, 251–52; difficulty of, postwar, 253–55; reunions and, 236, 237, 238; uncertainty faced by, 233, 235, 239
fear, x, 7, 15, 20, 21, 23, 30, 32, 35, 38, 47, 63–64; of execution, 146, 147, 177–78, 224–25; of "friendly" fire, 140, 160, 178, 182, 184, 185, 193; hellships and, 178, 182, 184, 185; long-term effects of, 251; youth as protection from, 25
firebombing campaign on Japan, 27, 130, 138, 145
food, 8, 60, 62, 132–33, 177, 265; civilians and, 81–82, 158, 168, 171, 173; conflicts about, 104–5, 119–23, 127; desperation for, 9, 185, 196, 199; dreams of, 117; forced marches and, 150, 155–57, 160, 162–64; in Japanese camps and, 67–68, 123–25; liberation and, 205, 207, 209–10, 215, 217, 219, 220, 222, 223, 225, 228, 232; Red Cross packages and, 83, 118, 119, 151; sharing of, 70–71, 190, 198; smuggling of, 80–81; theft of, 111, 112, 120–22, 126–29
forced laborers (civilian), 65, 66, 171, 173
forced marches (Germany), 165–75, 202, 210, 214; challenges of, 153–55, 159; deaths during, 150, 164; health problems and, 153, 155, 161, 164; rationale for, 149; Russian attacks and, 165–69; shortage of food and, 151–52, 157, 160, 162, 163
forgiveness, postwar, 260–64, 268
Formosa, 41, 69–70, 90, 125, 176, 178, 188, 190
Fourth Armored Division, 19
Fourth Ranger Battalion, 43
France, 16–18, 19, 42, 54, 59, 61, 79, 84, 94, 214, 241; Camp Lucky Strike in, 230, 232
Frederick, Carolyn, 251
Frederick, Don, 43–44, 92, 251, 271
Fukuoka Camp, 193

Galbraith, Stan, 71–72, 99–100, 113, 124, 258, 271
Gall, Ernest, 91–92, 205–6, 271
Geneva Convention, vii, x, 39, 41, 64, 78, 107, 137, 149
Gerhold, Melvin, 154–55
Germany, viii, xi, *xviii–xix*, 6, 39, 42–43, 58, 130, 136; capture of prisoners in, 22–26, 29–30, 31, 40; collapse of, near war's end, 150, 155, Geneva Convention and, 78, 107, 149; hospitals in, 57, 59; liberation and, 204–17; prison camps in, xiii, 5, 40–41, 44–46, 51–56, 60–63, 105, 108–12, 116–23, 131–37; return of ex-POWs to, 262, 264–65; work details in, 64–66. *See also* forced marches (Germany)
GI Bill, 264
Glischinski, Frank, 114, 196
Görlitz, Germany. *See* Stalag VII-A
Great Britain, 4, 88, 203, 214, 283
Great Escape, The (film), 78
Gross Tychow, Poland. *See* Stalag Luft IV
Guam, 85, 230
guards, 191, 197, 200, 224, 251; brutality and sadism of, 82–84, 87, 88, 89–91, 131, 260; civilian, 200; compassion among, 79–81, 90; end of war and, 203, 208, 209, 211, *212*, 220, 225, 262; forced marches and, 161–62, 168–69; in German camps, 78–83; in Japanese camps, 85–91; prisoner relationships with, 156, 191, 194–95, 197; punishment and, 89; retribution against, 211, 212–13; variability of, 77, 85, 86, 194–95
Gunvalson, Russ, 108–9, 214, 271

Hague Conventions, vii
Haider, Ed, 56, 82, 271
Hakodate, Japan, 3, 191, 219
Hall, Bill, 20–21, 85, 108, 206–7, 216–17, 271; evacuation of camp and, 165, 167, 168–69

Hammelburg, Germany. *See* Stalag XIII-C
health problems, 6, 51, 52, 108, 138, 203, 214; deaths in Pacific camps and, 75–76; on hellships, 179, 180; importance of mental state and, 73; long-term effects and, 231, 233–24, 246–47, 249; primitive treatments for, 72–74, 256; sense of helplessness about, 115; tropical, 12, 75, 193
Heer, Robert (Bob), 69–70, 125–26, 127, 190–92, *229*, 271
hellships, 176–77; conditions on, 178–84; psychological pressures and, 179, 181–83; survivors of, 191–201; torpedo attacks and, 185–90
Hertz, Marcus, 135, *136*, 137, 207, 252, 272
Heydekrug, Germany. *See* Stalag Luft VI
Hideki, Tojo, 41, 280
historical record, viii, ix
hokaku beihei (special prisoners), 130, 131, 138–48
Hokkaido, Japan, 191, 193, 219
Honshu, Japan, 191, 193, 196, 199
Hornet (aircraft carrier), 26, 183
hospitals, 59, 82, 113, 133, 214; evacuation and, 214–15; military, 57, 59, 229; prison, 17, 108
Houston (cruiser), 14, 115, 218; survivor of, 239, 280
humor, 14, 41, 61, 62, 208
Hungary, 34–36, 253
hunger, 9, 105, 117, 155–58, 160–64, 185, 204, 214; effect on mental state, 128; extreme behavior and, 120–21, 122–23, 127–28; in German camps, 116–23; in Japanese camps, 123–29, 138, 195–96; Red Cross packages and, 83, 118, 119

infantry, 16, 17, 19, 20, 59, 121
interrogation, 39–40, 54, 58, 130, 279; brutality and, 84, 131; German captors and, 42–47; Japanese captors and, 47–51, 138; preparedness for, 45–46
interviewees, viii, xi-xiii, 269–78
Isles, George, 132
Italy, vii, 66, 82, 96, 97, 98, 99, 174, 175, 251

Japan, vii, viii, xi, *xxi*, 28, 40, 87, 128, 224; atomic strikes on, 203, 222, 223; end of war and, 128, 177, 283; Geneva Convention not ratified by, 41; nationalism of, 7; prisoners working in private industry and, 177, 191–201; return of ex-POWs to, 262–64; risk of lynch justice in, 30–38
Japanese Army, 77
Java, 14, 71, 124
Jerome, Jerry, 165, 169, *175*
Jewish American POWs, 130, 134–37
Johnson, Hook, 126
Jordan, Jim, 21, 108
Joswick, Earl, 84, 272
jungle camps, 71–74, 89–90, 124

Kami-Gumi company, 198
Kamioka, Japan, 193–96, 220–21; return of prisoner of war to, 263–64
Kasten, Hans, 135
Kempeitai (Japanese military police), 28, 40, 127, 240, 267, 279; treatment of "special prisoners" and, 131, 138–40, 142–43, 146–48
King, Charles, 96, 97, *98*, 99, 272
Kingery, Hugh, 108–9
Kline, John, 159–61, 214, 237, 258–59, 272
Knobel, Bob, 79–80, 84, 118–19, 155, 209, 272
Kobayashi, Yasuo, 50–51, 138, 147, 280
Kohnke, Herb, 65, 66, 135, 211–12, 272
Kopp, Alois (Al), 14–15, *239*, 261–62, 265–66, 272; *Houston* survivor, 115; on liberation, 218; on postwar adjustment, 243–44
Koshiol, Milton, 19, 272
Krems, Austria. *See* Stalag XVII-B
Kruse, Vernon (Vern), 4, 42–43, *60*, 91, 110–11, *172*, *175*, 236, 272; on liberation and chaos, 165–66, 167–68, 170–71, 173–74
Kuptsow Aaron, 33, 137, 206, 241–42, 268, 272
Kurvers, Harold, 7, 76, 123–24, 183, 193, 230, 273
Küstrin, Germany. *See* Stalag III-C

Larson, Alf, 9, 178–79, 196, 222, 228, 236–37, 273; on Pacific work detail, 101–3, 115–16, 197–98
Lazarett (camp hospital), 214
Lewis, Dick, 29–30, *58*, 209–10, 257–58, 266, 273; on German military hospitals, 57, 59
liberation, 19, 202, 220–21, 224–25; anticipation of, 204–5; chaos and, 208, 209–10, 217–18; delays in camp evacuation and, 215–17; in Europe, 204–17; excitement and, 206–8, 227–30; in Pacific, 203, 218–29; retribution and, 211–14, 219, 222. *See also* repatriation

lice. *See* vermin
Limburg, Germany. *See* Stalag XII-A
Linc, Frank, 23–24, 45–46, 62, 63, 212–13, 273
Lopez, Ignacio, 120
Luckenwalde, Germany. *See* Stalag III-A
Lucky Strike. *See* Camp Lucky Strike
Luftwaffe, 39, 40; camp system of, 279–80
Luoma, Edwin, *52*, 273
Luzon, Philippines, 41, 100, 101, 178, 230
Lynch, Jessica, 251
lynch justice, x, 6, 28, 30–35, 49; increased risk in Japan, 36–38, 224

MacArthur, Douglas, 12, 100, 193, 230, 259
MacArthur, General Douglas, 226, 228
McOmis, Jim, 11–12
Magnuson, Harry, 127–28, 139–40, *145*, 146, 148, 238–39
Maibara, Japan, 199, 221, 222
Makepeace, Ray, *13*, 128–29, 220, 273; on hellship experience, 179–83; on slave labor in Pacific, 193–96
Malaybalay prison camp (Pacific), *69*, *100*, *114*
Malinta Tunnel (Philippines), 13
Manchuria, 66, 176, 217–18; Japanese prison camps in, 41
Manila, Philippines, 128, 178, 204; departure of hellships from, 180, 183, 188; tent camp for liberated POWs and, 228–29
Mansfield, Dick, 127, 139
Marine Corps veterans, 13, 195, 196
Martinson, Kelly, *30*, 204–5, 273
Meader, Les, *158*, 273
Mexican American prisoners of war, 131–32
Michelsen, Robert (Bob), 49–51, 138, 139, 146–47, 267, 274; on hunger, 127, 128; on liberation, 225, 226, 227–28
Miller, Earl, 238, 274
Miller, Walter, 217–18, 274
Mindanao, Philippines, 69
missing in action (MIA) notification, 233, 235, 237
Missouri (battleship), 228
Mitsui Company mine, 193
Moji, Japan, 178, 182, 183, 185, 193, 196
Moosburg, Germany. *See* Stalag VII-A
Morrett, John, 185, 186, 187, 274
Mühlberg, Elbe. *See* Stalag IV-B
Mukden, Manchuria, 217

Nagatomo, Yoshitada, 70
Nagoya, Japan, 36, 142, 192, 193, 235
Naples, Italy, 175
Navy, U.S., 145–46, 225, 226, 244
Naze, Glen, 22, 119, 151, 244, 274
Nazis, 130, 133–34, 260
Nenadich, Sam, *152*, 245–46, 274
Neubrandenburg, Germany. *See* Stalag II-A
Nichols Field, Luzon, 66–67
Niigata, Japan, 28, 199, 200–201, 222
90th Infantry Division, 174
92nd Garage facility, Corregidor, 12–14
Nissyo Maru (passenger-cargo auxiliary), 179–83, 193
Nomachi, Japan. *See* Camp Nomachi
Norman, Caldon (Cal), 3–4, 16–17, 262, 274
Norris, Donald and Marion, *248*
Noto Maru (freighter), 178–79, 196
Nuremberg, Germany. *See* Stalag XIII-D

Odessa (Black Sea port), 169, 173, 175, 236
Oflag (prison camps for officers), 40, 64, 92, 279
Oflag 64 (Poland), 92
Ofuna. *See* Camp Ofuna
Okinawa, Japan, 230
Oliver, Glenn, 66–68, 74–75, 187–90, 198, 199, 221, 274
Omori, Japan. *See* Camp Omori
100th Infantry Division, 16
101st Airborne, 18
106th Infantry Division, 52, 95, 121, 159, 161, 163
131st Field Artillery, 71, 280
194th Tank Battalion, 7
Oryoku Maru (passenger-cargo ship), 183–85, 283
Osaka, Japan, 221, 222
Ozark (ship), used for repatriation, 230

Pacific, the, viii, x, xi, 5–15, 77, 105; deaths of prisoners in, 75–76; hunger of prisoners and, 123–29; impossibility of escape and, 78, 99–103; interrogations in, 39–40, 47–51; prison camps in, xiii, 5, 41–42, 85–91, 112–16; treatment of airmen in, 130–31, 138–48; war's end in, 203, 217–30; work details in, 66–74
Paddle (submarine), 185
Palawan Island, Philippines, 68–69, 103, 114, 188
paratroopers, 18, 21, 56, 78, 82, 120, 218, 299

Patton, General George, 19
Pearson, Lyle, 109, 274
Pebley, Bill, 16
Peterson, Dale, *43*, 107, 274
Peterson, Paul, 122–23, 159, 163–64, 214–15, 267, 275
Pfaffinger, Richard (Dick), 46–47, 93–94, 120, 275
P-40 Warhawk (fighter aircraft), 116
P-51S Mustang (fighter aircraft), 31, 204
Pflueger, Ted, 47–48, 275
Philippines, *xx*, 7–14, 41, 100, 178, 230, 236; evacuation from, 183; prison camps in, 41, 66–70, 74–76
Poland, 91, 92, 136, 169–73
Porwoll, Ken, 201, 222–23, 229, 246, 255, 268, 275; on Bataan, 10–12; on Luzon work details, 68; on slave labor in Japan, 199–200
post-traumatic stress disorder (PTSD), 204, 244, 245, 248
postwar adjustment, 233–34, 238; attitudes of POWs and, 261–62; difficulties of, 242–44; guilt and, 240–41; healing processes and, 246–47; help from VA and, 246; recurring dreams and, 249–51; role of talking and, 251–59; strain on marriages and, 245, 248–49
Price, Bill, 36–37, 142–43, 224–25, 227, 234–36, 242–43, 275
prison camp conditions, 44–47, 93–94, 110–12, 114, *118;* boredom and, 59–63; danger from Allied bombing and, 63–64, 140, 141, 145–46; end of war and, 40–41, 147–48, 159; lack of evidence about, vii–viii; misery of, 6, 8–10, 13–14, 51–56, 71, 127–28, 131, 138–40, 142–44; overcrowding and, 54, 109, 110, 115, 139. *See also* abuse of prisoners; hunger
Prisoner of War Medal, 234
prisoner of war support groups, 258–59
prisoners of war: numbers of, vii, ix, xiii, 6–7, 39, 42, 165, 176; respect of enemy soldiers for, 18, 21–22, 43. *See also* psychological pressures on prisoners; relationships among prisoners
prisoner transports, 10, 59, 82, 146; to Berga, 130, 135; difficulty of, at war's end, 202, 203, 220–21; repatriation and, 225, 226, 230; work details and, 190–91, 196. *See also* hellships
psychological pressures on prisoners, 138–39, 155, 190; extreme, on hellships, 177, 179–83; guilt and, 11–12, 240–41; lack of understanding about, 204, 244; need to stay optimistic and, 106, 112; postwar, 234, 242–43, 245, 246–51; solitary confinement and, 142–43; support of VA and, 257–59; *See also* fear; interrogation
punishment, 102–3, 122–23; Geneva Convention and, 78; Japanese Army and, 77; Japanese guards and, 86–87, 89–90, 126; ten-man groups and, 78, 101–3

Recovered Allied Military Personnel (RAMPs), 203–4, 214, 228, 230, 233; processing at Camp Lucky Strike and, 231–32
Red Army (Soviet soldiers), 165–70, 174, *205*, 206–7, 215–16; forced marches and, 151, 153; German refugees and, 157–58, 213; in Manchuria, 217–18; reputation for violence and, 149, 171, 173
Red Cross, 137; end of war and, 151–52, 155, 207, 229, 230, 232; parcels, 60, 61, 63, 83, 104, 111, 112, 118, 128, 163; rare in Pacific camps, 105; sharing of, 116–17, 119; shortage of, 81
refugees, 79, 157–58, 171
relationships among prisoners, 9, 10, 11–12, 110–11, 144, 175; conflicts and, 104–5, 116, 119, 127, 128; hardships a test for, 159, 160, 177, 181; importance of friendship and, 38, 106, 108–9, 113–15, 154–55, 163, 190; secondary to survival, 12, 186
repatriation, 169, 203, 215, 233–34; from Europe, 231–32; from Pacific, 228–30; reunions with loved ones and, 235–40
retribution, 202, 203, 210, 211, 219, 225; against guards, 84, 212, 213, 222; fear of, 149; for theft of food, 105, 120–21, 122–23, 126; self-destructive nature of, 268. *See also* lynch justice
revenge. *See* retribution
Ring, Bob, 51, 127
Ringgenberg, Jack, *21*, 110, 120–21, 275
Rinko Coal Yard, Niigata, Japan, 199
Ritchie, Richard, 159, 161, *162*, 163, 275
Ritzman, Wilfred, *208*
roll call, 53–54, 86, 87, 94, 100, 102, 137
Roslansky, Marvin, 85, *195*, 230, 275
Royal Corps of Signals unit, *88*
rumors, 7, 149, 152, 207, 220, 222

Sabbatini, Abraham, *69*, *192*, 275
sabotage, 198
Sagan, Poland. *See* Stalag Luft III
Saigon, Vietnam, 218
San Fernando, Philippines, forced march to, 7, 8, 10
Schleppegrell, Bill, 22–23, 46, 110, 117, 213, 248, 264–65, 275
Schleppegrell, Norma, 248
Schmidt, Alvin, *166*, 169, 174, 276
Schoonover, Hewitt (Lex), 95–96, 121–22, 266, 276; on IX-B Bad Orb, 51–53, 111–12, 116–17
Schrenk, Lester (Les), 54–56, 82–83, 117, 265, 276; forced march and, 153–54; hunger and, 157; liberation and, 207–8
sea transport. *See* hellships
security, 53, 80
Shaw, LeRoy, 53, 61–62, 84, 213, 276
Shinyo Maru (ship), 185, 186, 187
Shogren, Rodney, 25, 31, 158, 276
Shortell, Bill, 108
Silverlieb, Irving (Irv), 101, 193, 219, 237–38, 242, 256, 262–63, 276
65th Infantry Division, 17
slave labor in Japan, 190–92, 198–201; in machine shops, 197; in mines, 193–96; survivors of, 220–21, 222–23, 255
Smith, Jr., Luther H., 133, 247, 276
Snell, Charlie, 240
solitary confinement, 44, 46, 47, 131, 140–43, 224, 250
Soviet soldiers. *See* Red Army
Soviet Union, vii, 169, 172, 202
Spann, Buster, 113
Sprong, Arnold, 60–61, 64, 80–81, *134*, 232, 260, 262, 276
Stalag II-A Neubrandenburg, 81, 215, 260
Stalag III-A Luckenwalde, 43–44, 169, 206, 216
Stalag III-C Küstrin: POWs from, 54, 60, 91, 110, 164, 167, 169, 175
Stalag IV-B Mühlberg, 60–61, 120, 122, 134, 159, 213, 214
Stalag VII-A Moosburg, 84, 207, 209, 212–13, 284; anticipation of liberation and, 204–5
Stalag VIII-A Görlitz, 122, 159, 161, 163, 214
Stalag IX-A Ziegenhain, 108–9, 214
Stalag IX-B Bad Orb, 52–53, 96, 108–9, 121, 130, 214, 266; anti-Semitism at, 134–35; food at, 116–17, 119; overcrowded conditions and, 51, 111–12
Stalag XI-B Fallingbostel, 159, 164, 214
Stalag XII-A Limburg, 59, 60, 108, 159
Stalag XIII-C Hammelburg, 19, 65, 135
Stalag XIII-D Nuremberg, 62–63, 132
Stalag XVII-B Krems, Austria, 40, 95, 131, 132, 158
Stalag Luft I Barth, 60–61, *80*, 93, 105, 110, 120, 249; liberation of, *205*, 206, 213; segregation of Jewish prisoners at, 137; overcrowded conditions at, *109*, *111*
Stalag Luft III Sagan, 62, *63*, 93, 118, 136, 207
Stalag Luft IV Gross Tychow, 40, 61, 119, 155, 207, 209, 210, 245; abusive guards at, 82–84; evacuation of, 151; friendly guard at, 79–80; hunger and, 117–18; roll calls and, 53–54
Stalag Luft VI Heydekrug, 54–55, 117, 155
Stalags (camps for enlisted men and noncommissioned officers), 40, 104
Stalin, Joseph, 202
starvation. *See* hunger
stigma, of being an ex-POW, 257
submarines, 48, 90, 141, 144, 176, 178, 182, 187, 188
sugarcane, 8, 70, 90
suicide, 243, 267; thoughts of, on hellships, 179, 180
surrender; of Germany, 202; of Italy, 96; of Japan, 203, 223–24, 228; of prisoners 5, 19, 21, 28, 39; seen as shameful, 7, 77
survival, 10, 11–12, 19, 48, 136, 179; forced marches and, 159–64; importance of attitude of mind for, 12, 41, 139, 142, 155, 160, 182, 266–67; in jungle camps, 71–74; role of good fortune in, 267; at sea, 184–90; sharing of resources for, 181, 190, 198–99
Swanson, Howard, 13–14, 128, 220, 250, 263–64, 276; on importance of friendships, 113–14; on hellships, 179–83; on slave labor in Japan, 193, 194–95, 196

Taga Maru (ship), *199*
Taiko Maru (ship), 190
Takamatsu, Japan, 195
Takao, Formosa, 182, 183
talking about POW experience, 239–40; disbelief of listeners and, 255–56; healing and, 246, 257–59; lack of encouragement and, 236, 238, 253; reluctance and, 248, 251–52, 254

Tang (submarine), 48, 90, 141, 144
Tarsau, Thailand, 71, 113
Taylor, Lewis, *229*
ten-man groups, 78, 101–3
Thailand, 71, 90, 113, 176
theft, 104–5, 110–12, 120, 126–29; desperation for food and, 121–22
Third Army (American), 204
thirst, 8, 9, 13–14, 180, 190, 265
332nd Fighter Group, 31
371st Fighter Group, 22
Toelle, Ray, 27–29, 87–88, 250, 276
Tokyo, 192, 264; bombing of, 138, 142, 145, 191; Camp Omori on outskirts of, 143, 223–25; Kempeitai headquarters in, 131, 138, 139
Tokyo Bay, 146–47, 226
Tokyo Trolley (bomber), 239, 240
torture, 48, 131. *See also* abuse of prisoners
Toyama, Japan (Camp Number 7), 192
transit camps, 40
tunnel projects, 93–94
29th Infantry Division, 20

United States, 5, 202, 265; German captor's knowledge of, 43; Japanese interrogator educated in, 40
Utashinai, Hokkaido, Japan, 193

Van Every, Harold, *93*, 277
Velasquez, Simon, 94–95, 131, *132*, 277
vermin, 53, 55–56, 131, 193
Veterans Administration (VA), 234, 241, 244, 246, 257, 258

Wade, Floyd, 198
Wakayama, Japan, 198, 221, 222
Wake Island, 230; veterans of, 237, 242, 256
Wakefield, Gerald, 68–69, 103, *231*, *242*, 277
war's end, 202–4, 224; air-dropped messages about, 218, 219; in Europe, 205–17; in Pacific, 218–30; rumors of, 222. *See also* liberation
Warsaw, Poland, 170, 171
water, 15; prisoners deprived of, 9, 13–14, 71, 177, 180, 181, 185, 265; torture with, 48
WCCO Radio, Minneapolis, 227
Weber, Reuben, 19, 42, 215–16, 260, 277
Wehrmacht (German Army), 26, 40, 149, 168, 261
Whittaker, James (Jim), 70–71, *88*, 89–90, 112–11, 124–25, 229, 277
Williams, Dave, 14–15
Winter, Ray, *121*, 277
Woehrle, Charles, 118, 252–53, 277
Wohlferd, Glenn, *86*, 217, 277
work details, 41, 79, 80, 101–2, 144–45; death and, 75–76; end of war and, 223–24; in Europe, 64–66, 91, 280; exhaustion and, 68–69; health problems and, 72–74; in Japanese private industry, 177; in Pacific, 67–75; punishment and, 67; slave labor in Japan and, 190–201
World War II, 5, 202–3; desire for victorious narrative of, ix; human stories of, viii, xiv
wounded men, 18, 25, 27–28, 29, 115, 127, 174; abused in Japanese custody, 15, 50–51, 87–88; in hospitals, 17, 57, 59, 133
Wundzettel (wound tag), *16*

Yangizawa, Kennichi, 50–51, 147, 280
Yokkaichi, Japan, 192
Yokohama, Japan, 86, 204

Zamboanga, Luzon, 185
Zentsuji, Japan, 85, 195, 230
Ziegenhain, Germany. *See* Stalag IX-A

Illustration Credits

National Archives: ii–iii, 8, 13
Keith Williams: xviii–xxi
James Fager family: 4, 235
Cal Norman: 17
Jack Ringgenberg: 21
Deborah Daniels and Greg Hadley: 28
Kelly Martinson: 30
Dale Peterson: 43, 60, 80, 107, 109, 111, 118, 205
Edwin Luoma family: 52
Dick Lewis: 58
Frank Linc: 63
Abraham and Robert Sabbatini: 69, 100, 114, 192
Glenn Wohlferd: 86
Jim Whittaker: 88
Harold Van Every: 93
Charles King: 98
Ray Winter: 121
Simon Velasquez: 132
Arnold Sprong: 134
Marcus Hertz: 136, 252
Bob Michelsen: 139
Harry Magnuson: 145
Sam Nenadich: 152
Les Meader: 158
Richard Ritchie: 162
Alvin Schmidt: 166
Vern Kruse: 172, 175
Marvin Roslansky: 195
Harold Brick: 208
David Claypool: 210, 212
Naval Historical Foundation: 226
Bob Heer: 229
Jameson Wakefield and Pixie Mumford: 231, 242
Alois Kopp: 239
Marion Norris: 248
Sam Alle: 254
Trevor Saylor: 298

The author with ex-POW Charles King at the June 2007 dedication of the Minnesota World War II memorial in St. Paul